HELLENIC STUDIES 16

THE POWER OF THETIS
and Selected Essays

Recent Titles in the Hellenic Studies Series

http://chs.harvard.edu/publications

THE POWER OF THETIS
and Selected Essays

Laura M. Slatkin

CENTER FOR HELLENIC STUDIES
Trustees for Harvard University
Washington, D.C.
Distributed by Harvard University Press
Cambridge, Massachusetts, and London, England
2011

The Power of Thetis and Selected Essays by Laura M. Slatkin
Copyright © 2011 Center for Hellenic Studies, Trustees for Harvard University
All Rights Reserved.
Published by Center for Hellenic Studies, Trustees for Harvard University, Washington, DC.
Distributed by Harvard University Press, Cambridge, Massachusetts, and
    London, England
Printed in Ann Arbor, MI by Edwards Brothers, Inc.

EDITORIAL TEAM
Senior Advisers: W. Robert Connor, Gloria Ferrari Pinney, Albert Henrichs,
    James O'Donnell, Bernd Seidensticker
Editorial Board: Gregory Nagy (Editor-in-Chief), Christopher Blackwell,
    Casey Dué (Executive Editor), Mary Ebbott (Executive Editor), Scott Johnson, Olga
    Levaniouk, Anne Mahoney, Leonard Muellner
Production Manager for Publications: Jill Curry Robbins
Web Producer: Mark Tomasko
Cover design: Joni Godlove
Production: Kristin Murphy Romano

The following essays are reprinted with the kind permission of their publishers:
"Measuring Authority, Authoritative Measures: Hesiod's Works and Days," in *The Moral
    Authority of Nature*, ed. L. Daston and F. Vidal (Chicago: 2004), 25-49.
"The Wrath of Thetis," *Transactions of the American Philological Association* 116 (1986): 1-24.
"Composition by Theme and the Mêtis of the *Odyssey*," in *Reading the Odyssey*,
    ed. S. L. Schein (Princeton: 1996), 223-237.
"Les amis mortels," *L'Écrit du Temps* 19 (1988): 119-32.
"Genre and Generation in the *Odyssey*," *MÉTIS* 1 (1987): 259-268.

LIBRARY OF CONGRESS CATALOGING-IN-PUBLICATION DATA:
Slatkin, Laura M.
The power of Thetis and selected essays / by Laura Slatkin.
    p. cm. -- (Hellenic studies ; 16)
Includes bibliographical references and index.
ISBN 978-0-674-02143-3 (alk. paper)
1. Homer. Iliad. 2. Thetis (Greek mythology) in literature. 3. Epic poetry, Greek--History
and criticism. 4. Trojan War--Literature and the war. I. Title. II. Series.
    PA4037.S494 2011
    883'.01--dc22

                                                                                2010049330

To C.A.S.
and to the memory of
R.L.S. and C.E.S.

Acknowledgments

WHEN *THE POWER OF THETIS* WAS FIRST PUBLISHED, I noted that for a short book, it boasted a long list of people to thank. Although that study, recast in the pages that follow, has not gotten longer, over the intervening years the list of friends and colleagues who have contributed to my thinking on its subject—and other topics in Homeric poetics that developed alongside it—has expanded exponentially; only a catalogue poem could do it justice. I am fortunate to have the opportunity to reiterate my thanks here, however inadequately, to those early interlocutors, whose comradeship and scholarly work continue to inspire and encourage my efforts, along with those of so many other Homerists. In this regard, it is a privilege to thank first and foremost Leonard Muellner and Gregory Nagy, without whom this volume would not have been imagined, much less completed; as a student of archaic notions of *metron*, I can confidently say that their intellectual and personal generosity, deservedly legendary, are beyond measure. To their colleagues at the Center for Hellenic Studies, who patiently and scrupulously shepherded this collection through to its final form, and particularly to Jill Curry Robbins, I offer my sincere thanks as well.

I owe renewed gratitude in addition to Margaret Carroll, and to Jeannie Carlier, Carolyn Dewald, Lillian Doherty, Helene Foley, Douglas Frame, Andrée Hayum, Richard Holway, Richard Janko, Seth Schein, Robert Tannenbaum, and Froma Zeitlin, each of whom has offered salutary advice and criticism over the years. I can only hope that they still find something of merit in these pages to justify all the help they provided.

Similarly, I think with continuing appreciation of the kindly provocations of the late Norman O. Brown, the encouragement of the late Helen Bacon, and the irreplaceable, wise counsel of the late John H. Finley, Jr. My admiration for the wide-ranging work of the late Nicole Loraux, who enlarged the horizons of my thinking on the *Iliad*, will, I hope, be suggested by the last chapter in this volume.

In discussions that followed the appearance of the original study, I benefited from the thoughtful responses of Andrew Becker, David Bouvier, Jenny Strauss Clay, Andrew Ford, and Renate Schlesier. That the interpretive and method-ological questions raised by a consideration of the *Iliad*'s Thetis were deepened and fruitfully transformed in the important work of Jonathan Burgess, Casey

Dué, Mary Ebbott, Margalit Finkelberg, John Miles Foley, J. Marks, Kenneth Mayer, Sheila Murnaghan, and Corinne Pache, has been an especially rewarding outcome of that initial investigation.

For stimulating perspectives that advanced my inquiries into the areas touched on in the essays included here, I am happy to thank Danielle Allen, Lorraine Daston, Marcel Detienne, Chris Faraone, Rachel Friedman, Marilyn A. Katz, Jinyo Kim, Leslie Kurke, Françoise Létoublon, James Redfield, and Mark Usher. I am grateful as well for the incisive suggestions of Caroline Alexander, Carin Calabrese, Antoine Compagnon, Olga Davidson, Rachel Eisendrath, Peter Euben, Denis Feeney, Alan Fishbone, Mary-Kay Gamel, Simon Goldhill, François Hartog, Brad Inwood, Sharon James, Bruce King, David Konstan, Eleanor Leach, John Lynch, Laura McClure, Gary Miles, Ramona Naddaff, Michael Nagler, Piero Pucci, Dale Sinos, Greg Thalmann, Fernando Vidal, and Marc Witkin.

Heartfelt thanks to Ann Bergren and Nancy Felson for their wisdom over many years and for the pleasure of our work together, and to Richard Sacks, who has been my steadfast companion in the exploration of early Greek poetry; their acute scrutiny greatly improved the contents of this book. And I owe deep gratitude, as always, to those penetrating readers, Sara Bershtel, Liz Irwin, and Amy Johnson, and to Pat Easterling for her incomparable, illuminating guidance; their friendship has been a lasting treasure. My reading of Hesiod owes more than I can say to Gloria Ferrari's insights and conversation; in keeping with her taking the ritual measure of the cosmos, her star has been a beacon through many seasons, for me and for others venturing into the terrain of archaic Greece.

A volume that includes reflections on early representations of reciprocity and exchange is a fitting place to record what I owe to Maureen McLane, whose collaborative spirit—and practice—set a new standard for *xenia*. Her judicious, galvanizing critical engagement with the material in this book has clarified and enriched my thinking about both archaic and contemporary poetics and pointed the way to future projects that bridge the two; I look forward to renewing this debt.

It remains to thank Carole Slatkin: her solidarity and unstinting support have been an indispensable, lifelong gift, as well as a precious remembrance of the heartening confidence of our late parents.

Contents

Introduction to this Volume

*T*HE *POWER OF THETIS* and the several essays included here are minimally
revised (including some updated footnotes) from the form in which
they were first published or presented. They thus stand as a record
of their own moment in Homeric studies, a moment that they both reflect
and, I hope, helped to further. The late decades of the twentieth century saw
a general reckoning among Homerists with the powerful heuristic provided
by the fieldwork of Parry and Lord as it was brought to bear upon research
developed by 'neo-analysis'—an approach through which the *Iliad* and the
Odyssey were studied not as singular unities but rather as narratives shaping
themselves in relation to traditional myth and to material given narrative
form in the Epic Cycle.[1] The transformative encounter of oralist and neoanalyst perspectives on the *Iliad*'s adaptation of pre-existing materials and
recombination of mythological motifs reinforced an awareness of the scope
of oral poetics and attuned students more closely to its supple resources.[2] In
its attention to the complex *hearing* that the *Iliad* encourages—a hearing of
tradition within and against the highly shaped and selected texture of the
poem—*The Power of Thetis* aspired to join this conversation and the broader,
increasingly nuanced and resonating choral hearing of the poem: hearing
within, around, before, and between the very specific poetic power of
the *Iliad*.

The narratological interests pursued by literary scholars and anthropologists also informed *The Power of Thetis* and the essays included here (e.g.,
"Composition by Theme and the *Mêtis* of the *Odyssey*"); so too did literary
studies on intertextuality, which—when generalized and liberated from exclusively textual and literary notions of *poiêsis*—proved fruitful for exploring
what I called in *The Power of Thetis* the "superbly overdetermined" workings of

---

[1] See the full discussion in Burgess 2006. For early examples, see Fenik 1964 and Kakridis 1949.
[2] Nagy 1979, 1990.

the *Iliad*. Scholars have turned closer attention to the gaps and contradictions in ancient narrative,[3] as well as to the interrelations among narrative traditions and mythological variants. In ongoing work subsequent to *The Power of Thetis*, I have aimed to put Homeric and Hesiodic works in conversation—or, more precisely, to reanimate the profound conversation embedded within and between them; for in these poems we can discern complex, sometimes mutually exclusive, systems of relation, which I have tended to call "intertropologic" relations, for lack of a more elegant term. If the *Iliad* and *Odyssey* shape themselves in relation to tradition, so too do the Homeric poems shape themselves in relation to Hesiodic narratives and ideologies: an underlying premise of my work—shared with many others—is that ancient Greek narrative is productively approached as a complex, interrelated, dynamic system.[4]

Such an approach may appear to err too much on the side of a synchronic systems-analysis (or neo-structuralist) approach to metaphor, trope, pattern, and formula, and by no means do I wish to downplay the historical problematics that scholars still debate regarding these poems.[5] Although the essays included here tend toward the literary side of analysis, this collection aims to engage with kindred work in "cultural poetics": the intersection of cultural anthropology, work on the poetics of Archaic Greek narrative, and historically grounded accounts of the economies embedded in and represented by epic form the background matrix for my thinking.[6]

Some years ago, in dialogue with the work noted below, I began to reflect on the language of exchange in the *Iliad*, most specifically as it emerges in the discourse of combat. At the moment of final confrontation, enemy warriors repeatedly imagine their fatal struggle as a negotiation and death as part of an imminent bargain.[7] In response to the Trojan Poulydamas' boast that he has killed Prothoënor, an Argive warrior, the Greek Ajax, in turn, kills a Trojan fighter and replies, "Consider, Poulydamas, whether this man's death

---

[3] Burgess 2001, Clay 1997, Felson 1994, Katz 1991, Peradotto 1990, Pucci 1987.

[4] Ballabriga 1998, Burgess 2001, Danek 1998, Finkelberg 1988, Foley 1991, Hunter 2005, Malkin 1998, Muellner 1996, Nagy 1979, Petegorsky 1982.

[5] See the considerations laid out in Morris 1986.

[6] A founding figure in this realm of inquiry in the early twentieth century was L. Gernet, whose work was fundamental for his student, J.-P. Vernant, and Vernant's own students and associates. Innovative research in recent years has helped us to uncover the cultural preoccupations encoded in ancient narrative: especially illuminating studies have been those of M. Detienne; W. Donlan; C. Dougherty; D. Frame; F. Hartog; L. Kurke; B. Lincoln; N. Loraux; I. Malkin; L. Muellner; G. Nagy; P. Vidal-Naquet, F. Zeitlin.

[7] *Iliad* 13.446.

isn't equivalent in exchange for (*anti*) Prothoënor?"[8] We might adduce any number of structurally similar transactions; those invoked in battlefield insults were the starting point for this investigation ("Les Amis Mortels," this volume).

Meditating on these dialogues led me to conclude that the discourse of the battlefield encodes and presupposes a conceptual ground, its features often marked by the term ἀντί 'in exchange for'. Warriors not only threaten but also taunt one another, and when they do so they express their intention to pay the enemy back or to exact payment from him. These dialogues invite us to see in the poem a pervasive figurative system of exchange: Is this man's death an adequate exchange for that one's? Is Agamemnon's seizure of Briseis worth Achilles' wrath? Is *timê* sufficient recompense for fighting in the forefront of battle?[9] Is *kleos* sufficient recompense for the death of the warrior hero? Battlefield dialogues thus simultaneously take the rhetorical form of agonistic exchange and introduce the conceptual problem of equivalence. They usher us into the problematic of commensurability, which is the deepest structuring principle—the foundational problematic—underlying the various orders of exchange (of goods, women, words, blows, lives) in the poem.

Throughout the *Iliad*, the equivalence on which exchange is based is repeatedly presented not as a given but as a problem, a matching or measuring to be contended, worked out, fought over, thought through. Warriors on the battlefield refer to their cohort as *philoi*, a term that expresses the bonds of equality among the heroes, their horizontal equivalence or exchangeability one for one.[10] Yet, however equal they are in their collaboration on the field of battle, the heroes are also inserted into a hierarchical social order, which

---

[8] *Iliad* 14.470ff.
[9] *Iliad* 12.310ff.
[10] *Iliad* 9.197–198:

> "χαίρετον· ἦ φίλοι ἄνδρες ἱκάνετον—ἦ τι μάλα χρεώ—
> οἵ μοι σκυζομένῳ περ Ἀχαιῶν φίλτατοί ἐστον."

Iliad 9.628–631:

> αὐτὰρ Ἀχιλλεὺς
> ἄγριον ἐν στήθεσσι θέτο μεγαλήτορα θυμὸν
> σχέτλιος, οὐδὲ μετατρέπεται φιλότητος ἑταίρων
> τῆς ᾗ μιν παρὰ νηυσὶν ἐτίομεν ἔξοχον ἄλλων...

Iliad 11.284–287:

> Ἕκτωρ δ' ὡς ἐνόησ' Ἀγαμέμνονα νόσφι κιόντα
> Τρωσί τε καὶ Λυκίοισιν ἐκέκλετο μακρὸν ἀΰσας·
> Τρῶες καὶ Λύκιοι καὶ Δάρδανοι ἀγχιμαχηταὶ
> ἀνέρες ἔστε, φίλοι, μνήσασθε δὲ θούριδος ἀλκῆς.

the poem presents as coexisting with their lateral warrior bonds. This project is concerned in part with the tension between orders (e.g., vertical v. horizontal bonds), with the way the *Iliad* refuses to simplify or settle the claims of any pole of disputed valuation.[11] The poem begins with the question of whose authority shall prevail—Agamemnon's polemical assertion of what Donna Wilson calls "fixed-rank" authority versus Achilles' model of fluid, agonistic authority.[12] Their dispute introduces questions of judging, calibrating, and transacting: questions that invite us, as they invited its earliest auditors, to consider what "equal" means. For what should be unambiguous—that this "A" is equal to that "B," that "A" is owed for "B," or even that "A" and "B" might be compared—is not. In the course of the poem, whenever a hero is called "equal to a god," it is precisely when he is about to be vulnerable, that is, when he is revealed to be exactly *not* a god.[13] To invoke the language of *isos* is in the *Iliad* to invoke its opposite or, more precisely, to destabilize the transparency of the equation, the congruence of the conjunctions. As Jakobson and his successors have taught us, figural comparisons—similes, metaphors, and more extended tropes—bear within them the shadow of disjunction, which the surface conjunction of terms apparently belies. If in the *Iliad* someone is said to be like a god only if he is, in fact, not a god, then we see a similar double movement encoded in every transaction at the level of social exchange and valuation: a woman might be worth two tripods or four oxen,[14] and in that sense "equal to" those items, but that is only because she is not tripods or oxen.

This is not to rehearse the logic of exchange value in its archaic moment; I hope rather to point to a mode of reflection often pursued in these pages. The exchanges and imagined equivalences presented and interrogated in the

---

Iliad 15.560–562:

Ἀργείους δ' ὄτρυνε μέγας Τελαμώνιος Αἴας·
ὦ φίλοι, ἀνέρες ἔστε, καὶ αἰδῶ θέσθ' ἐνὶ θυμῷ,
ἀλλήλους τ' αἰδεῖσθε κατὰ κρατερὰς ὑσμίνας.

[11] For a brilliant analysis of warrior *philia*, see Loraux 1997; also Vernant 1968, Sinos 1980, King 1997, and Kim 2000.

[12] See Wilson 2002: ". . . we have in the *Iliad* two different ideological models for determining social hierarchies and leadership: a zero-sum fluid model based on *timê* in which a social hierarchy, hence a best (*aristos*), is negotiated through ritualized conflict, and a fixed-rank model in which the best is politically authenticated and maintains his power in part through redistribution of spoils" (36). Wilson's book pursues many of the same themes and problematics pointed to here; her work represents a valuable furthering of the scholarship on Iliadic reciprocity and exchange thematics.

[13] Daraki 1980, Sacks 1987, Nagy 1979:161–163, Muellner 1996:12–13.

[14] E.g., *Iliad* 23.702–705.

Iliad partake simultaneously of linguistic/figural operations and ideational movements. The problematic of commensurability finds its systematic expression in those figures and tropes in the *Iliad* that themselves encode matching operations—the figural/ideational complex of *anti* for example, or that evoked by *isos* or *philotês*.

The *Iliad* explores the highest mortal stakes of equivalence and commensurability. The poem maps one territory for conceptualizing balance and equivalence, encouraging us to ask what the basis of sameness is in the poem. Achilles says, for example, that he regarded Patroklos as equal to his own life.[15] We should wonder: 'Equal' how? Through what "general equivalent" (to invoke a Marxian diction)? (Any metaphor, any simile might be read as introducing a problem of matching: *Is* my love like a red, red rose? *Is* Achilles god-like? And if so, in what ways?) To ask what underlies the much-discussed existential crisis of Achilles is to be led to the poem's crisis of measure, of commensurability, of value and values.

My question has been, what is the *ground* for such exchange language, or exchange ideation? My work has required, in part, an extended defamiliarization of the logic of equivalence: in this sense such a reading responds to the logic of the *Iliad*, which itself consistently interrogates equivalence. As my discussion thus far suggests, this study arises partly out of an anatomy of language and partly out of a focus on Iliadic situations: crises of exchange, of judgment, of measurement, of value. Throughout the poem we see that crises of exchange, for example in *Iliad* 1, are also simultaneously crises of cognition.

As examples, we might consider two famous moments in the *Iliad*: the exchange of armor between Glaukos and Diomedes in Book 6 and Hektor's recognition of the scales of Zeus at Book 16.658. Especially suggestive along these lines is a passage in *Iliad* 19 in which the scales of Zeus recur, this time in advice from Odysseus, who urges Achilles not to send men into battle hungry: "Let your heart endure to listen to my words. When there is battle men suddenly have their fill of it / When the bronze scatters on the ground the straw in most numbers / and the harvest is most thin, when Zeus has poised his balance / Zeus who is *tamiês polemoio* 'steward of war'" (216ff.).[16]

---

[15] *Iliad* 18.80–82:
ἀλλὰ τί μοι τῶν ἦδος, ἐπεὶ φίλος ὤλεθ᾽ ἑταῖρος
Πάτροκλος, τὸν ἐγὼ περὶ πάντων τῖον ἑταίρων,
ἶσον ἐμῇ κεφαλῇ·
[16] Translation is that of Lattimore 1953–1956.

Contemplating these images and scenes, I have felt, along with other readers, that in them we might find some central basis for understanding the poetics of the *Iliad*. By "poetics" I mean, in the widest sense, the discursive and figural parameters of the imagination—the terms in which the poem imagines its subject, figures its thought, thinks its figures. What we have in the *Iliad*, we might say—echoing many critics committed to the coherence, richness, and systematic complexity of the poem[17]—is a poem thinking. In invoking "poetics," we could as well invoke "the discourse of the poem." Considered as discourse, the poem offers a self-regulating linguistic, figurative, and ideational system. What I have wished to track in the following pages are the deep structural and tropological movements in the *Iliad*.

Such preoccupations have led me to explore more deeply not only the *Iliad* but also, and necessarily, the larger corpus of early Greek poetry. If we shift our frame to include Hesiod (or, as Gloria Ferrari has brilliantly done, Alcman[18]), we see that the problematic of matching, contending, measuring, and balancing cuts across the Archaic corpus. So it has proved fruitful to engage as well with Hesiod's *Works and Days*, and intermittently with other Archaic poems, through which I hope to suggest both the figural and ideational movements *within* each work and also the movements of tropes that are resonant *across* the corpus of Archaic Greek poetry.

My interest in cultural poetics, in each poem and in the collective corpus as a kind of systematic working through, may be seen as indebted to the stimulating work of what has been called the 'Paris School' of classicists, especially the writings of Jean-Pierre Vernant, Pierre Vidal-Naquet, Marcel Detienne, and Nicole Loraux.[19] These scholars have carefully articulated various levels of concern encoded in cultural texts, for example, the relation among specific orders of being; they have taught us to be particularly alert to axes of sameness and difference and to the organization of these axes hori-

---

[17] See, for example, van Wees 1992, who takes as his first methodological assumption the coherence of the poem, arguing against those who adhere to a "patchwork" theory of the *Iliad* (15): "First, one should reconstruct the heroic world as a whole..." (9); "we shall see that a variety of traditional material has in fact been welded into a consistent image of the practices and norms of Akhaian warfare" (168). The most rigorous and elegant accounts of the poem and its workings—however different their thematic and linguistic preoccupations—have addressed the poem as a totality.

[18] Ferrari 2008.

[19] For a representative selection of some of the work of these scholars, see Loraux 2001; for a discussion of the historical development of the 'Paris School', see F. Zeitlin's introduction to Vernant 1991. For a polemical account of some aspects of the interface of Classics and structuralism in post-war French thought, see Leonard 2005.

zontally, so to speak (viz. warriors contending), as well as vertically (beasts below men below gods). Their acute analyses of critical categories of thought have provided one kind of model for my reading and approach ("Genre and Generation in the *Odyssey*," this volume), as they have for so many classicists on this side of the ocean.[20]

It has sometimes been charged that structuralist readings of texts, myths, or situations all too often lend themselves to the production of a rigid *combinatoire* or grid of binaries, and that there can be a crude structuralism is certainly true. The work of the scholars mentioned above is, however, nothing but subtle. (For an appreciation, see the final essay in this volume, "Remembering Nicole Loraux Remembering Athens.") The essays in this volume do not offer an analytic formalism; my unit of analysis is typically not the term or the concept but rather the *movement* of the trope—thus my somewhat cumbersome invoking of "figural/ideational complexes" and movements. To find structuring principles in the *Iliad*, or in Hesiod's *Works and Days*, to take each poem provisionally as a self-enclosed (but not rigid) system: these seem to me the methodological presumptions least likely to distort the poem, depending of course on the mix you take as evidence for the structure. I assume one looks at the language of the poem for evidence.

Taking poetic language as our evidentiary base helps us to trace the development by which key phrases and concepts of Archaic poetry—*homoios*, *isos*, etc.—are translated into political language in the Classical period.[21] Archaic metaphors have an afterlife, another life in the *polis*: in tragedy, in the funeral oration, in the courts. The ideational complexes around measuring and exchanging also inform pre-Socratic philosophy, which I hope to explore further in a discussion of *dikê* from Hesiod to Heraclitus.[22]

As previously suggested, over the past two decades, "exchange," both as an economic mechanism and a linguistic-symbolic transaction, has become a fertile *topos* for classicists, as it had earlier for anthropologists, sociologists, and other students of culture. Sitta von Reden's *Exchange in Ancient Greece* is an example of this interest; she observes that the "shift of interest from production to exchange is an attempt to overcome the cultural parochialism in which economic history traditionally unfolds."[23] She, like Hans van Wees in

---

[20] At the start of my current project, I found support for my concerns in Loraux 1987.

[21] Among scholars who have pursued this line of inquiry, see von Reden 1995, Allen 2000, Loraux 1981, Vidal-Naquet 1981, and Vernant 1965.

[22] See, for example, Heraclitus fr. 9 D-K: Ἥλιος οὐχ ὑπερβήσεται μέτρα· εἰ δὲ μή, / Ἐρινύες μιν Δίκης ἐπίκουροι ἐξευρήσουσιν.

[23] Von Reden 1995:4.

his compelling *Status Warriors*, takes up and extends the discussion advanced by M. I. Finley concerning the representation of economic life in ancient Greek poetry.[24] A half-century of anthropological and economic work, partly inspired by Marcel Mauss's discussion of gift-economies, has informed attention to ancient Greek poetry as evoking an "embedded economy," in Karl Polanyi's terms: that is, the ancient Greek epics can be seen as representing or indexing a community in which "the economic" is not yet disaggregated from social, political, and ritual forms of life. I should reiterate here that my discussions of exchange language do not ground themselves in, or rely on, extended analyses of, say, "the gift" or "the commodity form," nor do they explore historical questions;[25] ancient Greek poetry appears here, not as a possible archive for historians (as it does, in the first instance, for van Wees), but as a field of representation and cognition, provisionally a world unto itself. This is a methodological restriction of the field of inquiry that I hope will bear fruit.

Sitta von Reden helpfully observes that "exchange was a model of thought in ancient Greece itself," yet she proceeds, "Conceiving of the world in terms of pairs of opposites and polarities, the Greeks expressed fundamental ideas about society and nature in terms of exchange."[26] "Exchange," however, need not be a structure of polarities and opposites; it can be, to shift the metaphor, a network of tropes, mobile and complex, irreducible to binaries: thus the need for poetics—for an analysis of the movement of tropes and thought.

---

[24] For van Wees's divergence from Finley, which is based on his rejection of what he sees as Finley's misguided attempt to isolate fantasy from fact in the poem, see 1992:9; for von Reden's relation to Finley's work as well as to Mauss on the gift, see her introduction, 1995:1–9. See also Finley 1954, Mauss 1925, and Polanyi 1944.

[25] And here this project diverges quite profoundly in conception from von Reden 1995, in which distinctions between "gift" and "commodity" structure her analysis, and distinctions between public and private exchange are diagnostic: see, for example, her Introduction, 1995:7, and Chapter 1: "The Scope of Gift Exchange." It does not detract from the value of von Reden's book to observe that the deployment of categories like gift, commodity, and property may at times impose retroactively a political-economical analytic and ideology that is partially foreign to the world of the poems: on the deformation caused by such "exporting" of concepts, understood to be in themselves historical and ideological formations requiring critique, see Baudrillard 1975. His "central argument" states: "Does the capitalist economy retrospectively illuminate medieval, ancient, and primitive societies? No" (86–87). So too, he suggests, the categories of the analysis and critique of capital—production, commodity-form, and so on—have limited explanatory power.

[26] Von Reden 1995:1.

With the discourse of exchange in mind, we see that, as represented in the poem, the warriors' entry into battle confirms relationships that are presumed to be reciprocal. B. Fenik's thorough analysis in *Typical Battle Scenes* establishes that a warrior typically enters the battle when a friend or relative is killed, wounded, or under siege. Fenik shows that this entry—often a figure's spotlit moment in the narrative—is, typically, explicitly motivated by anger, pity, or grief: warriors go into battle to protect, to rescue, or to avenge. Although the recompense offered for fighting is measured in material goods as an index of *timê*, neither the narrative nor the warriors adduce *timê* (or even *kleos*) as motivation at the point at which they take their lives in their hands.[27] What Achilles does in venturing into battle after the death of Patroklos is thus perfectly typical—an enlargement of the poem's patterning, not a deviation. If Achilles is understood to be an intensification of the paradigmatic and essential warrior predicament, this suggests that the discovery of incommensurability the poem enacts through him is always there systematically—embedded, so to speak, in the cultural logic the poem everywhere elaborates.

An impressive recent examination of this cultural logic is Donna Wilson's *Ransom, Revenge and Heroic Identity in the Iliad*.[28] Wilson's book offers a persuasive analysis of what she calls "the monumental compensation theme" of the poem,[29] focused in particular on the social and semantic fields of *apoina* (ransom) and *poinê* (reparation or revenge), insisting that they belong to a "unified social and semantic network"—a network the poem and its characters ceaselessly interrogate: "compensation thus emerges as the locus of a struggle for dominance based on a strategy of competing definitions and aggressive arrogation of roles."[30] Her book rightly proposes "compensation as a coherent system": "the poetics of compensation, or the collocation of formulaic and traditional elements, proves to be bound up with the politics, or social relations and power structures, of reciprocity in Homeric society."[31] Wilson sharpens our grasp of the several systems of economy operative in

---

[27] We see in the dialogue between Glaukos and Sarpedon at *Iliad* 12.310ff. an idealizing version of cultural motive delivered in a kind of backformation; see van Wees 1992 on the legitimacy of acquisition as a motive for raiding and battle.

[28] Wilson 2002.

[29] Wilson 2002:10.

[30] Wilson 2002:10.

[31] Wilson 2002:15 systematically tracks "when a character manipulates the *poetics* of compensation"—Agamemnon polemically offering Achilles *apoina*, not *poinê*, for example; Lykaon's plea—his remembrance of previous *apoina*—moving Achilles instead into giving a bleak *poinê*; Priam's supplication for *apoina* and Achilles' acceptance, the profoundly significant resolution of the *poinê/apoina* problematic.

the poem, and her systematic analysis rescues us from excessively psychologizing and modernizing accounts of heroic identity.

It is important to observe that Iliadic emotions are social, not private, however individually and somatically located the representation of emotional experience.[32] To put it another way, it is a mistake to understand pity, anger, or grief as opposed to the cultural value of *kleos*; pity, anger, and grief partake just as profoundly of the social-symbolic code. Jean Baudrillard is one of the theorists who has taught us not to reduce "the symbolic" to "the psychological": my discussion of Archaic poetics tries to bear that lesson in mind, focusing as it does on the logic of representation. Iliadic representation of subjectivity is always social, even and perhaps most profoundly when the poem locates cultural conflict or contradiction in an individual, most famously in Achilles. Bonds of reciprocity underlie and propel affect; exchange language structures the representation of emotion as much as the representation of combat or trade or sacrifice. Baudrillard writes: "*The symbolic must never be confused with the psychological. The symbolic sets up a relation of exchange in which the respective positions cannot be autonomized.*"[33] Every position implies a relation and thus a process. Extending this insight to Archaic poetry, we observe that there is no singular hero, there are heroes and contexts: one may be the *Best of the Achaeans*[34]—one is never solely the best; there is no solitary farmer in Hesiod—there are neighbors and brothers, getting along badly or well as they may; there is no unilateral sentence of justice—there is measuring, weighing, balancing.

The *Iliad* sustains a many-sided exploration of its constitutive predicaments, diagnosing its own impasses. In the founding dispute of Book 1, when Agamemnon declares that he is going to take Briseis, claiming that he is owed her for the loss of Chryseis, Achilles moves immediately to the question, why are we here? From Achilles' perspective, what is being violated in the imminent seizure of Briseis is the imperative of reciprocity; yet Agamemnon articulates his claim through an apparently similar language of owed honor and goods. By shifting the plane of the immediate dispute to the broadest question of the war, Achilles orients us to reciprocity as a system: the Achaeans have come to Troy because they have acknowledged and honored their reciprocal obligations to the sons of Atreus. Agamemnon, by contrast, looks at the

---

[32] On the cultural and historical specificity of the map of emotions in the *Iliad*, see Muellner 1996. For the status, dispersion, and figuration of pity in the poem, see Kim 2000.

[33] Baudrillard 1975:102-103.

[34] Nagy 1979.

local transaction, considering Briseis as rightful compensation for the loss of Chryseis.

We confront here not only a dispute about authority but more profoundly an impasse between levels of analysis—Agamemnon preoccupied with the immediate exchange; Achilles countering with a vision of the larger, cultural system of exchange that enables and subsumes all particular transactions. Achilles' question introduces a significant element into exchange language and exchange dispute: the dimension of temporality. For, in the oath on the scepter or when he contemplates his two alternative *kêres,* Achilles considers the long view. Through Achilles the poem constantly signals its awareness that reciprocity as both a material and a social-symbolic system exists *in time* and *over time.* In Book 1, Achilles declares that prizes should not be redivided or redistributed *now;* he assures Agamemnon that if he waits until the war's end he will be recompensed three times over. The mindfulness of temporality here is both Achilles' and the poem's. Thus we see that disputes over exchanges have as much to do with their *timing* as their *contents.*

As the *Iliad* thinks through the complexities of exchange, we see that the poem imagines its system of reciprocity not as a series of static, algebraic operations—this death for that one, this woman for that one, this insult for that one—but rather an experience of transactions *in and through time.* This temporal element forces all actors to take the measure of their predicaments: not only what would suffice, but *when.* Satisfaction that comes too late is not, of course, satisfaction; payback too early may similarly disappoint. The deep structure of cultural reciprocity—whether positive (*philotês*) or the negative reciprocity of debt or death-as-payback—must be seen, then, as requiring the ongoing work of measuring, thinking, *figuring.*

This temporalization of exchange is equally prominent in Hesiod. Mindful of the temporal element that renders exchange something other than a simple equation, something more than a spatialization or an image (e.g., the scales of Zeus), we can begin to understand a somewhat opaque pronouncement in *Works and Days:* Hesiod's accusation that the *dorophagoi basilees*—fools that they are—do not know "how much more the half is than the whole" (νήπιοι, οὐδὲ ἴσασιν ὅσῳ πλέον ἥμισυ παντός, 40). This culminating charge against these eminences, appearing at the very outset of the *Works and Days,* is a striking but curious rebuke. The much-discussed line has vexed many a commentator,[35] and I do not offer a solution to their vexation here. But what is clear from Hesiod's assertion is that quantifying or taking

---

[35] West 1978 and Verdenius 1985.

the measure of something is no simple operation, that the sum total which the process of measuring yields will not be transparently self-evident—may, in fact, be counter-intuitive: how can the half be more than the whole? Beyond and through this perplexity, this problem of measuring, we shall see that there is a connection between figuring this out and acting ethically, and—what is more—that there is an association between reckoning and power.

It is these notions that I have been concerned with over the past years, in thinking about why it matters that the *basileis* don't know how things add up—that is, in thinking about the role of measuring, and its contribution to the representation of exchange, in the *Works and Days*. I suggest that the paradox of the half being greater than the whole, as stated, draws attention to a problem that has fundamental and pervasive application in the *Works and Days*: namely, the meaning of equivalence, proportionality, and equilibrium and their function in social relations—considered in a register that is at the same time figurative *and* pragmatic.

Like *The Power of Thetis*, the essays in this volume are marked by their time of composition. I hope that the readings in these pages will be of use to students of early Greek epic, and that readers will accept them as conditioned, contingent offerings on a common field.

Works Cited

Allen, D. S. 2000. *The World of Prometheus: The Politics of Punishing in Democratic Athens*. Princeton.

Ballabriga, A. 1998. *Les fictions d'Homère: l'invention mythologique et cosmographique dans l'Odysée*. Paris.

Baudrillard, J. 1975. *The Mirror of Production*. Trans. M. Poster. St. Louis.

Burgess, J. S. 2001. *The Tradition of the Trojan War in Homer and the Epic Cycle*. Baltimore.

———. 2006. "Neoanalysis, Orality, and Intertextuality: An Examination of Homeric Motif Transference." *Oral Traditions* 21:148–189.

Clay, J. S. 1983. *The Wrath of Athena: Gods and Men in the Odyssey*. Princeton.

Danek, G. 1998. *Epos und Zitat: Studien zu den Quellen der Odyssee*. Wiener Studien, Beiheft 22. Vienna.

Daraki, M. 1980. "Le héros à *menos* et le héros *daimoni isos*. Une polarité homérique." *Annali della Scuola Normale Superiore di Pisa* III:10 (1):1–24.

Donlan, W. 1980. *The Aristocratic Ideal in Ancient Greece: Attitudes of Superiority from Homer to the End of the Fifth Century.* Lawrence, KS.

Dougherty, C. and L. Kurke, eds. 1993. *Cultural Poetics in Archaic Greece: Cult, Performance, Politics.* Cambridge.

Felson, N. 1994. *Regarding Penelope: From Character to Poetics.* Princeton.

Fenik, B. 1964. *"Iliad X" and the "Rhesus": The Myth.* Collection Latomus 73. Brussels.

———. 1968. *Typical Battle Scenes in the Iliad: Studies in the Narrative Techniques of Homeric Battle Description.* Hermes, Einzelschriften 21. Wiesbaden.

Ferrari, G. 2008. *Alcman and the Cosmos of Sparta.* Chicago.

Finkelberg, M. 2002. "Homer and the Bottomless Well of the Past." *Scripta Classica Israelica* 21:243-50.

Finley, M. I. 1954. *The World of Odysseus.* Harmondsworth, UK.

Foley, J. M. 1991. *Immanent Art: From Structure to Meaning in Traditional Oral Epic.* Bloomington, IN.

Frame, D. 1978. *The Myth of Return in Early Greek Epic.* New Haven.

Gernet, L. 1955. *Droit et société dans la Grèce ancienne.* Publications de l'Institut de droit romain de l'Université de Paris 13. Paris.

———. 1968. *Anthropologie de la Grèce antique.* Paris.

Hartog, F. 1996. *Mémoire d'Ulysse. Récits sur la frontière en Grèce ancienne.* Paris.

Hunter, R., ed. 2005. *The Hesiodic Catalogue of Women: Constructions and Reconstructions.* Cambridge.

Kakridis, J. T. 1949. *Homeric Researches.* Skrifter utgivna av Kungliga Humanistiska vetenskapssamfundet i Lund 45. Lund, Sweden. Reprint 1987.

Katz, M. A. 1991. *Penelope's Renown: Meaning and Indeterminacy in the Odyssey.* Princeton.

Kim, J. 2000. *The Pity of Achilles: Oral Style and the Unity of the Iliad.* Lanham, MD.

King, B. 1997. *The End of Adventure.* Doctoral dissertation, University of Chicago.

Kurke, L. 1999. *Coins, Bodies, Games and Gold: The Politics of Meaning in Archaic Greece.* Princeton.

Lattimore, R. 1951. *The Iliad of Homer.* Chicago.

Leonard, M. 2005. *Athens in Paris: Ancient Greece and the Political in Post-war French Thought*. Oxford.

Loraux, N. 1981. *L'Invention d'Athènes: histoire de l'oraison funèbre dans la "cité classique."* Civilisations et sociétés 65. Paris.

———. 1987. "Le lien de la division." *Le cahier du collège international de philosophie* 4:101–123. Paris.

———. 1997. "La politique des frères." In *La cité divisée: l'oubli dans la mémoire d'Athènes*. 197–215. Paris.

Loraux, N., G. Nagy, and L. Slatkin, eds. 2001. *Antiquities*. Trans. A. Goldhammer. New Press Postwar French Thought Series 3. New York.

Lord, A. B. 1960. *The Singer of Tales*. Harvard Studies in Comparative Literature 24. Cambridge, MA.

———. 1991. *Epic Singers and Oral Tradition*. Ithaca.

———. 1995. *The Singer Resumes the Tale*. Ithaca.

Malkin, I. 1998. *The Returns of Odysseus: Colonization and Ethnicity*. Berkeley.

Mauss, M. 1925. *Essai sur le don. Forme et raison de l'echange dans les sociétés archaiques*. Paris.

Morris, I. 1986. "The Use and Abuse of Homer." *Classical Antiquity* 5:81–138.

Muellner, L. 1976. *The Meaning of Homeric Eukhomai through its Formulas*. Innsbrucker Beiträge zur Sprachwissenschaft 13. Innsbruck.

———. 1996. *The Anger of Achilles: Mênis in Greek Epic*. Ithaca.

Nagy, G. 1979. *The Best of the Achaeans: Concepts of the Hero in Archaic Greek Poetry*. Baltimore.

———. 1990. *Greek Mythology and Poetics*. Ithaca.

———. 1996. *Homeric Questions*. Austin.

Peradotto, J. 1990. *Man in the Middle Voice: Name and Narration in the Odyssey*. Princeton.

Petegorsky, D. 1982. *Context and Evocation: Studies in Early Greek and Sanskrit Poetry*. Doctoral dissertation, University of California, Berkeley.

Polanyi, K. 1944. *The Great Transformation*. New York.

Pucci, P. 1987. *Odysseus Polutropos: Intertextual Readings in the Odyssey and the Iliad*. Cornell Studies in Classical Philology 46. Ithaca.

Reden, S. von. 1995. *Exchange in Ancient Greece*. London.

Sacks, R. 1987. *The Traditional Phrase in Homer: Two Studies in Form, Meaning and Interpretation.* Columbia Studies in the Classical Tradition 14. Leiden.

Sinos, D. 1980. *Achilles, Patroklos, and the Meaning of Philos.* Innsbrucker Beiträge zur Sprachwissenschaft 29. Innsbruck.

Verdenius, W. J. 1985. *A Commentary on Hesiod: Works and Days, vv. 1–382.* Mnemosyne, bibliotheca classica Batava. Supplementum 86. Leiden.

Vernant, J.-P. 1965. *Mythe et pensée chez les Grecs: Etudes de psychologie historique.* Paris.

———, ed. 1968. *Problèmes de la guerre en Grèce ancienne.* Civilisations et sociétés 11. Paris.

———. 1974. *Mythe et société en Grèce ancienne.* Paris.

———. 1988. *Myth and Society in Ancient Greece.* New York.

———. 1991. *Mortals and Immortals: Collected Essays.* Ed. F. Zeitlin. Princeton.

Vidal-Naquet, P. 1981. *Le chasseur noir: Formes de pensée et formes de société dans le monde grec.* Paris.

Wees, H. van. 1992. *Status Warriors: War, Violence, and Society in Homer and History.* Dutch Monographs on Ancient History and Archaeology 9. Amsterdam.

West, M. L., ed. 1978. *Hesiod: Works and Days.* Oxford.

Wilson, D. 2002. *Ransom, Revenge and Heroic Identity in the Iliad.* Cambridge.

Zeitlin. F. 1996. *Playing the Other: Gender and Society in Classical Greek Literature.* Chicago.

Part I

The Power of Thetis
Allusion and Interpretation in the *Iliad*

Preface

A S EVERY ERA FINDS ITS OWN REASONS for reading the *Iliad* and the *Odyssey* and discovers its own meaning in them, so it must participate in the ongoing process of discriminating Homeric thought, attitudes, values, ideology from its own, rather than assimilating Homer to itself. The attempt to establish a context within which to read Homeric poetry must naturally draw on the indispensable efforts of archaeologists, historians, anthropologists, linguists, and specialists in ancient religion in order to provide appropriate bearings for analysis. This is obvious enough when we consider social and political institutions, economic configurations, or technology, areas in which the differences between our world and that of early Greece are apparent. Modes of perception and cognition, as reflected in literature, are more difficult to distinguish and identify.

The challenge to define as fully as possible the cultural environment in which a work of literature was produced presents itself with every examination of an ancient text. In the case of the extraordinarily complex phenomenon of Attic drama the task is perhaps facilitated by the survival of more complete documentation about the conditions, if not of its genesis, at least of its evolution and reception during the fifth century, as well as by contemporary commentary on it, as in the plays of Aristophanes. Drama, moreover, has continued to flourish as an art form with many of its conventions intact, and through our own experience of it in practice we appreciate much about how it realizes its aesthetic effects and meaning. Still, modern understanding of ancient drama is handicapped by ignorance of many of its integral features, such as music and dance. It is true nonetheless that readers of these works offer powerful and stimulating analyses of them; and it is by no means certain that if we were suddenly to find ourselves enlightened about ancient music and choreography we would need to alter our readings of the plays in a radical way. But a new awareness of these dimensions would entitle us to reconsider the plays interpretively, because it would mean that we would be able to hear and see them as their audiences did, to gauge more responsively the scope and complexity of their achievement.

Is there anything comparable that, as readers of Homer, we do not "hear" and "see"? The researches of Milman Parry and Albert Lord and others who have studied the mechanics and artistry of Homeric verse making have pioneered an awareness of its essential oral characteristics and altered our perception of the bases of its formal structure. Formulas, type-scenes, repeated episodes, have been fruitfully mapped; but the oral, traditional poet depends as well on other compositional techniques and resources alien to a literate culture, which are crucial to an understanding of the meaning of his poem.

Direct attention needs to be paid to the oral poet's orchestration of the mythology out of which his narrative is composed. The poet, it appears, constructs his narrative using myths that are not related in full, but only in part. Why should this be so? Is he inventing, but abridging, limiting the compass of his inventions? Is he attempting novelties and abandoning them unelaborated? Are these preparatory sketches awaiting further development? How are we to understand the poet's use of those fragments within the larger story?

The mythological corpus on which the poet draws, taken together, constitutes an internally logical and coherent system, accessible as such to the audience. The poet inherits as his repertory a system, extensive and flexible, whose components are familiar, in their manifold variant forms, to his listeners. For an audience that knows the mythological range of each character, divine or human not only through this epic song but through other songs, epic and nonepic the poet does not spell out the myth in its entirety but locates a character within it through allusion or oblique reference.

He thereby incorporates into his narrative another discourse, one that makes its appearance on the surface of the poem through oblique references, ellipses, or digressions, evoking for his audience themes that orient or supplement the events of the poem in particular ways. What becomes instrumental in this mode of composition is not only what the poet articulates by way of bringing a given myth (with its associated themes) into play, in relation to his narrative, but also what is left unsaid; for his audience would hear this as well.

In the continuously reversible shift of emphasis from explicit to implicit meaning, how does the poet activate the implicit? For an audience to whom this fundamental compositional resource is foreign or to whom the myths in their essential multivalence, flexibility, and systematicity are unfamiliar, the task of hearing as Homer's audience did requires the apparently paradoxical task of listening for what is unspoken.

Introduction

THE HOMERIC POEMS, as I hope to show, constitute acts of interpretation as well as acts of creation. The elucidation of their oral nature has taught us to look at Homeric composition not as a matter of rigidly prescribed transmission of inviolate requirements, but as a choice among alternative arrangements of fundamental compositional elements—formulas, diction, "themes," type-scenes—that allow for modification within established contours.[1]

---

[1] Milman Parry's pioneering studies of the oral nature of the poems are reprinted and translated in Adam Parry's edition of his father's collected papers, published as *The Making of Homeric Verse* (Oxford, 1971); the fullest exposition of M. Parry and Albert Lord's seminal discoveries based on their fieldwork in Yugoslavia on living oral epic is in Lord's *The Singer of Tales* (Cambridge, Mass., 1960; reprint, New York, 1965). On "theme," the term by which Lord, following Parry, designated "the groups of ideas regularly used in telling a tale," see Lord's "Composition by Theme in Homer and Southslavic Epos," *TAPA* 82 (1951): 71–80, and his *Singer of Tales*, 68–98. On the dynamics of the oral poet's choice, Lord's writings are fundamental; see *Singer of Tales*, 13–29, esp. 98–123. Significant contributions to an understanding of particular aspects of the process have been numerous. Among them one might cite, as a sample, the studies of A. Hoekstra, *Homeric Modifications of Formulaic Prototypes: Studies in the Development of Greek Epic Diction* (Amsterdam, 1964); J. Russo, "The Structural Formula in Homeric Verse," *YCS* 20 (1966): 217–40; J. B. Hainsworth, *The Flexibility of the Homeric Formula* (Oxford, 1968); M. Nagler, *Spontaneity and Tradition: A Study in the Oral Art of Homer* (Berkeley, 1974); M. Edwards, "Some Stylistic Notes on *Iliad* XVIII," *AJP* 89 (1968): 257–83; N. Postlethwaite, "Formula and Formulaic: Some Evidence from the Homeric Hymns," *Phoenix* 33 (1979): 1–18; R. Janko, *Homer, Hesiod and the Hymns: Diachronic Development in Epic Diction* (Cambridge, 1982); and M. Cantilena, *Ricerche sulla dizione epica* (Rome, 1982). R. Sacks, *The Traditional Phrase in Homer: Two Studies in Form, Meaning, and Interpretation* (Leiden, 1987), contributes an important discussion of the significance of context as a factor in the adaptability of traditional phraseology. On the modification of structural elements beyond the epithet system—motifs, "themes," or type-scenes (first examined in detail by W. Arend, *Die typischen Szenen bei Homer* [Berlin, 1933])—instructive works are many, including (in addition to those of Lord) B. Fenik, *Typical Battle Scenes in the Iliad: Studies in the Narrative Technique of Homeric Battle Description*, Hermes Einzelschriften 21 (Wiesbaden, 1968); D. Lohmann, *Die Komposition der Reden in der Ilias* (Berlin, 1970); T. Krischer, *Formale Konventionen der homerischen Epik* (Munich, 1971); C. P. Segal, *The Theme of the Mutilation of the Corpse in the Iliad* (Leiden, 1971); M. Edwards, "Type-scenes and Homeric Hospitality," *TAPA* 105 (1975): 51–72; as well as Nagler, *Spontaneity and Tradition*.

The process of participating in a poetic tradition, far from being a simple matter of inflexible dependence on antecedents, has emerged, on the contrary, as a process of selection at every stage.

On another level, but analogously, I propose, the *Iliad* and the *Odyssey* interpret the mythological material they inherit. As we shall see, they select not only from among different myths—combining those chosen into a narrative within which certain central concerns illustrated by the myths are allowed full development—but also from among different variants and aspects of a single myth. As with rearrangements of formulas or themes, alternative combinations of the features of a myth are possible and equally legitimate, the choices serving to reveal the framework imposed on its subject matter by traditional genre requirements of heroic epic.[2]

But just as an individual formula implies a system of formulaic usage—in each instance expresses not only its individual "essential idea" but a principle of "formularity"[3]—and just as any type-scene involves a recognized pattern, so, I will argue, a particular version of a myth is part of a larger whole that invites shaping, focusing, and integrating within a narrative structure, but that, however partially represented, can be invoked in all its dimensions. The epic

[2] Homeric epic, in its pan-Hellenic ambition, tends, for example, to exclude overt reference to distinctly local religious phenomena. As G. Nagy has shown in *The Best of the Achaeans* (Baltimore, 1979), elements in myth that refer to hero-cult are abridged or suppressed in the epic narrative. See D. Sinos, *Achilles, Patroklos, and the Meaning of Philos* (Innsbruck, 1980), esp. 13–36, 47–52, for further elucidation of the consequences of this restriction in the *Iliad* and for the manner in which Homeric poetry "offers us clear proof by way of dictional analysis that its epic tradition does indeed contain elemental vestiges of cult and references to the heroes of cult in a manner necessarily modified to fit the strict generic ordering of the language of epic" (15).

[3] M. Parry's definition of the formula, given first in *L'épithète traditionelle dans Homère* (Paris, 1928), was restated in "Studies in the Epic Technique of Oral Versemaking," *HSCP* 41 (1930) as "a group of words which is regularly employed under the same metrical conditions, to express a given essential idea" (80). See Cantilena, *Dizione epica*, 36–73, for a balanced recent appraisal of the major contributions to the debate about the nature of the formula. For evaluations of the limitations of Parry's definition, with discussion of the general problem of definition and terminology, see the papers in B. Stolz and R. Shannon, eds., *Oral Theory and the Formula* (Ann Arbor, Mich., 1976) by P. Kiparsky (pp. 73–104), J. Russo (pp. 31–54), and G. Nagy (pp. 239–257, now rewritten in id., *Greek Mythology and Poetics* [Ithaca, N.Y., 1990], 18–35); also A. Parry's introduction to *The Making of Homeric Verse*, esp. xxii–lxii. M. Edwards, "Homer and the Oral Tradition: The Formula, Part I," *Oral Tradition* 1/2 (1986): 171–230, and "Part II," *Oral Tradition* 3/1–2 (1988): 11–60, provide a judicious survey of the vast bibliography on the formula. For fundamental considerations of the relationship of a given formula to the larger compositional system, see Lord, *Singer of Tales*, 30–67, esp. 36–45 and 65–66; and the far-reaching generative approach of M. Nagler, "Towards a Generative View of the Oral Formula," *TAPA* 98 (1967): 269–311; as well as id., *Spontaneity and Tradition*, esp. chaps. 1 and 2.

audience's knowledge of the alternative possibilities allows the poet to build his narrative by deriving meaning not only from what the poem includes but also from what it conspicuously excludes. A telling instance of this is the *Iliad*'s treatment of the Judgment of Paris. Presupposed by the poem and implicit in its plot, where it underlies divine as well as human alignments,[4] the Judgment of Paris would, however, remain an obscure reference, occurring as it does in a single allusion at the end of the poem (24.25–30)—if we were not able to look to sources outside Homer to recover the content of the myth and thus to appreciate the *Iliad*'s particular use and placement of it.[5] The epic can highlight or suppress attributes associated with a particular character, allowing their meaning to be colored by the specific narrative context, thus revising or manipulating its audience's expectations. And, in a complementary movement, it can appropriate the resonance of mythological variants that the narrative context may not explicitly accommodate. In adapting specific features in this way, the poem acts traditionally; it does not violate tradition (although it may be violating one particular tradition) but remains within it, exploiting its possibilities and using traditionality as an instrument of meaning.[6]

The discovery that the dynamics of selection and combination, modification and revision, are intrinsic to participation in an oral poetic tradition— that is, are traditional operations themselves—applies, as I will argue in the present study, to the relationship the epic has with the mythology that is its medium, from which it derives both its identity as part of a system and its distinctive individuality. But if one suggests that modifications of formula, phrase, or type-scene find an analogy in the poem's handling of mythological variants, it is important to stress that no aboriginal prototype of a myth exists that can claim priority over other versions.[7]

This study will examine the processes by which Homeric epic draws on the full mythological range of each character in the development of that character's role and its relation to the poem's central ideas. An especially

---

[4] See M. Davies, "The Judgement of Paris and *Iliad* XXIV," *JHS* 101 (1981): 56–62.

[5] See K. Reinhardt's important "Das Parisurteil" in *Tradition und Geist* (Göttingen, 1960), 16–36, first published as vol. 11 of *Wissenschaft und Gegenwart* (Frankfurt, 1938).

[6] How enlightening an awareness of this process can be is powerfully demonstrated by the work of J. Th. Kakridis, *Homeric Researches* (Lund, 1949), whose analyses of the adaptation of motifs are informed by close familiarity with modern Greek folktale and song-making traditions; see in particular pp. 1–42, 106–48.

[7] As has been most effectively illustrated by Claude Lévi-Strauss's meticulous analyses; in *The Raw and the Cooked* (New York, 1969; reprint, 1975), see especially his discussion of the essential "multiplicity" of myths at pp. 12ff., 199ff., 332ff. See as well M. Detienne, *Dionysus mis à mort* (Paris, 1977), 23ff.

revealing example is the figure of Thetis. Her role in the *Iliad* (which has not previously been the subject of any special critical scrutiny) presents a number of enduringly enigmatic and apparently contradictory features that need to be considered in any interpretive approach to the poem, especially because the poem's use of her has important implications for its view of its principal character, Achilles, and hence of its dominant themes. The *Iliad*'s treatment of Thetis offers a crucial instance of the way in which its narrative incorporates traditional material from mythology that does not overtly reflect the subject matter of heroic poetry. To what end does it do so? How does the resonance of this material contribute a wider context and meaning to the *Iliad*'s central themes? Such a study thus aims to make a contribution to Homeric poetics, in that unraveling the functional identity of a figure like Thetis leads necessarily to the larger enterprise of determining what is and is not compatible with Homeric epic's definition of its subject matter and realm of function—its boundaries as a genre. In pursuing this inquiry, it will be useful to compare how features of Thetis's mythology are exploited by independently inherited poetic traditions, such as those of lyric poetry and the Epic Cycle.

In defining Thetis through a selective presentation of her mythology, the *Iliad* makes explicit, emphatic use of her attributes as a nurturing mother—a *kourotrophos*—and protector. To put it another way, this aspect of Thetis's mythology—her maternal, protective power—which is adapted by the *Iliad*, makes possible one of the poem's central ideas: the vulnerability of even the greatest of the heroes. Semidivine as Achilles is, death is inevitable even for him. At the same time, as we shall see, the *Iliad* returns us to Thetis's role in the theogonic myth of succession. In its superbly overdetermined economy, the *Iliad* shapes Thetis as thoroughly from the perspective of its hero's response and ultimate mortal concerns as it delineates his human dilemma against the dimension of a particular divine genealogy. The formal accommodation of Thetis's mythology within epic is recapitulated in the shape of the Homeric *Iliad*. In defining Thetis, therefore, the poem defines itself.

The discovery of the oral and traditional nature of the Homeric poems, and our increased grasp of the extraordinary complexity and refinement of their oral evolution, has prompted the suggestion that we need a new poetics in order to read them. J. A. Notopoulos, for example, whose work represented an important contribution to the early discussion of oral epic, urged the founding of a new, "non-Aristotelian" criticism of Homer. In fact, what may be called for, as Richard Janko has argued, is a more complete appreciation of the old poetics.[8]

What we need is not to produce our own new basis for reading Homer, but to recover as much as possible what an ancient "reading" might have been based on; or rather we might say that to gain greater access to what Homer's audience heard in the epics—that is, to return to the oldest way of hearing Homer—would be, paradoxically, to achieve for ourselves new grounds for interpreting the *Iliad* and *Odyssey*. Just as basic etymological studies of single words (using modern tools of linguistic reconstruction) have brought us closer to the meaning of traditional diction, and finally of Homeric themes,[9] similarly, by uncovering the constituent components of a single Iliadic character we may come closer to understanding how the *Iliad* conjoined these elements and what the Homeric audience recognized in the depiction of that character.

In our pursuit of the poetic archaeology of Homer, small fragments of evidence will prove indispensable. If careful excavation and comparative analysis of relevant testimony outside the *Iliad* can show us how to fit together disparate pieces of a mythopoeic entity like Thetis—as we proceed on the assumption that they were once intact, and recognizably so—then even a single successful linkage can show us where to look for further interlocking connections. It can help us to see the shape of the whole structure; it may even turn out to be a cornerstone.

The Epic Cycle has emerged as our most productive (if controversial) resource for understanding the "uniqueness of Homer."[10] The search for the sources of the *Iliad*, as it was pursued, with exceptional imagination and industry, by scholars in the middle decades of this century, focused attention

---

[8] J. A. Notopoulos, "Studies in Early Greek Poetry," *HSCP* 68 (1964): 1–77, esp. 54–65. See now the discussion in R. Janko, *The Iliad: A Commentary, Vol. IV: Books 13–16* (Cambridge, 1992), xi, for the most recent statement of his view.

[9] In particular the exemplary studies by E. Benveniste, *Le vocabulaire des institutions indo-européennes I, II* (Paris, 1969); also R. Schmitt, *Dichtung und Dichtersprache in indogermanischer Zeit* (Wiesbaden, 1967). See the notable contributions of D. Frame, *The Myth of Return in Early Greek Epic* (New Haven, 1978); A. L. Bergren, *The Etymology and Usage of ΠΕΙΡΑΡ in Early Greek Poetry*, American Classical Studies 2, American Philological Association (New York, 1975); as well as L. C. Muellner, *The Meaning of Homeric EYXOMAI through its Formulas* (Innsbruck, 1976); F. Mawet, *Le vocabulaire homérique de la douleur* (Brussels, 1979); Sacks, *Traditional Phrase in Homer*; and S. Edmunds, *Homeric Nēpios* (New York, 1990), all of which develop a careful analysis of semantic field and contextual restrictions to supplement etymological reconstruction.

[10] The phrase is J. Griffin's; see his article "The Epic Cycle and the Uniqueness of Homer," *JHS* 97 (1977): 39–53.

on the lost poems of the Epic Cycle—whose contents are known to us only indirectly, in a summary dating to the second century A.D.[11]—as the crucial clue to finding "das Homerische in Homer."[12] This goal remained elusive to those concerned with specifying the *Iliad*'s literary origins within the Cycle poems' sequence of narratives, as sketched by Proclus's summary, from the genesis of the Trojan War to its aftermath; but their scholarly investigations were stimulating in the scrutiny to which they subjected puzzling and obscure passages of the *Iliad*.[13] And although their efforts to reconstruct the *Iliad*'s specific literary prototypes were inconclusive, their discussions of the common features shared by the *Iliad* and the Cycle poems were fruitful, because in attempting to establish which work constituted model and which transformation or revision the "neoanalyst" approach gave important consideration to the general question of the *Iliad*'s adaptation of preexisting traditional material, such as that inherited by the Cycle poems and (despite their later date) embedded in them.[14]

Especially illuminating along these lines was the work of J. Th. Kakridis, whose studies in the morphology and transformation of story patterns are

---

[11] For the plot summaries of the Cycle poems contained in Proclus's *Chrestomathia*, and testimonia and fragments, see T. W. Allen, ed., *Hymns, Epic Cycle*, vol. 5 of *Homeri Opera* (Oxford, 1912), 93–143.

[12] Georg Schoeck, *Ilias und Aethiopis: Kyklische Motive in homerischer Brechung* (Zurich, 1961), 10.

[13] In fact, the "neoanalyst" approach could have been indispensable in sidestepping debates that equated originality with pure invention, had it not been concerned with pinning down specific textual prototypes for the *Iliad*. The principal exponents of "neoanalysis" include H. Pestalozzi, *Die Achilleis als Quelle der Ilias* (Erlenbach-Zurich, 1945); W. Kullmann, *Die Quellen der Ilias*, Hermes Einzelschriften 14 (Wiesbaden, 1960); W. Schadewaldt, *Von Homers Welt und Werk*, 2d ed. (Stuttgart, 1952), 155ff.; as well as Kakridis, *Homeric Researches*; and Schoeck, *Ilias und Aethiopis*. A discussion of some of the results of the neoanalytic method is contained in K. Reinhardt, *Die Ilias und ihr Dichter* (Göttingen, 1961), 349ff. For recent expositions of the approach as a whole, see A. Heubeck, *Die homerische Frage* (Darmstadt, 1974; reprint, 1988), 40ff.; and W. Kullmann, "Zur Methode der Neoanalyse in der Homerforschung," *Wiener Studien* n.s. 15 (1981): 5–42; a critical assessment is offered by A. Dihle, *Homer-Probleme* (Opladen, 1970); see esp. pp. 19–44 in the latter.

[14] A. Severyns, *Le cycle épique dans l'école d'Aristarque* (Liège, 1928), 313, dates the *Aethiopis* to the eighth century, but even an approximate dating for the Cycle cannot be secure. See Nagy, *Best of the Achaeans*, 42–43. The Cycle exhibits linguistic and stylistic features that indicate that it is in certain respects less developed, or more primitive, than the *Iliad* and *Odyssey* (the *enthen* phenomenon, for example); similarly, the composition of the Cycle poems was not monumental (so the interlocking of their stories suggests). On these features, see the useful contribution of Notopoulos, "Early Greek Oral Poetry," esp. 27–41, which demonstrates the orality of the Cycle poems and arrives independently at the same conclusions as Kakridis, *Homeric Researches*, esp. 90. See as well the discussion in C. H. Whitman, *Homer and the Heroic Tradition* (Cambridge, Mass., 1958), 181–82.

grounded in solid ethnographic empiricism.[15] Subsequent researches showed in detail that the Cycle poems inherit traditions contingent to our *Iliad* and *Odyssey* and preserve story patterns, motifs, and type-scenes that are as archaic as the material in the Homeric poems, to which they are related collaterally, rather than by descent.[16] The Cycle poems and the *Iliad* offer invaluable mutual perspective on the recombination of elements deriving from a common source in myth, which makes possible the continuous evolution of themes and characters appropriate to individual epic treatments—a dynamic process that must be understood as a function not only of the individual genius of a given practitioner of oral poetry, but of the "many centuries of what must have been the most refined sort of elite performer/audience interaction,"[17] through which the focus and central concerns of poetic entities like the *Iliad* and the *Odyssey* could develop, reflecting the developing consciousness of their culture.

Similarly, as we shall see, an important source of comparative evidence offering insight into the themes of the *Iliad* is choral lyric poetry, where treatment of closely related mythic material provides the possibility of recovering archaic poetic traditions not overtly employed by Homer.[18] As Emile Benveniste has demonstrated, we may even see preserved in Pindar poetic traditions whose Indo-European provenance is clearly discernible.[19] On a similar basis, evidence from Hesiodic poetry proves indispensable.[20]

Because the contents of myth must necessarily be adapted to the restrictions and demands of poetic form, such apparently disparate evidence can shed valuable light on the criteria involved in heroic epic's generic regulation of its content. It may illuminate, moreover, any given epic's idiosyncratic handling of content, beyond the first level of adaptation to the formal conventions of epic, to convey the particular ideas and themes of a particular composition— a process that comparison with epic other than the *Iliad* also shows us. It is

---

[15] See note 6 above.

[16] Most important is the early research of Bernard Fenik; see especially his *Iliad X and the Rhesus: The Myth* (Brussels, 1964) and *Typical Battle Scenes*; also Kullman, *Quellen der Ilias*.

[17] Nagy, *Best of the Achaeans*, 79. For a discussion of the relationship between the *Iliad* and the Cycle poems in the realm of character development, see Whitman, *Homer and the Heroic Tradition*, 154–80.

[18] See the discussion of traces of the *kourotrophos*, as confirmed by Pindar, in Sinos, *Meaning of Philos*.

[19] See Benveniste's discussion of *Pythian* 3.40–55 in "La doctrine médicale des Indo-Européens," *RHR* 130 (1945): 5–12.

[20] See G. P. Edwards, *The Language of Hesiod in Its Traditional Context* (Oxford, 1971); and H. Koller, "Das kitharodische Prooimion: Eine formgeschichtliche Untersuchung," *Philologus* 100 (1956): 159–206.

essential to bear in mind these two operative levels of selection in order to escape the automatic conclusion that traditional material that does not have an overt role in the *Iliad* was "not known" to Homer, and, rather, to perceive that either the genre did not encompass it or the thematic development of a particular epic composition did not appropriate it as directly functional. From the latter perspective, as we shall see, the *Aethiopis* is especially interesting for the student of the *Iliad*, featuring as it does an alternative development of the theme of the hero's acquisition of immortality through his mother.

Thus, as noted above, the *Iliad* all but ignores that not inconsequential piece of Iliadic prehistory, the Judgment of Paris; and yet, as we discover in Book 24—although not until then—the Judgment of Paris is indeed known to Homer, but carefully contained in a brief reference.

Similarly, we may note that neither the *Iliad* nor the *Odyssey* overtly includes or elaborates theogonic mythology, although the myth of the struggle for divine sovereignty is a fundamental and pervasive one.[21] But the poems' references to "Zeus, son of Kronos" (as well as to other divine relations) make clear that the *Iliad* and the *Odyssey* assume a divine order dependent upon the myth of succession in heaven. We owe our familiarity with the content of that myth to Hesiod's *Theogony*; without it we would be unaware of the developed "history" of the Olympians implicit in the *Iliad*'s use of Zeus's patronymic.[22] Comparably, it has been shown that the reference to the wall built by the Achaeans in *Iliad* 12 evokes a complex myth of destruction to which even the myth of the Flood has been assimilated; yet we would have no awareness of such a myth without the *Cypria* and the Hesiodic *Catalogue*, as well as comparative evidence from the Near East.[23] In such instances, without a knowledge of mythological material from outside the *Iliad* and the *Odyssey*, not only would we not be able to identify what lies behind the allusions, but we would not even recognize that they are allusions.

For a clearer understanding of Homeric poetics we need to see that the exclusion of such traditional mythological material, or its displacement into more or less oblique references (rather than overt exposition), including its subordination within digressions, is a defining principle by which the *Iliad* demarcates its subject and orients the audience toward its treatment of its themes. Consider the vivid example of this illustrated by the observation

---

[21] See S. Littleton, "The Kingship in Heaven Theme," in *Myth and Law among the Indo-Europeans*, ed. J. Puhvel (Berkeley, 1970), 83–121, esp. 85–93.

[22] See L. M. Slatkin, "Genre and Generation in the *Odyssey*," this volume, pp157–166.

[23] See R. Scodel, "The Achaean Wall and the Myth of Destruction," *HSCP* 86 (1982): 33–50. For further discussion, see pp93–94.

known as Monro's Law, so called after the editor who formulated it in his 1901 edition of the *Odyssey*: that the *Odyssey* "never repeats or refers to any incident related in the *Iliad*."[24] It is scarcely possible to imagine that the *Odyssey* was composed without the slightest knowledge of the *Iliad* and its tradition, given its reliance throughout on the Trojan story for its own background.[25] It is certainly more likely that this "exclusion" of the *Iliad* is part of a deliberate narrative strategy that serves the *Odyssey*'s goal of staking out its own poetic territory in relation to the *Iliad*, according to its own bearings.

It is a reasonable surmise, then, that numerous allusions to traditional material may go unidentified by the modern reader unless special effort is made to locate them. If we make the effort, we will be able to discern both foreground and background in the poems' use of mythology and gain a clearer picture of how that mythology is integrated or subsumed. In this way, we will be able to avoid not only denying to Homer knowledge that we did not realize he possessed, but also—and just as importantly—ascribing to him supposed "inventions" that are in fact part of a received heritage and have been employed to be recognized as such. Thus we may achieve a fuller sense of how the epics' specific relation to tradition informs their self-definition.

---

[24] D. B. Monro, ed., *Homer's Odyssey*, vol. 2, books 13–24 (Oxford, 1901), 325.
[25] D. L. Page imagined this, however. See *The Homeric Odyssey* (Oxford, 1955), 158. For a perspective that refutes Page's argument, see Nagy, *Best of the Achaeans*, chap. 1, esp. 20ff.

CHAPTER 1
The Helplessness of Thetis

In a key passage in Book 1 of the *Iliad* Achilles, in order to obtain from Zeus the favor that will determine the trajectory of the plot, invokes not Athena or Hera, those powerful, inveterate pro-Greeks, but his mother. The *Iliad*'s presentation of Thetis, as we recall, is of a subsidiary deity who is characterized by helplessness and by impotent grief. Her presentation of herself is as the epitome of sorrow and vulnerability in the face of her son's mortality. Consider her lament to her Nereid sisters at 18.54–62.

ὤ μοι ἐγὼ δειλή, ὤ μοι δυσαριστοτόκεια,
ἥ τ' ἐπεὶ ἄρ τέκον υἱὸν ἀμύμονά τε κρατερόν τε
ἔξοχον ἡρώων· ὃ δ' ἀνέδραμεν ἔρνεϊ ἶσος·
τὸν μὲν ἐγὼ θρέψασα, φυτὸν ὡς γουνῷ ἀλωῆς,
νηυσὶν ἐπιπροέηκα κορωνίσιν Ἴλιον εἴσω
Τρωσὶ μαχησόμενον· τὸν δ' οὐχ ὑποδέξομαι αὖτις
οἴκαδε νοστήσαντα δόμον Πηλήϊον εἴσω.
ὄφρα δέ μοι ζώει καὶ ὁρᾷ φάος ἠελίοιο
ἄχνυται, οὐδέ τί οἱ δύναμαι χραισμῆσαι ἰοῦσα.

Alas for my sorrow, alas for my wretched-best-childbearing,
since I bore a child faultless and powerful,
preeminent among heroes; and he grew like a young shoot,
I nourished him like a tree on an orchard's slope,
I sent him forth with the curved ships to Ilion
to fight the Trojans. But never again shall I welcome him
returning home to the house of Peleus.
Still, while he lives and looks on the sunlight
he grieves, and I, going to him, am all unable to help him.

We can hardly fail to question, then, why a figure of evidently minor stature—whose appearances in the poem are few—serves such a crucial function in its plot. Why, that is, does the poem assign to Thetis the awesome role of persuading Zeus to set in motion the events of the *Iliad*, to invert the inevitable course of the fall of Troy? Our initial answer to this might be, because Achilles is her son, and this poem is his story; but a methodologically more fruitful way of posing the question is, why has the *Iliad* taken as its hero the son of Thetis?

Let us begin by recalling the specific terms of Achilles' appeal to his mother in Book 1. He asks Thetis to make his request of Zeus, reminding her of how she saved Zeus when the other Olympians wished to bind him:

ἀλλὰ σύ, εἰ δύνασαί γε, περίσχεο παιδὸς ἑῆος·
ἐλθοῦσ' Οὔλυμπόνδε Δία λίσαι, εἴ ποτε δή τι
ἢ ἔπει ὤνησας κραδίην Διὸς ἠὲ καὶ ἔργῳ.
πολλάκι γάρ σεο πατρὸς ἐνὶ μεγάροισιν ἄκουσα
εὐχομένης, ὅτ' ἔφησθα κελαινεφέϊ Κρονίωνι
οἴη ἐν ἀθανάτοισιν ἀεικέα λοιγὸν ἀμῦναι,
ὁππότε μιν ξυνδῆσαι Ὀλύμπιοι ἤθελον ἄλλοι,
Ἥρη τ' ἠδὲ Ποσειδάων καὶ Παλλὰς Ἀθήνη·
ἀλλὰ σὺ τόν γ' ἐλθοῦσα, θεά, ὑπελύσαο δεσμῶν,
ὦχ' ἑκατόγχειρον καλέσασ' ἐς μακρὸν Ὄλυμπον,
ὃν Βριάρεων καλέουσι θεοί, ἄνδρες δέ τε πάντες
Αἰγαίων'—ὃ γὰρ αὖτε βίην οὗ πατρὸς ἀμείνων—
ὅς ῥα παρὰ Κρονίωνι καθέζετο κύδεϊ γαίων·
τὸν καὶ ὑπέδεισαν μάκαρες θεοὶ οὐδ' ἔτ' ἔδησαν.
τῶν νῦν μιν μνήσασα παρέζεο καὶ λαβὲ γούνων,
αἴ κέν πως ἐθέλησιν ἐπὶ Τρώεσσιν ἀρῆξαι,
τοὺς δὲ κατὰ πρύμνας τε καὶ ἀμφ' ἅλα ἔλσαι Ἀχαιοὺς
κτεινομένους, ἵνα πάντες ἐπαύρωνται βασιλῆος,
γνῷ δὲ καὶ Ἀτρεΐδης εὐρὺ κρείων Ἀγαμέμνων
ἣν ἄτην, ὅ τ' ἄριστον Ἀχαιῶν οὐδὲν ἔτεισεν.

(1.393–412)

But you, if you are able to, protect your own son:
going to Olympos, pray to Zeus, if in fact you ever
aided the heart of Zeus by word or action.
For I have often heard you in my father's halls
avowing it, when you declared that from Kronos'
            son of the dark clouds
you alone among the immortals warded off unseemly destruction
at the time when the other Olympians wanted to bind him,
Hera and Poseidon and Pallas Athena;

but you went, goddess, and set him free from his bonds,
quickly summoning the hundred-handed one to high Olympos,
the one whom the gods call Briareos, but all men call
Aigaion—for he is greater in strength than his father—
who, rejoicing in his glory, sat beside the son of Kronos.
And the blessed gods feared him, and ceased binding Zeus.
Reminding him of these things now sit beside him
    and take his knees,
in the hope that he may somehow be willing to help the Trojans
and the others—the Achaeans—to force against the ships' sterns
    and around the sea
as they are slaughtered, so that they may all benefit
    from their king,
and so that the son of Atreus, wide-ruling
    Agamemnon, may realize
his disastrous folly, that he did not honor the best of
    the Achaeans.

Here we see the *Iliad* alluding to aspects of Thetis's mythology that it does not elaborate and that do not overtly reflect the subject matter of heroic poetry. Why does it do so? The question is twofold: why does it allude to Thetis's power, and why does its reference remain only an allusion? Why does it, moreover, present us with an apparent contradiction: if the mother of Achilles is so helpless, why was she able to rescue Zeus; and if she rescued Zeus, why is she now so helpless? Why does the *Iliad* remind us of Thetis's efficacious power in another context while it presents her to us in an attitude of lamentation and grief without recourse?

In order to establish the proper framework for answering these questions, we begin our poetic archaeology. If we can set the Homeric use of Thetis into the perspective of her mythology, we may be led, as suggested earlier, to a deeper comprehension of Homeric poetics as well as to a richer appreciation of the specific themes associated with Achilles' divine origin. Our best initial index of comparison with the *Iliad*'s Thetis is afforded by Thetis's role in another epic treatment, the Cycle's *Aethiopis*, where we are presented not only with Thetis and Achilles but with a strikingly similar relationship, namely that of the divine Dawn Eos and her son Memnon.

The heroic identity of the Trojan ally Memnon was established in the *Aethiopis*, whose now-lost five books related his single combat against

Achilles, among other events.[1] In the *Aethiopis*, the confrontation between Achilles and Memnon seems to have made use of the same narrative features that characterize the climactic duel of *Iliad* 22: the contest followed upon the death of Achilles' close friend at the hands of his chief Trojan adversary and was preceded by Thetis's prophecy of the outcome.

In the *Aethiopis* Achilles avenged the killing of Nestor's son Antilokhos, whose death at the hands of Memnon is referred to at *Odyssey* 4.187–88. Proclus's summary of this section goes as follows:

Μέμνων δὲ ὁ Ἠοῦς υἱὸς ἔχων ἡφαιστότευκτον πανοπλίαν παραγίνεται τοῖς Τρωσὶ βοηθήσων· καὶ Θέτις τῷ παιδὶ τὰ κατὰ τὸν Μέμνονα προλέγει. καὶ συμβολῆς γενομένης Ἀντίλοχος ὑπὸ Μέμνονος ἀναιρεῖται, ἔπειτα Ἀχιλλεὺς Μέμνονα κτείνει· καὶ τούτῳ μὲν Ἠὼς παρὰ Διὸς αἰτησαμένη ἀθανασίαν δίδωσι.[2]

So Memnon, the son of Eos, wearing armor made by Hephaistos, arrives to aid the Trojans; and Thetis prophesies to her son things about Memnon. In the encounter that takes place Antilokhos is killed by Memnon, whereupon Achilles kills Memnon. Then Eos, having asked Zeus for immortality for Memnon, bestows it on him.

Memnon, although functioning in a role like Hector's, is a mirror image of the Iliadic Achilles. The association of these two heroes, not principally as adversaries but as parallel figures, is reflected in the poetry of Pindar, who more than once describes Memnon in terms appropriate to Achilles in the *Iliad*—singularly so, as they are the terms Achilles uses of himself—calling him Μέμνονος οὐκ ἀπονοστήσαντος ("Memnon who did not return home again").[3] Preeminent among his allies, bearing armor made by Hephaistos, Memnon is the child of a divine mother, Eos, and a mortal father, Tithonos. This last feature was apparently given emphasis by the narrative shape of the *Aethiopis*: the actual presence of the two goddesses Eos and Thetis on the field of battle, contrasting the

---

[1] See Proclus's summary in Allen, *Homeri opera*, vol. 5, 106. For a discussion of the range of its contents, see Severyns, *Cycle épique*, 313–27; also G. L. Huxley, *Greek Epic Poetry: From Eumelos to Panyassis* (London, 1969), 144–49. On the structure and style of the Cycle, see Kullmann, *Quellen der Ilias*, 204ff., esp. 212–14.

[2] See Allen, *Homeri Opera*, vol. 5, 106.

[3] *Nem.* 6.50. See also *Ol.* 2.83 and *Nem.* 3.63. References are to the Oxford edition of Pindar by C. M. Bowra (1947; reprint, 1961).

mortal vulnerability of the opponents with their equal heritage from the mother's immortal line, may have generated the poem's narrative tension.[4] What the *Iliad* treats as a unique and isolating phenomenon, the *Aethiopis* developed along alternative traditional lines, giving prominence to the theme of mortal-immortal duality by doubling its embodiment, in the two heroes Memnon and Achilles.

Iconographic evidence supplements the version of the myth given by the *Aethiopis*. The symmetry of the two heroes is reflected in numerous examples of archaic pictorial art.[5] Vase paintings illustrating the *monomachia* of Memnon and Achilles significantly portray Eos and Thetis facing each other, each at her son's side.[6] The parallelism persists even in the outcome of the duel, although ultimately one hero will win and the other will lose. Vase painting corroborates the existence, in the tradition also shared by the *Aethiopis*, of a *kêrostasia* in which Hermes weighs the *kêres* of Memnon and Achilles in the presence of Eos and Thetis.[7] In the *Aethiopis*, the paired

---

[4] To precisely what effect the *Aethiopis* used this traditional parallelism is of course a matter for speculation; in any case, as the iconographic evidence indicates (see note 6 below), the poem very likely transmitted this inherited confrontation without special innovation. W. Burkert, *Greek Religion* (Cambridge, Mass., 1985), 121, observes, "When Achilles fights with Memnon, the two divine mothers, Thetis and Eos, rush to the scene—this was probably the subject of a pre-*Iliad* epic song."

[5] Pausanias (3.18.12) reports that their confrontation in single combat was depicted on the decorated throne in the sanctuary at Amyklae in Laconia. See the discussion in A. Schneider, *Der troische Sagenkreis in der ältesten griechischen Kunst* (Leipzig, 1886), 143ff; also Pestalozzi, *Achilleis als Quelle der Ilias*, 11.

[6] In his important study *The Iliad in Early Greek Art* (Copenhagen, 1967), K. Friis Johansen, referring to "a well-known type of picture that was very popular in early Greek art, a conventional monomachy framed by two standing female figures," points out that "there can be no doubt that this type was originally invented for the fight between Achilles and Memnon in the presence of their mothers Thetis and Eos" (200–201). According to Pausanias (5.19.2), the scene was also represented on the relief-decorated chest of Kypselos at Olympia: the two heroes duel, each with his mother at his side. M. E. Clark and W. D. E. Coulson discuss the iconography of the *Aethiopis* and its adaptations in painting, as well as the poem's relation to the *Iliad*, in "Memnon and Sarpedon," *MH* 35 (1978): 65–73. See also K. Schefold, *Myth and Legend in Early Greek Art* (London, 1966), 45, together with plate 10 (Athens National Museum 3961.911).

[7] On the iconography of this subject, see *RE* 23.2 (1959), 1442, s.v. "Psychostasie" (E. Wust); G. E. Lung, "Memnon: Archäologische Studien zur *Aethiopis*" (Diss., Bonn, 1912), 14–19; and the discussion in Johansen, *Iliad in Early Greek Art*, 261. The weighing of the fates of Memnon and Achilles is not specifically mentioned by Proclus in his summary, although it provided the subject for Aeschylus' lost play *Psychostasia*, as we learn from schol. A ad 8.70 and Eust. 8. 73.699.31, among others. For views in support of its existence in the *Aethiopis*, see Clark and Coulson, "Memnon and Sarpedon"; B. C. Dietrich, "The Judgment of Zeus," *RhM* 107 (1964): 97–125, esp. 112–14; Severyns, *Cycle épique*, 318–19.

mothers are equated in their involvement in the struggle, each present to protect her son.

The efforts of Thetis and Eos in the *Aethiopis* are essentially identical. In only one respect are Thetis and Eos distinguished in Proclus's summary of the *Aethiopis*. Unlike Eos, Thetis communicates to Achilles some foreknowledge about his adversary: τὰ κατὰ τὸν Μέμνονα προλέγει ("Thetis prophesies to her son about Memnon"). In the reconstruction of the "Memnonis" proposed by neoanalytic studies, Thetis here foretells Achilles' imminent death, which is to follow upon his slaying of Memnon. According to this hypothesis, Thetis's prophetic warning here is the cause of Achilles' abstention from battle, which he will reenter only after the death of his friend Antilokhos.[8] This cannot be a conclusive reading, of course; nevertheless, we can appreciate what prompted it: the certain existence of a scene in the *Aethiopis* in which, at the very least, Thetis intervened with her divine foresight and maternal solicitude on behalf of her son's safety.

Eos requests of Zeus, and obtains, immortality for Memnon. Thetis does not actually ask Zeus for immortality for Achilles; but she herself "having snatched her son away from the pyre, transports him to the White Island."[9] Like Elysion, the White Island represents the refuge of immortality for heroes, where they live on once they have not avoided but—even better—transcended death.[10]

The *Aethiopis*, then, emphasized the hero's divine heritage as a way of separating him from ordinary human existence and his access to communication with the gods as a way of resolving the conflict between heroic stature and mortal limitation.

---

[8] Schoeck, *Ilias und Aethiopis*, 38–48, contributes the interesting observation that the *Iliad* makes reference to a prophecy from Thetis precisely at those junctures where the question of Achilles' return to battle arises, e.g., 11.790ff.; 16.36–50. He argues that the *Iliad* in this way adverts to a "Memnonis" prototype, in which Thetis's prophecy was the specific cause of Achilles' absence from battle; that is, Achilles absented himself from battle at his mother's request.

[9] See Allen, *Homeri opera*, vol. 5, 106.

[10] The use of the White Island motif, like that of Elysion at *Odyssey* 4.563, is an acknowledgment of the religious and social phenomenon of the hero-cult, which is generally excluded from direct reference in epic. E. Rohde, *Psyche: Seelencult und Unsterblichkeitsglaube der Griechen*, vol. 2, 4th ed. (Freiburg, 1898; Tübingen, 1907), 371, calls Leuke a "Sonderelysion" for Achilles. Rohde offers a discussion of the thematic equivalence of Leuke, Elysion, and the Isles of the Blessed on pp. 365–78. On Elysion as a cult concept, see W. Burkert, "Elysion," *Glotta* 39 (1961): 208–13; and Th. Hadzisteliou Price, "Hero-Cult and Homer," *Historia* 22 (1973): 133–34. On the traditional poetic diction of "snatching," or abducting, used (at least by Proclus) to describe Thetis's action here, see note 28 below.

The tradition represented by the *Aethiopis* and by our iconographic examples thus posits an identity not only between Achilles and Memnon but between Thetis and Eos, based on their roles as immortal guardians and protectors of their mortal children. From a narrative standpoint this parallelism is more than an instance of the Cycle's fondness for repetition or doublets.[11] The *Aethiopis* shows us not a recapitulation of a prior situation by a subsequent one, but a rendering of the mythological equation between the two figures as a simultaneous juxtaposition, a mirroring, in which each reflects, and must assume the dimensions of, her counterpart.

The virtual identity of the two mothers asserted by the tradition transmitted by the *Aethiopis* as well as by pictorial representations reinforces the uniqueness of Thetis in the *Iliad*, the incomparable singularity of her position, to which the poem explicitly calls attention at 18.429–34:

> Ἥφαιστ', ἦ ἄρα δή τις, ὅσαι θεαί εἰσ' ἐν Ὀλύμπῳ,
> τοσσάδ' ἐνὶ φρεσὶν ᾗσιν ἀνέσχετο κήδεα λυγρά,
> ὅσσ' ἐμοὶ ἐκ πασέων Κρονίδης Ζεὺς ἄλγε' ἔδωκεν;
> ἐκ μέν μ' ἀλλάων ἁλιάων ἀνδρὶ δάμασσεν,
> Αἰακίδῃ Πηλῆϊ, καὶ ἔτλην ἀνέρος εὐνὴν
> πολλὰ μάλ' οὐκ ἐθέλουσα.

> Hephaistos, is there anyone, of all the goddesses on Olympos,
> who has endured so many baneful sorrows in her heart,
> as many as the griefs Zeus the son of Kronos has
>   given me beyond all others?
> Of all the daughters of the sea he forced on me a mortal man,
> Aiakos' son Peleus, and I endured the bed of a mortal man
> Utterly unwilling though I was.

But if the *Iliad* treats Thetis's position as unparalleled, then an examination of its treatment in the light of the sources of the Thetis-Eos equation can serve as an introduction to the *Iliad*'s process of interpreting and selectively shaping its mythology, preserving for us aspects of Thetis that elucidate her role in the *Iliad* even when Eos is not present to help evoke them.

Comparative evidence indicates the connection of several female deities who are notable in Greek and Indic mythologies to the prototype of an Indo-

---

[11] E. Howald examines doubling as a feature of the evolution and transmission of myth in *Der Mythos als Dichtung* (Zurich, 1937); on doublets in the Cycle in particular, see Howald's *Der Dichter der Ilias* (Erlenbach-Zurich, 1946), 125.

European Dawn goddess, *Ausos.[12] The representatives of this important Indo-European figure who most closely assume her functions in their respective poetic traditions are Indic Uṣas and Greek Eos. The shared attributes of these Greek and Indic Dawn goddesses, which link them to their prototype, yield a still more productive legacy in Greek epic, however, where they are inherited by Aphrodite, among others.

In analyzing the elements that Aphrodite and Eos share and that identify them (with Uṣas) as descendants of the Indo-European Dawn goddess, we recognize motifs that are significant in the story of Thetis.[13] Chief among these is the association of the immortal goddess with a mortal lover.[14] Like Uṣas in the Vedic hymns, Eos unites with various lovers, among whom Tithonos is prominent in epic; Aphrodite has union with several, notably Anchises; and Thetis is joined to Peleus. Although the outcome of a love relationship between immortal and mortal may be benign, the potential for extraordinary pathos in such a story is clear. In these instances the inherent tension resulting from the juxtaposition of immortal and mortal is involved with a specific and fundamental connection between the timeless goddesses and time itself.

The function of the Dawn goddess in Indo-European religious traditions, and hence the inherited function of Eos, is the model for this connection. Eos brings the day into being: in a sense she creates time, as at *Odyssey* 5.390:

ἀλλ' ὅτε δὴ τρίτον ἦμαρ ἐϋπλόκαμος τέλεσ' Ἠώς

but when beautiful-haired Dawn had accomplished the third day

As she brings the day into existence and, in effect, controls time, time controls the lives of men, by aging them; yet the goddess herself is unaging,

---

[12] On the etymology of Attic Ἔως (= Ionic Ἠώς), see P. Chantraine, *Dictionnaire étymologique de la langue grecque* (Paris, 1968), 394–95.

[13] The evidence for the Indo-European origins of Aphrodite, Eos, and Uṣas is presented in D. D. Boedeker, *Aphrodite's Entry into Greek Epic* (Leiden, 1974), whose subject is Greek epic's integration of Aphrodite's inherited features, through diction and theme, into its development of her character and role. See also the observations in P. Friedrich, *The Meaning of Aphrodite* (Chicago, 1978), who holds that "the Proto-Indo-European goddess of dawn was one of several main sources for the Greek Aphrodite" (31).

[14] Boedeker, *Aphrodite's Entry*, 67, notes: "The tradition of the mortal lover of the Dawn-goddess is an old one; in Greek epic it is surely the most obvious aspect of Eos' mythology. Comparative evidence from the Ṛg-Veda indicates that this feature of solar mythology dates back to common Indo-European, although in Greek myth it may have been amplified beyond its original importance." See also C. P. Segal, "The Homeric Hymn to Aphrodite: A Structuralist Approach," *CW* 67 (1974): 205–12.

ever-renewed.[15] Eos's epithet ἠριγένεια (*êrigeneia*, "early-born") expresses
the contrast between the consequences for men of her activity, and her own
freedom from those consequences. From the human point of view, she is not
simply immortal; she is the agent of the process by which the meaning of
mortality is fulfilled.

Eos and her lovers serve as the model for goddess-mortal relationships,
with their essential antithesis between the timelessness of the goddess and
the temporality of her lover.[16] Eos and her lovers are even cited by characters
within epic as exemplary of such relationships. Aphrodite herself tells Eos's
story (*Hymn. Hom. Aphr.* 218–38); Kalypso knows it as well, even though, as
the *Odyssey* points out, she lives very far away (*Od.* 5.121); and both compare
it to their own stories. The marriage of Thetis to Peleus exhibits the same
antithetical pattern. Because Eos typifies such goddess-mortal relationships,
Thetis is perceived synchronically as being connected with her, as in the
Aethiopis, and thus shares diction-al features associated with her—although
Thetis cannot definitively be shown, as Eos has been, to be a direct descendant, or hypostasis, of the Indo-European Dawn goddess; their relationship is
structurally homologous, rather than historical.

In Greek epic, the themes attached to the goddess and her mortal lover
are recapitulated, with much greater emphasis, in the relationship between
the goddess and her son, the offspring of her union with her mortal lover. Eos
and Memnon, as an instance of this, reinforce the Eos-Thetis parallel. But in
the case of Eos, the pattern of whose relationship with Tithonos is repeated
in part with Memnon—when she requests and obtains his immortality—the
erotic aspect of her mythology dominates. Thetis's erotic aspect, discernible
(as we shall see) in the tradition followed by Pindar and Aeschylus, where
both mortal and immortal partners woo her, is subordinated to her maternal
aspect, as she appears in the *Iliad*.

In the *Iliad*, the collocation of Thetis's activities with early morning may
reflect the association with Eos and her time-related function, inherited from
Indo-European tradition. At 18.136, Thetis tells Achilles that she will seek
armor from Hephaistos for him at dawn: ἠῶθεν γὰρ νεῦμαι ἅμ' ἠελίῳ ἀνιόντι
("for I shall return at dawn, with the sun's rising").[17] At 1.497, when Thetis

---

[15] On the similarly ambivalent nature of the Indic Dawn goddess Uṣas, see A. K. Coomaraswamy, "The
Darker Side of Dawn," *Smithsonian Miscellaneous Collections* 94.1 (1935): 1–18, esp. 4–6.
[16] See Boedeker, *Aphrodite's Entry*, 69.
[17] This association is recalled by Apollonius (*Argon.* 4.841).

travels to Olympos to ask Zeus for the favor on behalf of Achilles, the adjective ἠερίη (*êeriê*) is used to describe her:

> ἥ γ᾽ ἀνεδύσετο κῦμα θαλάσσης.
> ἠερίη δ᾽ ἀνέβη μέγαν οὐρανὸν Οὔλυμπόν τε.
>
> (1.496–97)

> she rose from the sea's wave
> and early in the morning ascended to the great sky and Olympos.

Later, Hera rebukes Zeus for conferring with Thetis at the latter's request, saying:

> νῦν δ᾽ αἰνῶς δείδοικα κατὰ φρένα μή σε παρείπῃ
> ἀργυρόπεζα Θέτις θυγάτηρ ἁλίοιο γέροντος·
> ἠερίη γὰρ σοί γε παρέζετο καὶ λάβε γούνων.
>
> (1.555–57)

> But now I fear dreadfully that she won you over,
> silver-footed Thetis, daughter of the old man of the sea,
> for early in the morning she sat with you and clasped your knees.

Apart from being used of Thetis, ἠερίη occurs in the *Iliad* only once (3.7). Like Eos's epithet ἠριγένεια (*êrigeneia*, "early-born"), it may be related to ἦρι (*êri*).[18] The use of ἠερίη and Thetis's early morning travels may evoke her ties to *Êôs êrigeneia* and the connection of their power with time, the defining fact of human life.

The reason that such diction and the motifs to which it is attached have worked their way into the narrative is to be found in the themes of the epic as a whole.[19] A preeminent concern of our *Iliad* is the problem of mortality.

---

[18] See the discussion in Chantraine, *Dictionnaire étymologique*, 407. Chantraine observes that the usage of ἠερίη reflects alternative etymologies, both of which are susceptible to this morphology: *aer* and *awer*. These would yield separate meanings, either "early in the morning" or "mistlike." Both are appropriate to Thetis. She does much of her traveling at dawn, but she also rises from the sea ἠΰτ᾽ ὀμίχλη ("like a mist") at 1.359. In its epic usage in association with Thetis, ἠερίη has the resonance of both meanings, not as ambiguous but as surcharged with meaning: its association with her conflates the two possibilities. Schoeck, *Ilias und Aethiopis*, 41, comments, "Schon im Altertum war es strittig, ob ἠερίη hier [1.497] 'in der Morgenfrühe' oder 'wie Luft' heisse. Es ist denkbar, daß Homer selber mit den zwei Bedeutungen spielt." On the connection of these motifs with Okeanos, see Boedeker, *Aphrodite's Entry*, 69ff.

[19] On the relationship between the words ἥρως ("hero") and ὥρα ("season, seasonality"), see W. Pötscher, "Hera und Heros," *RhM* 104 (1961): 302–55; on the association of the hero and

While it is characteristic of epic not to confine its thematic expression to its principal character, the *Iliad* centers definitively in the monumental figure of Achilles, whose life represents the fullest embodiment of this theme.[20] In our *Iliad*, the mainspring of Achilles' developing sense of values is his consciousness of the brevity of human life, and especially the extreme brevity that the war enforces. He finds the meaning of any situation by measuring it against the irreducible fact of the brevity of life. In the course of the poem, the value that he assigns to such meaning will be transformed. Because his life will be short, his dishonor at the hands of Agamemnon is initially seen to be all the more important; later, with Achilles' increased perspective on what it means to have a short life, honor from Agamemnon will have no value for him.

From the outset, the *Iliad* presents Achilles as possessing a powerful, personal sense of his own mortality. His first assertion of this is to Thetis, when he originally invokes her assistance at 1.352:

μῆτερ, ἐπεί μ' ἔτεκές γε μινυνθάδιόν περ ἐόντα

Mother, since you did bear me to be short-lived.

That the adjective μινυνθάδιος (*minunthadios,* "short-lived") is not just a neutral term for describing anyone mortal but is highly charged and refers pointedly to Achilles' own imminent death is evident from its other occurrences in the poem. Elsewhere only Lykaon calls himself *minunthadios* (21.84), when he is about to die at Achilles' hands. At 15.612, Hektor is said to be "about to be" *minunthadios,* which the subsequent lines make explicit:[21]

---

[20] ὥρα as a fundamental theme in Greek myth, see Sinos, *Meaning of Philos,* 13–26.

Just as the *Odyssey* is concerned with many variations on the theme of return to home and self—including the "homecomings" of Penelope, Agamemnon, Menelaos, Nestor, and Odysseus's companions—yet focuses on the *nostos* of Odysseus, so the *Iliad* presents numerous individual histories to illustrate the encompassing view expressed at 6.146–49:

οἵη περ φύλλων γενεή, τοίη δὲ καὶ ἀνδρῶν.
φύλλα τὰ μέν τ' ἄνεμος χαμάδις χέει, ἄλλα δέ θ' ὕλη
τηλεθόωσα φύει, ἔαρος δ' ἐπιγίγνεται ὥρη·
ὣς ἀνδρῶν γενεὴ ἣ μὲν φύει ἣ δ' ἀπολήγει.

As is the generation of leaves, so is that of men.
The wind showers the leaves to the ground,
but the budding wood blossoms, and the season of Spring arrives.
So one generation of men flourishes and the other fades away.

[21] Hektor and Lykaon are the two characters to whom Achilles expresses the necessity of recognizing and accepting death; as he himself has done it, so they must do it as well. The adjective is used otherwise only of two Trojan warriors, Simoeisios and Hippothoos, at the precise point at which each meets his death (4.478 = 17.302).

μινυνθάδιος γὰρ ἔμελλεν
ἔσσεσθ’· ἤδη γάρ οἱ ἐπόρνυε μόρσιμον ἦμαρ
Παλλὰς Ἀθηναίη ὑπὸ Πηλεΐδαο βίηφιν.

(15.612–14)

So Hektor was to be *minunthadios*;
for now Pallas Athena was already driving his death day
upon him, beneath the strength of the son of Peleus.

Thetis's reply in Book 1 more than confirms the insight that ultimately, in Book 24, enables Achilles to place his brief existence in the context of others' lives—but through which, initially, he is isolated as epic poetry isolates no other single hero. His role and his self-perception converge, whereby the plot of the *Iliad* is multiply determined. Thetis's response at 1.416,

ἐπεί νύ τοι αἶσα μίνυνθά περ, οὔ τι μάλα δήν

since now your destiny is brief, of no length,

uniquely then speaks of an αἶσα (*aisa*, "destiny, allotment") that is brief, as though Achilles' *aisa*—his final goal, that which is destined for him in the end—were precisely identical with the process by which it is attained. Elsewhere, *aisa* is either the literal end of life (as at 24.428, 750) or it is the principle of destiny, the index of whether one's actions are appropriate to one's nature. A hero can act either *kata* or *huper aisan*—"according to" or "beyond, in contravention of" *aisa*—or he can have an evil *aisa*, but only Achilles has a *brief aisa*—a destiny that is nothing other than the span of his life.[22]

Equally remarkable is Thetis's use of the compound ὠκύμορος (*ôkumoros*), as her lament continues:

νῦν δ’ ἅμα τ’ ὠκύμορος καὶ ὀϊζυρὸς περὶ πάντων
ἔπλεο·

(1.417–18)

For now you are swift in fate and wretched beyond all men.

Like *aisa*, the word *ôkumoros* acquires a new meaning when used of Achilles. Its principal meaning appears at 15.441, where Ajax uses it of the arrows belonging to the archer Teucer:

---

[22] See page 84.

> ποῦ νύ τοι ἰοὶ
> ὠκύμοροι καὶ τόξον, ὅ τοι πόρε Φοῖβος Ἀπόλλων;
>
> (15.440–41)

> Where now are your arrows
> of quick death and the bow that Phoibos Apollo gave you?

Here the original meaning, "bringing swift death," is evident.[23] But elsewhere in the poem this adjective is applied only to Achilles and only by Thetis, who repeats it at 18.95, replying or prophesying in response to Achilles' declaration to avenge Patroklos's death:

> ὠκύμορος δή μοι, τέκος, ἔσσεαι, οἷ᾽ ἀγορεύεις·

> Then you will be swift in fate, my child, from what you say.

Later in Book 18, requesting the aid of Hephaistos, she says:

> αἴ κ᾽ ἐθέλησθα
> υἱεῖ ἐμῷ ὠκυμόρῳ δόμεν ἀσπίδα
>
> (18.457–58)

> if you are willing to give a shield to my son swift in fate.

Used of Achilles, the word describes not the agent but the victim of *moros*. In effect both functions are joined in Achilles, who participates in bringing about his own swift death. Because *moros* can mean destiny as well as death, *ôkumoros* characterizing Achilles could be said to mean "swiftly fated" and to denote the same idea expressed by *aisa minuntha*, namely, that for Achilles destiny is a synonym for life span.

Achilles, then, has special diction that distinguishes his experience as the limiting case of the experience of mortality. Its use by Thetis lays great stress on this; it is the essence of her appeal to Zeus:

> τίμησόν μοι υἱὸν, ὃς ὠκυμορώτατος ἄλλων
> ἔπλετ᾽·
>
> (1.505–6)

> Honor my son who is swiftest in death of all mortals.

---

[23] This meaning is confirmed by the *Odyssey*'s use of the adjective at 22.75, where it is used of the arrows aimed against the suitors by Odysseus.

The poem uses Thetis to view Achilles' life from a cosmic perspective that enhances its stature as it throws into relief its brevity. Her close connection with Achilles' recognition of his mortal condition—and with all the most human aspects of his nature—contrasts sharply with the role shared by Eos and Thetis in the *Aethiopis*, which emphasized their sons' access to divinity. It shows as well how Achilles has been developed in the *Iliad* beyond the stage in which he and Memnon were correspondingly parallel and minimally differentiated from each other.

The *Iliad* establishes Achilles as the limiting case of human brevity and thus insists on the disparity between his situation and the timelessness of Thetis.[24] Unlike the *Aethiopis*, however, the *Iliad* does so not in order to value more highly the acquisition of immortality but to define the boundaries of human life that it accepts as final. Thetis and her mythology are put to radically different use in the *Iliad*. Through her the *Iliad* offers not the immortality of the *Aethiopis*, but a conception of heroic stature as inseparable from human limitation and of heroic experience as a metaphor for the condition of mortality, with all its contradictions. No hero in the *Iliad* is given immortality, which would be utterly incompatible with such a perspective; the possibility is entirely absent. The premise of the poem, as conveyed through the characters' own perceptions, is that the idea of immortality expresses only the extreme of imagination against which the reality of human potential and limitation is measured and comprehended.[25]

Achilles' discovery of identity—of values, of morality—is inseparable from the apprehension of mortality; that discovery becomes necessary and has meaning only if immortality is precluded. The battle as a context for events to be celebrated in epic may well have originated as a setting for descriptions of extraordinary exploits involving physical prowess and designating a hierarchy of heroes. But where the life-and-death import of the action may in other epic treatments have been only a framework, in the *Iliad* it becomes the subject itself. The heroism of Achilles emerges not so much because his exploits distinguish him as because the battle serves as a setting in which every choice, every

---

[24] At 17.446ff. Zeus pities the horses of Peleus because, although immortal, they are yoked to the lives of men who, being mortal, are especially given over to suffering (ὀϊζυρώτεροι). But it is Achilles who has been called ὠκύμορος καὶ ὀϊζυρὸς περὶ πάντων, at 1.417; so that what mortals are by nature, Achilles is *most*.

[25] As expressed, for instance, in the famous speech of Sarpedon to Glaukos at 12.309–28. On this subject, see the penetrating discussion of Whitman, *Homer and the Heroic Tradition*, 181–220; see as well the insights in S. L. Schein, *The Mortal Hero: An Introduction to Homer's Iliad* (Berkeley, 1984), 67–84.

action, becomes all-important—an arena where one's life is most closely bound to the lives of others and where, for that reason, the definition of the self comes urgently into question. Prowess becomes peripheral to the crisis of the self relative to one's own expectations and the lives of others.

To speak of the evolution of the *Iliad*, therefore, is to speak of the growth of the idea of the hero. The very story the poem tells embodies that evolution, describing the coming into being of the new hero. It tells the story of the making of its own subject matter. This is what Thetis's request to Zeus in *Iliad* 1 signifies, in contrast to Eos's in the *Aethiopis*. For in this sense, what Thetis asks Zeus to give Achilles is the opportunity to become the hero of the *Iliad*, to create the terms by which heroism will be redefined.

The *Iliad* explores the theme of mortality precisely by evoking and transforming an important traditional motif in such a way that the transformation expresses the premise of the poem. Placed in the context of the tradition the *Iliad* evokes—the equation of Thetis and Eos seeking immortality for their sons— Thetis's appeals to Zeus and later to Hephaistos on behalf of Achilles' vulnerability can be understood as significant examples of how the poem develops its major theme.

Certain elements in the constellation of motifs common to the divinities sharing the mythology of the Dawn goddess are preserved by the *Iliad*; others are significantly reworked. The motif of the goddess's protection of the mortal hero she loves is a central traditional feature shared by the immortal mothers (and lovers) who inherit, or are assimilated to, the mythology of the Dawn goddess.[26] Its variations, apart from Eos and Thetis in the *Aethiopis*, include Kalypso in the *Odyssey* and Aphrodite in the *Homeric Hymn to Aphrodite* as well as in the *Iliad*.[27] This tradition is well known to the *Iliad*, where in two dramatic episodes Aphrodite acts to protect her favorites from imminent danger, snatching them away from battle at the crucial moment. In Book 3 she rescues Paris as he is about to be overpowered by Menelaos:

---

[26] Sinos, *Meaning of Philos*, has shown in detail that the *kourotrophos* or nurturing function of the goddess, revealed in the diction of vegetal growth, as, for example, at *Iliad* 18.437–38, is apparent in the relationship in cult between the *kourotrophos* goddess and the *kouros*. The protection motif is a correlate of this function in myth. See also R. Merkelbach, "ΚΟΡΟΣ," *ZPE* 8 (1971): 80; and P. Vidal-Naquet, "Le chasseur noir et l'origine de l'éphébie athénienne," *Économies-sociétés-civilisations* 23 (1968): 947–49.

[27] On the related attributes of these goddesses, see Boedeker, *Aphrodite's Entry*, 64–84. Apart from the Dawn goddess hypostases, Demeter in the *Homeric Hymn to Demeter* appears in the role of *kourotrophos* to Demophon; see the commentary ad 231–55 (esp. 237ff. with remarks on Achilles and Thetis) in N. J. Richardson, ed., *The Homeric Hymn to Demeter* (Oxford, 1974; reprint, 1979), 231ff.

τὸν δ' ἐξήρπαξ' Ἀφροδίτη
ῥεῖα μάλ' ὥς τε θεός, ἐκάλυψε δ' ἄρ' ἠέρι πολλῇ,
κὰδ δ' εἷσ' ἐν θαλάμῳ εὐώδεϊ κηώεντι.

(3.380–82)

But Aphrodite snatched him up
easily as a god may, and enclosed him in a dense mist
and put him down in his fragrant bedchamber.

In Book 5 it is Aeneas whom she saves, from the onslaught of Diomedes:

ἀμφὶ δ' ἑὸν φίλον υἱὸν ἐχεύατο πήχεε λευκώ,
πρόσθε δέ οἱ πέπλοιο φαεινοῦ πτύγμ' ἐκάλυψεν,
ἕρκος ἔμεν βελέων, μή τις Δαναῶν ταχυπώλων
χαλκὸν ἐνὶ στήθεσσι βαλὼν ἐκ θυμὸν ἕλοιτο.
Ἡ μὲν ἑὸν φίλον υἱὸν ὑπεξέφερεν πολέμοιο·

(5.314–18)

and around her dear son she threw her white arms,
and in front of him she wrapped a fold of her shining robe,
to be a shield against weapons, lest any of the
Danaans with quick horses
should take his life from him, striking bronze into his chest.
So she bore her dear son away from the battle.

To snatch a hero from danger, to protect him from death, however, offers a paradox of which the *Iliad* and *Odyssey* are conscious: that preserving a hero from death means denying him a heroic life.[28] Thus Kalypso, who compares her intention toward Odysseus with Eos's abduction of Orion,[29] wants by sequestering Odysseus to offer him immortality; but this would inevitably mean the loss of his goal, the impossibility of completing the travels, the denial of his identity. From a perspective that is as intrinsic to the *Odyssey* as to the *Iliad*, it would mean the extinction of heroic subject matter, the negation of epic. Kalypso, "the concealer," uses persuasive arguments in her attempt to hide Odysseus from mortality. Her ultimate failure measures

---

[28] For an analysis of the structure and diction of similar episodes of abduction and "preservation," especially the ambivalence inherent in such episodes' use of the particular terminology of snatching, kidnapping, and concealing, see Nagy, *Greek Mythology and Poetics*, 223–62, esp. 242–57. This same terminology (as transmitted by Proclus, at any rate) is used to designate Thetis's action in the *Aethiopis* in snatching Achilles from the pyre (N.B. the use of *anarpasasa*), after which she "preserves" him on the White Island.

[29] *Od.* 5.121–24.

the hero's commitment to his mortal existence—not, as she believes, the Olympian gods' jealousy, but their participation in human values.

Aphrodite, on the other hand, is a successful concealer, shielding her favorites by hiding them, Paris in the cloud of mist and Aeneas in her flowing robe.[30] She enters the battle swiftly at the critical moment to save the life of her son, or, in the case of Paris, her protégé:

Καί νύ κεν ἔνθ᾽ ἀπόλοιτο ἄναξ ἀνδρῶν Αἰνείας,
εἰ μὴ ἄρ᾽ ὀξὺ νόησε Διὸς θυγάτηρ Ἀφροδίτη,
μήτηρ, ἥ μιν ὑπ᾽ Ἀγχίσῃ τέκε βουκολέοντι·

(5.311–13)

And now Aeneas lord of men would have perished there
if the daughter of Zeus, Aphrodite, had not quickly noticed him,
his mother, who bore him to Anchises the oxherd.

She is expressly credited with protecting Aeneas from death, just as earlier she contrives Paris's escape from Menelaos at the fatal instant:

καί νύ κεν εἴρυσσέν τε καὶ ἄσπετον ἤρατο κῦδος,
εἰ μὴ ἄρ᾽ ὀξὺ νόησε Διὸς θυγάτηρ Ἀφροδίτη,
ἥ οἱ ῥῆξεν ἱμάντα βοὸς ἶφι κταμένοιο·

(3.373–75)

And now [Menelaos] would have dragged him off and won an
indelible triumph,
if the daughter of Zeus, Aphrodite, had not quickly noticed him.
She broke for him the oxhide chinstrap.

Thetis, like Kalypso and Aphrodite, is associated by the *Iliad* with impenetrable clouds and with veils and with concealment. But the *Iliad* does not pursue the parallelism of this aspect of their mythology. Thetis never spirits Achilles away from danger, and she never tempts him with immortality. On the contrary, it is she who states the human limits of his choice. Repeatedly, the absoluteness of the *Iliad*'s rejection of the idea of immortality emerges from its treatment, in relation to Achilles, of this protection motif, which figures so importantly in the immortal goddess-mortal lover or son stories and which has a preeminent place in Thetis's mythology.

---

[30] It is perhaps significant, however, that while both Aphrodite's beneficiaries do escape destruction and survive the *Iliad*, their individual heroism, from an epic standpoint, has been permanently compromised.

Thetis acts on behalf of Achilles in the *Iliad* only after asserting repeatedly the knowledge that he must die and finally, in Book 18, the certainty that it is to happen soon. It is only then, after establishing her awareness of Achilles' vulnerability, her understanding that he cannot be saved, that she makes her gesture toward protecting him. She asks Hephaistos to create new armor for him, to replace the old armor worn by Patroklos and lost to Hektor. In contrast to the rescue efforts by which Aphrodite removes her man from danger, Thetis "protects" Achilles by providing him with the means to reenter the battle from which he will not return. The shield, supreme implement of "safety," becomes the instrument of his fatality. In its implications, this favor from Hephaistos corresponds to the initial one requested of Zeus: much as Zeus's acquiescence to Thetis commits Achilles to his death at Troy, so Hephaistos's repayment of what he owes Thetis equips her son for destruction and brings him closer to it.[31]

The *Iliad*'s treatment of the *hoplopoiia* is underscored by the evident existence of a similar scene in the *Aethiopis* in which Memnon entered the battle wearing ἡφαιστότευκτον πανοπλίαν, prior to Eos's successful plea for his immortality. In the *Aethiopis*, apparently, Memnon's divine armor anticipated the successful intervention of divinity and was emblematic of its redemptive patronage. It confirmed Memnon's special relationship with the gods, which would make immortality possible for him.[32]

In the *Iliad*, the implement of protection made by Hephaistos at Thetis's request is the shield, which only Achilles can endure to look at when Thetis brings it to him. But it precisely does not fulfill for Achilles, as it did for Memnon, the promise of ultimate divine preservation through the agency of his mother.[33] The *Iliad*'s rejection of this outcome for Achilles, and hence for its conception of heroism, is expressly stated. Thetis prefaces her request of Hephaistos with a summary of the *Iliad* up to that juncture; the *Iliad*

---

[31] As we shall see below (p55), Thetis is similarly owed a favor by Dionysos, whom she is said to have rescued as she did Hephaistos. Strikingly, his *antidōron* equally does nothing other than attest to Achilles' mortality: it is the golden urn in which Achilles' bones will lie with those of Patroklos.

[32] See Griffin, "Epic Cycle and Uniqueness of Homer," 39–53, esp. 42–43 on immortality as a feature of the Cycle poems.

[33] Much has been written on the importance of a hero's armor as an emblem of his warrior identity; see Ph. J. Kakridis, "Achilleus Rüstung," *Hermes* 89 (1961): 288–97, esp. 292–93; on the shield in particular see W. Leaf, ed., *The Iliad*, vol. 1, 2d ed. (London, 1902), 470. In *The Arms of Achilles and Homeric Compositional Technique* (Leiden, 1975), R. Shannon makes these connections: "Peleus' spear links Achilles with his mortal ancestry; his new armor links him with his immortal parent and, through her, with Hephaistos, its forger, and his attribute, fire" (31).

recapitulates itself here from Thetis's viewpoint, so that it represents itself as a mother's narrative about her son:

> κούρην ἥν ἄρα οἱ γέρας ἔξελον υἷες Ἀχαιῶν,
> τὴν ἄψ ἐκ χειρῶν ἔλετο κρείων Ἀγαμέμνων.
> ἤτοι ὁ τῆς ἀχέων φρένας ἔφθιεν· αὐτὰρ Ἀχαιοὺς
> Τρῶες ἐπὶ πρύμνῃσιν ἐείλεον, οὐδὲ θύραζε
> εἴων ἐξιέναι· τὸν δὲ λίσσοντο γέροντες
> Ἀργείων, καὶ πολλὰ περικλυτὰ δῶρ' ὀνόμαζον.
> ἔνθ' αὐτὸς μὲν ἔπειτ' ἠναίνετο λοιγὸν ἀμῦναι,
> αὐτὰρ ὁ Πάτροκλον περὶ μὲν τὰ ἃ τεύχεα ἔσσε,
> πέμπε δέ μιν πόλεμόνδε, πολὺν δ' ἅμα λαὸν ὄπασσε.
> πᾶν δ' ἦμαρ μάρναντο περὶ Σκαιῇσι πύλῃσι·
> καί νύ κεν αὐτῆμαρ πόλιν ἔπραθον, εἰ μὴ Ἀπόλλων
> πολλὰ κακὰ ῥέξαντα Μενοιτίου ἄλκιμον υἱὸν
> ἔκταν' ἐνὶ προμάχοισι καὶ Ἕκτορι κῦδος ἔδωκε.

(18.444–56)

The girl whom the sons of the Achaeans picked out
          for him as a prize,
the ruler Agamemnon took back from his hands.
Grieving for her he was wearing away his heart; but
the Trojans hemmed in the Achaeans by the ships' sterns
and were not allowing them to go beyond; and the
          Achaean elders
beseeched him, and named many splendid gifts.
He himself then refused to ward off destruction,
but he dressed Patroklos in his armor
and sent him into battle, and supplied many people with him.
All day they fought around the Skaian gates,
and on that same day would have sacked the city, if
          Apollo had not
killed the powerful son of Menoitios when he had
          caused much harm,
in the front ranks, and given the victory to Hektor.

The Olympian reply, however compassionate, reconfirms the inevitability of Achilles' imminent death; divine collaboration on his behalf may honor him and enhance his stature, but it cannot save him and does not propose to. Hephaistos replies:

θάρσει· μή τοι ταῦτα μετὰ φρεσὶ σῇσι μελόντων.
αἲ γάρ μιν θανάτοιο δυσηχέος ὧδε δυναίμην
νόσφιν ἀποκρύψαι, ὅτε μιν μόρος αἰνὸς ἱκάνοι,
ὥς οἱ τεύχεα καλὰ παρέσσεται, οἷά τις αὖτε
ἀνθρώπων πολέων θαυμάσσεται, ὅς κεν ἴδηται.

$$\text{(18.463–67)}$$

Take heart; do not let these things distress your thoughts.
If only I were able to hide him away
from grievous death, when dire fate overtakes him,
as surely as there will be beautiful armor for him, such as
anyone among many mortal men will marvel at, whoever sees it.

Through Thetis the *Iliad* evokes this constellation of traditional elements—the divine armor, the protection motif—in order to violate conventional expectations of their potency, and it does so for the sake of the primacy of the theme of mortality, as Thetis's lament to the Nereids at 18.54–64 explicitly and deliberately reminds us:

ὤ μοι ἐγὼ δειλή, ὤ μοι δυσαριστοτόκεια,
ἥ τ' ἐπεὶ ἄρ τέκον υἱὸν ἀμύμονά τε κρατερόν τε
ἔξοχον ἡρώων· ὃ δ' ἀνέδραμεν ἔρνεϊ ἶσος·
τὸν μὲν ἐγὼ θρέψασα, φυτὸν ὣς γουνῷ ἀλωῆς,
νηυσὶν ἐπιπροέηκα κορωνίσιν Ἴλιον εἴσω
Τρωσὶ μαχησόμενον· τὸν δ' οὐχ ὑποδέξομαι αὖτις
οἴκαδε νοστήσαντα δόμον Πηλήϊον εἴσω.
ὄφρα δέ μοι ζώει καὶ ὁρᾷ φάος ἠελίοιο
ἄχνυται, οὐδέ τί οἱ δύναμαι χραισμῆσαι ἰοῦσα.
ἀλλ' εἶμ', ὄφρα ἴδωμι φίλον τέκος, ἠδ' ἐπακούσω
ὅττί μιν ἵκετο πένθος ἀπὸ πτολέμοιο μένοντα.

Alas for my sorrow, alas for my wretched-best-childbearing,
since I bore a child faultless and powerful,
preeminent among heroes; and he grew like a young shoot,
I nourished him like a tree on an orchard's slope,
I sent him forth with the curved ships to Ilion
to fight the Trojans. But never again shall I welcome him
returning home to the house of Peleus.
Still, while he lives and looks on the sunlight
he grieves, and I, going to him, am all unable to help him.

> But I shall go, so that I may see my dear child, and may hear
> what grief has come to him as he waits out the battle.

The semidivine hero is inextricably associated with nonhuman perfection and scope, but instead of conceiving of him as elevated by this into the realm of divinity, the *Iliad*'s vision is of an exacting mortal aspect that exerts its leveling effect on the immortal affiliations and expectations of the hero. These retain their authenticity, but no longer their overriding authority as guarantors of immortal stature.

There is thus an additional dimension to the poem's evocation and adaptation of the aspects of Thetis's mythology and attendant motifs discussed above. The "violation of expectations," which is so effective on a formal level, provides the material of Achilles' own experience, as the poem represents it. In the *Iliad*'s characterization, Achilles lives the violation of expectations, of the assumption of what it means to be the goddess's son: to be beyond compromise. Achilles' expectations, which this assumption underlies—of the inevitable success of Thetis's intervention with Zeus, of the unambiguous privilege of being τετιμῆσθαι Διὸς αἴσῃ (9.608), of the possibility of taking Troy with Patroklos alone—come to be understood as illusions, and the course of the *Iliad* describes their transformation. The poem uses Thetis to underscore our recognition of this, as she replies to Achilles' lament for Patroklos in Book 18 with an echo of their initial exchange in Book 1:

> τέκνον τί κλαίεις; τί δέ σε φρένας ἵκετο πένθος;
> ἐξαύδα, μὴ κεῦθε· τὰ μὲν δή τοι τετέλεσται
> ἐκ Διός, ὡς ἄρα δὴ πρίν γ' εὔχεο χεῖρας ἀνασχών
>
> (18.73–75)

> Child, why are you crying? What grief has come to your heart?
> Speak it, do not conceal it. Indeed, these things have been
>   accomplished for you
> by Zeus, just as you prayed for earlier, lifting up your hands

To which Achilles responds:

> μῆτερ ἐμή, τὰ μὲν ἄρ μοι Ὀλύμπιος ἐξετέλεσσεν·
> ἀλλὰ τί μοι τῶν ἦδος, ἐπεὶ φίλος ὤλεθ' ἑταῖρος
>
> (18.79–80)

> My mother, these things the Olympian brought to fulfillment;
> but what good is there in them for me, since my
>   dear companion is dead

The dislocation of which Achilles speaks here—and which constitutes his portion of suffering and of moral challenge—corresponds to the larger experience of the poem itself, in which individuals are compelled to revise drastically their formulations of their values and actions. Not only are the heroic code and the rationale of the war called into question, but central characters are repeatedly displayed in those moments of crisis that come to be recognized as typically Iliadic: the crisis of identity undermined by adamant revision of the expected and the familiar, a revision that assaults old roles and dissolves the continuity of the future. Helen on the walls of Troy or Hektor before them, Andromache preparing the bath, Patroklos storming the city: these figures are stamped with the poem's overriding theme. Achilles is preeminent among them, and his relation to this theme is both the most profound and the most fully documented of the poem. In its action the *Iliad* objectifies this preoccupation with inexorable events as a test of value, but the structure of the epic is studded with inner mirrors of this thematic concern. We read this larger question in every strategic violation of a "set" motif, as in the displaced outcome of the apparently traditional episode of the divine armoring.[34] The character of the particular altered expectation gives us its meaning, as the *Iliad*'s themes enforce it; the device of dislocation itself gives that meaning strength. Finally, the accumulation of characteristic incidents—sharing this revisionary quality of form and of theme—gradually establishes a distinctive tone that is yet another manifestation of the pervasive and unifying power of the determining themes. But the *Iliad* draws on tradition in order to assert as well as to alter convention, initiating its audience into an epic world at once familiar and unprecedented.

Thus the *Iliad*'s rejection of the possibility of Achilles' salvation through Thetis results in its emphasis on her helpless status, which is put into relief as a radical contrast to her part in the tradition of divine protectresses—one might even say, to her role as protectress *par excellence*; for the *Iliad*, in such provocative allusions as Achilles' speech at 1.394-412, depicts Thetis as the efficacious protectress not of heroes but of gods.[35]

---

[34] See the analysis of J. I. Armstrong, "The Arming Motif in the *Iliad*," *AJP* 79 (1958): 337-54.

[35] M. Lang, "Reverberation and Mythology in the *Iliad*," *Approaches to Homer*, ed. C. A. Rubino and C. W. Shelmerdine (Austin, 1983), 153-54, suggests that "hurlings out of heaven and rescues by Thetis seem to have been popular motifs," noting that Thetis "made a specialty of rescue (witness her deliverance of Zeus in 1.396ff., and her rescue of Dionysus in 6.130ff.)."

CHAPTER 2
The Power of Thetis

THE MOST STARTLING SILENCE in the voluble divine community of the *Iliad* is the absence of any reproach made to Thetis for her drastic intervention in the war. What accounts for Thetis's compelling influence over Zeus and, equally puzzling, for her freedom from recrimination or retaliation by the other Olympians? From the standpoint of characterization, of course, for Zeus to accede to Thetis's plea on behalf of Achilles means that the poet can both show Achilles worthy of human and divine *timê* and at the same time develop the figure of Hektor in order to render him as an adversary worthy of the invincible Achilles; but it soon becomes apparent that nowhere else in the course of the poem is there an instance of such far-reaching partisan activity on behalf of any of the other characters. Such efforts as any of the gods may make to assist either side inevitably meet with reprisals and vituperation from one or more of the divine supporters of the other party—as in the case, for example, of Hera and Ares at 5.755ff.

Zeus continually reiterates his refusal to brook any challenge to his promise to Thetis. All his threats against the other Olympians that assert his supremacy on Olympos occur in this context.[1] Indeed, attempts are made on the part of Hera, Athena, and Poseidon to contravene Zeus's accord with Thetis by aiding the Greeks; and Athena voices her frustration at being unable to crush Hector:

νῦν δ' ἐμὲ μὲν στυγέει, Θέτιδος δ' ἐξήνυσε βουλάς,
ἥ οἱ γούνατ' ἔκυσσε καὶ ἔλλαβε χειρὶ γενείου,
λισσομένη τιμῆσαι Ἀχιλλῆα πτολίπορθον.

(8.370–72)

But now [Zeus] is disgusted with me, and accomplishes
the plans of Thetis,

---

[1] These raise repeatedly the specter of the Titanomachy, e.g., 8.477ff.

who kissed his knees and took his chin in her hand,
begging him to give honor to Achilles the city-sacker.

Yet no complaint is made against Thetis herself; no mention is made of her less-than-Olympian status; no question is raised as to the appropriateness of her involvement in, as it were, the strategy of the war—in the way, for example, that Aphrodite's participation on behalf of Aeneas calls for caustic humor at her expense. How is the poem's audience to make sense of Thetis's extraordinary authority? It claims a divine consent—and consensus—that is significantly tacit.

In the previous chapter, I drew attention to the motifs and attributes common to myths about immortal goddesses who have mortal lovers. As a rule, the goddess's irresistible desire for her mortal partner is emphasized as the vital impetus for their union;[2] thus Kalypso memorably complains that the gods inevitably begrudge female divinities their mortal consorts, with perilous consequences for the latter. Thetis, by contrast, was not the ardent seducer of her mortal lover. Her mythology gives a wholly different cause for her uniting with Peleus, which the gods in no way begrudged. In *Iliad* 18 Thetis accounts for her uniquely grief-stricken condition:

> Ἥφαιστ᾽, ἦ ἄρα δή τις, ὅσαι θεαί εἰσ᾽ ἐν Ὀλύμπῳ,
> τοσσάδ᾽ ἐνὶ φρεσὶν ᾗσιν ἀνέσχετο κήδεα λυγρά,
> ὅσσ᾽ ἐμοὶ ἐκ πασέων Κρονίδης Ζεὺς ἄλγε᾽ ἔδωκεν;
> ἐκ μέν μ᾽ ἀλλάων ἁλιάων ἀνδρὶ δάμασσεν,
> Αἰακίδῃ Πηλῆϊ, καὶ ἔτλην ἀνέρος εὐνὴν
> πολλὰ μάλ᾽ οὐκ ἐθέλουσα.
>
> (18.429–34)

Hephaistos, is there anyone, of all the goddesses on Olympos,
who has endured so many baneful sorrows in her heart,
as many as the griefs Zeus the son of Kronos has
　　　given me beyond all others?
Of all the daughters of the sea he forced on me a mortal man,
Aiakos' son Peleus, and I endured the bed of a mortal man
utterly unwilling though I was.

Thetis did not choose Peleus, as Aphrodite chose Anchises; Peleus was chosen for her.

---

[2] So in the *Homeric Hymn to Aphrodite* (56–57), the goddess is overwhelmed with passion for Anchises.

To what does the epic allude in these lines? What myth is its audience intended to recognize? Can the *Iliad*'s reference here to the Olympians' endorsement—even enforcement—of Thetis's marriage to Peleus clarify its representation of their reluctance to challenge her, as she preempts the course of the entire war? To give these lines their full weight—indeed, even to begin to interpret them—means addressing other digressions that interrupt the narrative surface of the poem.

In the *Iliad* Thetis has a present and, prospectively, a future defined by the mortal condition of her son; as such she is known in her dependent attitude of sorrowing and caring. But the *Iliad* recognizes that she has a past as well and in recalling it at crucial points suggests a source for her role that is far more important than may initially appear.

How does the *Iliad* reveal a character's past? Typically, it does so through the character's own reminiscences and reflections on his previous achievements or position. Instead, Hephaistos gives the only first-person account of Thetis's previous activities, anterior to the time frame of the epic.

In Book 18, when Thetis arrives to request the new set of armor for Achilles, Hephaistos responds to the news of her presence with an account of how she saved him after Hera cast him out of Olympos:

> ἦ ῥά νύ μοι δεινή τε καὶ αἰδοίη θεὸς ἔνδον,
> ἥ μ' ἐσάωσ' ὅτε μ' ἄλγος ἀφίκετο τῆλε πεσόντα
> μητρὸς ἐμῆς ἰότητι κυνώπιδος, ἥ μ' ἐθέλησε
> κρύψαι χωλὸν ἐόντα· τότ' ἂν πάθον ἄλγεα θυμῷ,
> εἰ μή μ' Εὐρυνόμη τε Θέτις θ' ὑπεδέξατο κόλπῳ.
>
> (18.394–98)

> Truly then, an awesome and honored goddess is in my house,
> who saved me when pain overcame me after I had fallen far
> through the will of my bitch-faced mother, who wished
> to hide me for being lame. Then I would have
>   suffered much pain in my heart,
> if Eurynome and Thetis had not rescued me to their bosoms.[3]

---

[3] That Eurynome, who otherwise does not figure in Homeric epic, is named here as a participant in the rescue of Hephaistos may be explained by the particular context of Hephaistos's conversation with Charis. Elsewhere in Homer, Hephaistos is the husband of Aphrodite; but here Charis is his wife, as in the *Theogony* (945–46), where he is married to one of the Charites (there specifically Aglaia; Homer uses simply the generic Charis). And at *Theogony* 905ff., Hesiod identifies the Charites as the daughters of Eurynome. The inclusion of Hesiodic Eurynome, therefore, is owed to the presence of her Hesiodic child. Moreover, the mention

In Book 6 (130–37), there is another instance of Thetis preserving a god from disaster; it is, similarly, not related by her but in this case by Diomedes, who cites it as part of an example of how dangerous it is to fight with the gods. Diomedes describes how Lykourgos chased Dionysos with a cattle prod until Dionysos in terror leapt into the sea where he was sheltered by Thetis:[4]

οὐδὲ γὰρ οὐδὲ Δρύαντος υἱός, κρατερὸς Λυκόοργος,
δὴν ἦν, ὅς ῥα θεοῖσιν ἐπουρανίοισιν ἔριζεν·
ὅς ποτε μαινομένοιο Διωνύσοιο τιθήνας
σεῦε κατ᾽ ἠγάθεον Νυσήϊον· αἱ δ᾽ ἅμα πᾶσαι
θύσθλα χαμαὶ κατέχευαν ὑπ᾽ ἀνδροφόνοιο Λυκούργου
θεινόμεναι βουπλῆγι· Διώνυσος δὲ φοβηθεὶς
δύσεθ᾽ ἁλὸς κατὰ κῦμα, Θέτις δ᾽ ὑπεδέξατο κόλπῳ
δειδιότα·

(6.130–37)

No, for not even the son of Dryas, powerful Lykourgos,
lived long, who contended with the heavenly gods;
he who once drove the nurses of frenzied Dionysos
down the holy Nyseian mountain. And they all
scattered their wands to the ground, struck by man-slaughtering
Lykourgos, with a cattle prod; but Dionysos in panic
plunged under the sea's wave, and Thetis took him, terrified,
to her bosom.

Together with the episode described by Hephaistos in Book 18, this account associates Thetis in a divine past—uninvolved with human events— with a level of divine invulnerability extraordinary by Olympian standards. Where within the framework of the *Iliad* the ultimate recourse is to Zeus for protection,[5] here the poem seems to point to an alternative structure of cosmic relations, one that was neither overthrown by the Olympian order (insofar as Thetis—unlike, say, the Titans—still functions) nor upheld by it

---

of Eurynome here and perhaps even the presence of Charis are motivated by what emerges, as I hope to show below, as the *theogonic* context of references to Thetis's power. The *Homeric Hymn to Apollo* (319ff.) gives a similar account of Thetis's rescue of Hephaistos, including her Nereid sisters but singling out Thetis as his benefactor.

[4] For a discussion of the antiquity of this episode and the poet's assumption of his audience's familiarity with it see G. Aurelio Privitera, *Dionisio in Omero e nella poesia greca arcaica* (Rome, 1970), 57ff.

[5] As at 21.505ff., where Artemis retreats to Zeus when attacked and struck by Hera.

(insofar as no challenge to the Olympian order remains), but whose relation to it was otherwise resolved.

We do not have far to look for explicit confirmation of this in the poem. Once again, it does not come from Thetis; she does not refer to her own power. Rather, it is made part of Achilles' appeal to Zeus in Book 1, and it stands out in high relief because of the anomalous form of the plea. Why does Achilles convey his request to Zeus through his mother, rather than directly? Such a procedure is unknown elsewhere in the *Iliad*; and, after all, Achilles is capable of appealing to Zeus directly, as he does at length at 16.233ff. But at 1.396ff. he addresses Thetis:

> πολλάκι γάρ σεο πατρὸς ἐνὶ μεγάροισιν ἄκουσα
> εὐχομένης ὅτ' ἔφησθα κελαινεφέϊ Κρονίωνι
> οἴη ἐν ἀθανάτοισιν ἀεικέα λοιγὸν ἀμῦναι,
> ὁππότε μιν ξυνδῆσαι Ὀλύμπιοι ἤθελον ἄλλοι,
> Ἥρη τ' ἠδὲ Ποσειδάων καὶ Παλλὰς Ἀθήνη·
> ἀλλὰ σὺ τόν γ' ἐλθοῦσα, θεά, ὑπελύσαο δεσμῶν,
> ὦχ' ἑκατόγχειρον καλέσασ' ἐς μακρὸν Ὄλυμπον,
> ὃν Βριάρεων καλέουσι θεοί, ἄνδρες δέ τε πάντες
> Αἰγαίων',—ὃ γὰρ αὖτε βίην οὗ πατρὸς ἀμείνων—
> ὅς ῥα παρὰ Κρονίωνι καθέζετο κύδεϊ γαίων·
> τὸν καὶ ὑπέδεισαν μάκαρες θεοὶ οὐδ' ἔτ' ἔδησαν.
>
> (1.396–406)

For I have often heard you in my father's halls
avowing it, when you declared that from Kronos'
    son of the dark clouds
you alone among the immortals warded off unseemly
    destruction
at the time when the other Olympians wanted to
    bind him,
Hera and Poseidon and Pallas Athena;
but you went, goddess, and set him free from his bonds,
quickly summoning the hundred-handed one to high
    Olympos,
the one whom the gods call Briareos, but all men call
Aigaion—for he is greater in strength than his father—
who, rejoicing in his glory, sat beside the son of Kronos.
And the blessed gods feared him, and ceased binding
    Zeus.

A closer look at the context of this account helps to explain why Achilles enlists his mother as intermediary rather than addressing Zeus himself, as he does when he makes his prayer in Book 16.[6]

We become aware that Achilles' appeal is remarkable in a number of important ways when we note that the passage is introduced at 1.352 with the following lines:

μῆτερ, ἐπεί μ' ἔτεκές γε μινυνθάδιόν περ ἐόντα,
τιμήν πέρ μοι ὄφελλεν Ὀλύμπιος ἐγγυαλίξαι
Ζεὺς ὑψιβρεμέτης·

(1.352–54)

My mother, since you did bear me to be short-lived,
surely high-thundering Olympian Zeus ought to
grant me honor.

It has been established that the typical structure of prayers, as represented in archaic poetry, consists of an arrangement of distinct elements: the invocation of the god or goddess; the claim that the person praying is entitled to a favor on the basis of favors granted in the past or on the basis of a previous response that implies the existence of a contract between god and man based on past exchange of favors; and the specific request for a favor

---

[6] Lines 399–406 of Book 1 have troubled critics since antiquity: Zenodotus athetised the passage, evidently sharing the worry expressed in the scholia about the seemingly improbable alliance of rebellious gods, and preferring to read Φοῖβος Ἀπόλλων for Παλλὰς Ἀθήνη. The attempt to overthrow Zeus provided an opportunity for a variety of allegorical readings from different vantage points, including the meteorological; see schol. bT ad 399ff. and the discussion in F. Buffière, *Les mythes d Homère et la pensée grecque* (Paris, 1956), 173–79. Buffière writes, "Si bien que l'allégorie a dû venir de bonne heure au secours de ce texte scabreux, qui offensait doublement la divinité: car les dieux révoltés péchaient à la fois contre les lois de l'ordre et la paix des cieux, et contre les devoirs de l'entente familiale" (174). Thetis's power, however, was never in doubt; she was allegorized as the force ordering the universe: τὴν θέσιν καὶ φύσιν τοῦ πάντος. Some modern interpreters, less concerned about the particular *combinazione* of deities or the impropriety of their behavior, but more perplexed about the apparent absence of other references to the episode of the attempted binding, have identified this passage as an instance of Homeric "ad hoc invention"; see, for example, M. Willcock, "Mythological Paradeigma in the *Iliad*," CQ 58, n.s. 14 (1964): 141–54, and "Ad Hoc Invention in the *Iliad*," HSCP 81 (1977): 41–53. For an answer to "demonstrations" of "invention" on the poet's part, illustrating "the extent to which *paradeigmata* include inherited material" (Willcock, "Mythological Paradeigma," 147), see the convincing examination of this passage in Lang, "Reverberation and Mythology," in *Approaches to Homer*, eds. Rubino and Shelmerdine; also the discussion of inherited material about divine conflict in A. Heubeck, "Mythologische Vorstellungen des Alten Orients im archaischen Griechentum," *Gymnasium* 62 (1955): 508–25, on this passage, 519ff.

in return, including an implied or explicit statement of the relevance of the favor to the particular god's sphere. This arrangement constitutes a formal communication of reciprocal obligations between god and man.[7]

Achilles' prayer to his mother at 1.352ff. presents a variation on the formal restrictions governing prayers in Homeric poetry, as L. C. Muellner has shown. This is signaled by the substitution of δάκρυ χέων for εὐχόμενος, the participle that regularly accompanies the prayer of a man to a god (although not necessarily requests from one god to another). Muellner observes that

> Achilles is depressed and helpless, his prayer is sub-standard, and his goddess mother makes an instantaneous epiphany. To express Achilles' sadness with particular force, the poet has replaced ὣς ἔφατ᾽ εὐχόμενος with #ὣς φάτο δάκρυ χέων. The deletion of εὐχόμενος may be a covert statement that Achilles is less a man addressing a goddess than a god addressing a goddess, or, which is similar, a man addressing his mother who happens to be a goddess.[8]

Achilles' prayer to Thetis, as Muellner points out, omits the specific request for a favor. Curiously, we may note, it also lacks the element of a claim of entitlement to a favor implied by the "existence of a contract between god and man based on past exchange of favors."[9] All the requisite features, in fact, seem to be missing from Achilles' address to his mother; but they are present in the passage in which Achilles instructs her on how to approach Zeus.

The conventional form in which one god asks a favor of another does not include the reminder of a past favor or the promise of a future one on either part.[10] Conventionally, however, a god or goddess who makes a request of another god on behalf of a hero will recall the hero's past services to the god, as Apollo does for the sake of the dead Hektor at 24.33–34 or as Athena does on behalf of Odysseus at *Odyssey* 1.60–62.[11] But here, for Achilles' ritual

---

[7] I am paraphrasing here from the detailed discussion of the formal structure of Homeric prayers in Muellner, *Meaning of Homeric EYXOMAI*, 27–28. See as well H. Meyer, "Hymnische Stilelemente in der frühgriechischen Dichtung" (Diss., Cologne, 1933), esp. 9–16; E. Norden, *Agnostos Theos* (Leipzig, 1913), 143–76; M. Lang, "Reason and Purpose in Homeric Prayers," *CW* 68 (1975): 309–14.

[8] Muellner, *Meaning of Homeric EYXOMAI*, 23.

[9] Ibid., 28.

[10] E.g., Hera to Aphrodite at 14.190ff.; Hera to Hephaistos at 21.328ff.

[11] σχέτλιοί ἐστε, θεοί, δηλήμονες· οὔ νύ ποθ᾽ ὑμῖν
Ἕκτωρ μηρί᾽ ἔκηε βοῶν αἰγῶν τε τελείων;

(*Il.* 24.33–34)

You are relentless, you gods, and destructive: did Hektor

or other services to Zeus, is substituted the reminder of Thetis's earlier championing of Zeus. Instead of asking for a favor based on Achilles' past, she is to ask on the basis of her own. It can be no trivial service that is recalled in exchange for reversing the course of the war, with drastic results that Zeus can anticipate; Thetis need say no more than

Ζεῦ πάτερ, εἴ ποτε δή σε μετ' ἀθανάτοισιν ὄνησα
ἢ ἔπει ἢ ἔργῳ, τόδε μοι κρήηνον ἐέλδωρ·

(1.503–4)

Father Zeus, if I ever before helped you among the
immortals, in word or action, grant me this favor.

Achilles, however, specifies wherein Thetis's claim to favor lies:

πολλάκι γάρ σεο πατρὸς ἐνὶ μεγάροισιν ἄκουσα
εὐχομένης, ὅτ' ἔφησθα κελαινεφέϊ Κρονίωνι
οἴη ἐν ἀθανάτοισιν ἀεικέα λοιγὸν ἀμῦναι

(1.396–98)

For I have often heard you in my father's halls
avowing it, when you declared that from Kronos'
        son of the dark clouds
you alone among the immortals warded off unseemly destruction.

Thetis, the rescuer of Hephaistos and Dionysos, was first and foremost the rescuer of Zeus.

The most general, but most telling, statement of Thetis's power is expressed by the formula λοιγὸν ἀμῦναι—"ward off destruction."[12] The ability to λοιγὸν ἀμῦναι (or ἀμύνειν) within the *Iliad* is shared exclusively by Achilles, Apollo, and Zeus. Although others are put in a position to do so and make the attempt, only these three have the power to "ward off destruction," to be efficacious in restoring order to the world of the poem. Thetis alone, however, is

---

never burn the thighs of oxen and choice goats for you?

οὔ νύ τ' Ὀδυσσεὺς
Ἀργείων παρὰ νηυσὶ χαρίζετο ἱερὰ ῥέζων
Τροίῃ ἐν εὐρείῃ; τί νύ οἱ τόσον ὠδύσαο, Ζεῦ;

(*Od.* 1.60–62)

        Did Odysseus not
please you, making sacrifices by the Achaeans' ships
in wide Troy? Why are you so angry at him, Zeus?

[12] For a detailed discussion of the thematics of this formula, see Nagy, *Best of the Achaeans*, 74–78.

credited with having had such power in the divine realm, for she alone was able to ward off destruction from Zeus. She herself unbound Zeus, summoning the hundred-handed Briareos as a kind of guarantor or reminder of her power:

ἀλλὰ σὺ τόν γ' ἐλθοῦσα, θεά, ὑπελύσαο δεσμῶν,
ὦχ' ἑκατόγχειρον καλέσασ' ἐς μακρὸν Ὄλυμπον,
ὃν Βριάρεων καλέουσι θεοί, ἄνδρες δέ τε πάντες
Αἰγαίων'—ὁ γὰρ αὖτε βίην οὗ πατρὸς ἀμείνων—
ὅς ῥα παρὰ Κρονίωνι καθέζετο κύδεϊ γαίων·

(1.401–5)

but you went, goddess, and set him free from his bonds,
quickly summoning the hundred-handed one to high Olympos,
the one whom the gods call Briareos, but all men call
Aigaion—for he is greater in strength than his father—
who, rejoicing in his glory, sat beside the son of Kronos.

That Thetis saves Zeus from being bound deserves special attention; for the motif of binding on Olympos, together with the reference to Briareos, specifically evokes the succession myth and the divine genealogy on which it is founded.

The motif of binding is central to the account of the succession myth in the *Theogony*, recurring as one of the primary ways to assert divine sovereignty over a potential or actual challenger. Ouranos attempts to ensure his power over Briareos and his other children by binding them; ultimately they are freed by Zeus,[13] who in turn wants their allegiance in his own bid for hegemony. Their willingness to cooperate is based on their gratitude for being unbound:

"κέκλυτέ μευ Γαίης τε καὶ Οὐρανοῦ ἀγλαὰ τέκνα,
ὄφρ' εἴπω τά με θυμὸς ἐνὶ στήθεσσι κελεύει.
ἤδη γὰρ μάλα δηρὸν ἐναντίοι ἀλλήλοισι
νίκης καὶ κάρτευς πέρι μαρνάμεθ' ἤματα πάντα,
Τιτῆνές τε θεοὶ καὶ ὅσοι Κρόνου ἐκγενόμεσθα.
ὑμεῖς δὲ μεγάλην τε βίην καὶ χεῖρας ἀάπτους
φαίνετε Τιτήνεσσιν ἐναντίον ἐν δαῒ λυγρῇ,
μνησάμενοι φιλότητος ἐνηέος, ὅσσα παθόντες
ἐς φάος ἂψ ἀφίκεσθε δυσηλεγέος ὑπὸ δεσμοῦ
ἡμετέρας διὰ βουλὰς ὑπὸ ζόφου ἠερόεντος."
ὣς φάτο· τὸν δ' αἶψ' αὖτις ἀμείβετο Κόττος ἀμύμων·

---

[13] Hes. *Theog.* 501–2. References are to M. L. West, ed., *Hesiod: Theogony* (Oxford, 1966).

....

"σῇσι δ' ἐπιφροσύνῃσιν ὑπὸ ζόφου ἠερόεντος
ἄψορρον ἐξαῦτις ἀμειλίκτων ὑπὸ δεσμῶν
ἠλύθομεν..."

(Hes. *Theog.* 644–54; 658–60)

"Listen to me, radiant children of Gaia and Ouranos,
so that I may say what the spirit in my breast bids.
For a very long time have the Titan gods and all those born of
Kronos struggled with each other every day for
        victory and power.
But show your great strength and irresistible hands
against the Titans in painful battle, bearing in mind
our kindly friendship, and all the sufferings you returned from
into the light, back from wretched bondage
beneath the misty darkness, on account of our counsels."
Thus he spoke. And illustrious Kottos replied in turn:
"...Through your shrewdness, from beneath the misty darkness
we have come back again from our relentless bonds."

With the aid of Briareos and his brothers, the Olympians, once they have managed to overpower Kronos and the other Titans, bind them and cast them beneath the earth.[14]

Binding is the ultimate penalty in the divine realm, where by definition there is no death. It serves not to deprive an opponent of existence, but to render him impotent.[15] Once bound, a god cannot escape his bondage by himself, no matter how great his strength. In this sense it is not finally an expression of physical strength (although violence certainly enters into the Titanomachy), but of what has been called "terrible sovereignty."[16]

The attempt to bind Zeus recounted at 1.396ff. thus constitutes a mutinous effort at supplanting him and imposing a new divine regime—on

---

[14] Hes. *Theog.* 658ff.

[15] References to binding of gods in the *Iliad* include the account of the binding of Ares by Otos and Ephialtes at 5.385–91, of Hera by Zeus at 15.19–20, and Zeus's threat to the other gods at 13.17ff.

[16] On the metaphysical nature of binding, see M. Eliade, *Images and Symbols*, trans. P. Mairet (New York, 1969), chap. 3, "The 'God Who Binds' and the Symbolism of Knots," 92–124. On binding (and unbinding) as an expression and instrument of sovereignty, see the discussion, with thorough exposition of the comparative evidence, in G. Dumézil, *Ouranos-Varuna: Étude de mythologie comparée indo-européenne* (Paris, 1934), and *Mitra-Varuna*, 2d ed. (Paris, 1948), 71–85 (in English, trans. D. Coltman [New York, 1988], 95–111).

the pattern of his own overthrow of Kronos and the Titans. Thetis's act in rescuing Zeus is therefore nothing less than supreme: an act that restores the cosmic equilibrium. Once having loosed the bonds, she summons Briareos, not to perform, but simply to sit beside Zeus as a reminder of Zeus's final mastery in the succession myth struggle. Briareos and his brothers, in Hesiod (as later in Apollodorus), are never instigators, but agents; Thetis's power to summon the *hekatoncheir* ("hundred-handed one") here—beyond what the insurgent gods are capable of—recalls Zeus's own successful use of Briareos and his brothers. Not even a single one of Briareos's hands needs to be laid on the mutinous gods here: they are overwhelmed by the assertion of sovereignty implied by the presence of Briareos, rather than overpowered by him. In this sense, one can see Briareos's narrative function as a mirror of his dramatic function: he is a reminder. The binding element in itself is a sufficient allusion to the succession myth, so that Briareos is included as a multiplication of the motif.

Linked to this cosmic act on the part of Thetis is the phrase ὁ γὰρ αὖτε βίην οὗ πατρὸς ἀμείνων ("for he is greater in strength than his father")—a reference about which it has rightly been said that "much remains obscure."[17] Yet some light may be shed on this "obscure" phrase if we remind ourselves that the reference to the son who is greater than his father is significant for Thetis in a crucial dimension of her mythology.

The background of the fateful marriage alluded to in *Iliad* 18 is given in fuller form in Pindar's *Isthmian* 8, where Thetis's story is the ode's central myth.[18] *Isthmian* 8 recounts that Zeus and Poseidon were rivals for the hand of Thetis, each wishing to be her husband, for love possessed them. But the gods decided not to bring about either marriage, once they had heard from Themis that Thetis was destined to bear a son who would be greater than his father.[19] Therefore, Themis counseled, let Thetis marry a mortal instead

---

[17] G. S. Kirk, *The Iliad: A Commentary* (Cambridge, 1985), 95, ad 1.403–4. See pp. 93–95 for observations on 1.396–406. It has proved difficult even to construe 403–4; in what way does the phrase ὁ γὰρ αὖτε βίην οὗ πατρὸς ἀμείνων explain either of the *hekatoncheir*'s names? See the analysis by J. T. Hooker, "ΑΙΓΑΙΩΝ in Achilles' Plea to Thetis," *JHS* 100 (1980): 188–89, who does not consider the episode to be an invention of the poet, but rather "a fragment of a poetical tradition represented elsewhere in the *Iliad*" (188 n.4, with references). On the other hand, perhaps the phrase is not an etymological gloss, but rather explains the participial phrase in 402—that is, it does not give a reason for why Briareos is so named, but why Thetis summoned him.

[18] Other references to the marriage are found in *Pythian* 3, as well as in several odes written, like *Isthmian* 8, for Aeginetan victors: *Nem.* 3, *Nem.* 4, *Nem.* 5.

[19] C. M. Bowra, *Pindar* (Oxford, 1964), 88–89, observes that *Isthmian* 8 "is concerned with the

and see her son die in war. This divine prize should be given to Aiakos's son Peleus, the most reverent of men. The sons of Kronos agreed with Themis, and Zeus himself assented to the marriage of Thetis.

ταῦτα καὶ μακάρων ἐμέμναντ᾽ ἀγοραί,
Ζεὺς ὅτ᾽ ἀμφὶ Θέτιος ἀγλαός τ᾽ ἔρισαν Ποσειδὰν γάμῳ,
ἄλοχον εὐειδέα θέλων ἑκάτερος
ἑὰν ἔμμεν· ἔρως γὰρ ἔχεν.
ἀλλ᾽ οὔ σφιν ἄμβροτοι τέλεσαν εὐνὰν θεῶν πραπίδες,
ἐπεὶ θεσφάτων ἐπάκουσαν· εἶπεν
εὔβουλος ἐν μέσοισι Θέμις,
οὕνεκεν πεπρωμένον ἦν, φέρτερον πατέρος ἄνακτα γόνον τεκεῖν
ποντίαν θεόν, ὃς κεραυνοῦ τε κρέσσον ἄλλο βέλος
διώξει χερὶ τριόδοντός τ᾽ ἀμαιμακέτου, Δί τε μισγομέναν
ἢ Διὸς παρ᾽ ἀδελφεοῖσιν. "ἀλλὰ τὰ μέν
παύσατε· βροτέων δὲ λεχέων τυχοῖσα
υἱὸν εἰσιδέτω θανόντ᾽ ἐν πολέμῳ,
χεῖρας Ἄρεΐ τ᾽ ἐναλίγκιον στεροπαῖσί τ᾽ ἀκμὰν ποδῶν."
(Isthm. 8.29–38)

This the assembly of the Blessed Ones remembered,
When Zeus and glorious Poseidon
Strove to marry Thetis,
Each wishing that she
Should be his beautiful bride.
Love held them in his grip.
But the Gods' undying wisdom
Would not let the marriage be,

When they gave ear to the oracles. In their midst
Wise-counselling Themis said
That it was fated for the sea-goddess
To bear for son a prince
Stronger than his father,

---

consequences of what will happen if Thetis marries either Zeus or Poseidon. If she does, says Themis, it is πεπρωμένον that her son will be stronger than either. Here everything turns on the meaning of πεπρωμένον. It is clear that it is not a decision of the gods on Olympus, but something which is bound to happen unless they take avoiding action.... What Pindar means is that, the gods being what they are, such a union will inevitably bring forth a being stronger than they. The gods have their own nature, and this is a consequence of it."

> Who shall wield in his hand a different weapon
> More powerful than the thunderbolt
> Or the monstrous trident,
> If she wed Zeus or among the brothers of Zeus.
> "Put an end to this. Let her have a mortal wedlock
> And see dead in war her son
> With hands like the hands of Ares
> And feet like the lightning-flashes."[20]

Isthmian 8 thus reveals Thetis as a figure of cosmic capacity, whose existence promises profound consequences for the gods. Not only does she generate strife between Zeus and Poseidon because of their love for her, but her potential for bearing a son greater than his father threatens the entire divine order. The rivalry she arouses between Zeus and Poseidon because of their love for her is unprecedented, but her greatest power does not lie there. Themis advises Zeus and Poseidon against marriage with Thetis, not in terms suggesting that their competition over her would be dangerous, but rather that marriage between Thetis and any of the Olympians (Διὸς παρ' ἀδελφεοῖσιν, "among the brothers of Zeus") would be disastrous in itself. If the issue were simply that of ending a conflict between the brothers, that presumably could be resolved by assigning Thetis to either of them. Once married to either of them, Thetis would be settled and beyond the other's reach; the possibility of her subsequently—δίς ("a second time")—causing a similar rivalry would be unlikely. But Themis fears another "banishment," the effects of a *petalismos*.[21]

Themis, the guardian of social order, is apparently trying not simply to avert a quarrel prompted by sexual jealousy between the brothers (a quarrel that would always be reparable), but a catastrophic *neikos* on the scale of previous intergenerational succession struggles.[22] This is what Thetis has the power to engender.

---

[20] Translation from C. M. Bowra, trans., *The Odes of Pindar* (Harmondsworth, England, 1969), 52–53.

[21] On the diction of banishment in the succession myth, see Hes. *Theog.* 491, 820. On the interpretation of *Isthmian* 8.92, see the scholion as given in A. B. Drachmann, ed., *Scholia vetera in Pindari carmina* (Leipzig, 1927), 275.

[22] On the role of Themis, compare A. Köhnken, "Gods and Descendants of Aiakos in Pindar's Eighth Isthmian Ode," *BICS* 22 (1975): 33 n.19. Apollodorus (3.13.5) says that one version attributes to Themis and another to Prometheus the revelation of the secret that Thetis will bear a son greater than his father: τὸν ἐκ ταύτης γεννηθέντα οὐρανοῦ δυναστεύσειν. We may recall the rivalry between Hephaistos and Ares, as related in *Odyssey* 8, and the rapproche-

Thetis's overwhelming potential as *Isthmian* 8 reveals it lies at the heart of Aeschylus'(?) *Prometheus Bound*. In the tragedy, Gaia (there identified with Themis) has made known to her son Prometheus the secret of Zeus's future overthrow: that Thetis, whom Zeus plans to "marry," is destined to bear a child who will be mightier than his father.[23] It is this threat at which Prometheus hints, with increasing explicitness, throughout the tragedy, his private knowledge of which he asserts as the guarantee of his ability to stalemate Zeus.[24] Although we cannot be sure precisely how possession of this knowledge may have served Prometheus in the trilogy as a whole, we can say that the plot and dramatic tension of (at least) *Prometheus Bound* are organized around the Titan's knowing that Thetis is

---

ment of Hera and Aphrodite at *Iliad* 14.190ff. as examples of the reparability of quarrels arising from sexual jealousy. On the potential *neikos*:

Ζεὺς ... ἀμφὶ Θέτιος ἀγλαός τ' ἔρισαν Ποσειδᾶν γάμῳ,

. . . .

μηδὲ Νηρέος θυγάτηρ νεικέων πέ- ταλα δὶς ἐγγυαλιζέτω ἄμμιν·

(*Isthm.* 8.30, 47–48)

Zeus and shining Poseidon were rivals over the marriage of Thetis

. . . .

Let the daughter of Nereus not bring the petals of strife twice into our hands.

Note Themis's role in the *Cypria*, where *eris* also plays a crucial part. See Nagy, *Best of the Achaeans*, 253–75 and 309–16, on the overlapping semantics of *eris* and *neikos* and their implications for archaic Greek poetry.

[23] R. Reitzenstein, "Die Hochzeit des Peleus und der Thetis," *Hermes* 35 (1900): 73–105, argues that Pindar and Aeschylus depend on the same early source, while Apollodorus makes use of a different, though essentially compatible, "Hauptquelle" for the story of Thetis; see esp. pp. 74–75 and 74 n. 1. See as well the discussions in U. von Wilamowitz–Moellendorf, *Aischylos Interpretationen* (Berlin, 1914), 132ff.; F. Stoessl, *Die Trilogie des Aischylos: Formgesetze und Wege der Rekonstruktion* (Baden bei Wien, 1937), 146; and F Solmsen, *Hesiod and Aeschylus* (Ithaca, N.Y., 1949), 128ff., all of which argue for a common poetic source for Aeschylus's and Pindar's treatment of the dangerous marriage with Thetis. Solmsen (following Wilamowitz) points out that the reference to Poseidon at *PV* 922ff. is gratuitous in terms of the plot of the tragedy (Prometheus has nothing against Poseidon) but serves to evoke the tradition about Thetis and the brothers' courtship of her more fully. See also *RE* 19.1 (1937), 271–308, s.v. "Peleus" (A. Lesky); Lesky comments, "Es unterliegt keinem Bedenken, das Drama auf dieselbe Dichtung zurückzuführen wie Pind. Isthm. 8 und die besondere Rolle des Prometheus aus der Erfindung des Dichters zu erklären" (col. 296). D. J. Conacher, *Aeschylus' Prometheus Bound: A Literary Commentary* (Toronto, 1980), 15, notes, "The myth of Zeus' pursuit, in competition with his brother Poseidon, of the sea-nymph Thetis, was, of course, traditional, but its connection with the Prometheus myth appears to have been an Aeschylean adaptation."

[24] Aesch. *PV* 167ff., 515ff., 755ff., 907ff.

the answer to the only question that matters to Zeus.[25] The secret of Thetis is represented in *Prometheus Bound* as indispensable to Zeus's survival: his rule, his future, are hostage to her fatal power.

While the danger to Zeus posed by the attempt of Hera, Athena, and Poseidon (1.396ff.), therefore, was averted by Thetis, she herself presented the greatest challenge of all to his supremacy, according to the myth as recovered in Pindar and Aeschylus.[26] The phrase ὁ γὰρ αὖτε βίην οὗ πατρὸς ἀμείνων at *Iliad* 1.404 describes Achilles within that tradition and recalls his association with the theme of ongoing genealogy and generational strife.

The *Iliad*, then, gives us a seemingly inconsistent picture. How are we to reconcile Thetis's cosmic capacity, as alluded to in the *Iliad*'s digressions and as known to *Isthmian 8*, *Prometheus Bound*, and Apollodorus (and the traditions they follow), with what seems, for the most part, to be her limited status in

---

[25] Whether *Prometheus Bound* was part of a trilogy, and if so, what the trilogic sequence and plots of the other plays were, remains a matter for speculation. For a summary of views on the problem, see Stoessl, *Die Trilogie des Aischylos*, 114–56, esp. 122–24. For a discussion and reconstruction of the trilogy from the fragments (placing *P. Purphoros* first), see the appendix in M. Griffith, ed., *Aeschylus: Prometheus Bound* (Cambridge, 1983), 281–305. When and how did Prometheus divulge the secret of the dangerous marriage with Thetis? The scholion ad *PV* 167 indicates that Prometheus alerted Zeus as he was in full pursuit of Thetis in the Caucasus. According to Philodemus, *De pietate* (p. 41.4–15 Gomperz), Aeschylus made the revelation of Thetis's secret by Prometheus responsible for the latter's liberation (and for Thetis's marriage to a mortal); similarly, Hyginus (*Fab.* 64), who likewise explains that disclosure as the reason for Thetis's marriage to Peleus—although by this account the freeing of Prometheus followed only years (millennia?) later. Griffith, *Prometheus Bound*, 301, suggests that "the order of events (killing of eagle, revelation of secret, release of P.) is not certain but if [the scholion at 167 and a passage in Servius on Vergil Ecl. 6.42 about the killing of the eagle] are based on *Luomenos*, Thetis may have arrived, in flight from Zeus (like Io in *Desmotês*...), thus provoking the still-bound Prometheus to divulge the secret before it is too late; whereupon Zeus gave orders for him to be released.... Or else Zeus' pursuit of Thetis may have been merely narrated (e.g., by Heracles or Gê)." The safety both of Prometheus and of Zeus, then, depends on Thetis.

[26] It is necessary to proceed with the greatest caution when reading Pindar (or any later author) as evidence for traditions latent in Homeric poetry. Two considerations support the validity of doing so here. First, Pindar has been shown to preserve highly archaic material reaching back even to an Indo-European provenance, as illustrated in Benveniste's discussion of *Pythian 3* in "La doctrine médicale," 5–12. Second, as C. Greengard, *The Structure of Pindar's Epinician Odes* (Amsterdam, 1980), 35, has demonstrated, *Isthmian 8* "draws... heavily on the themes and movements of the *Iliad* tragedy." Greengard's comprehensive analysis concludes that "the diction itself of 1.8 is more than usually allusive to that of the *Iliad*" (36 n. 27). It seems reasonable to suppose that Pindar in *Isthmian 8* draws on mythology present in the *Iliad* in some form, and recoverable from it—even if deeply embedded and only allusively evident to us. See the discussion in Lesky's article on Peleus in *RE* 19.1 (1937), 271–308.

the *Iliad*? Our initial impression of her there is that she is a divinity of at best secondary importance, whose position is inferior to that of the major deities in the poem. Her expressed grief and reiterated helplessness in the face of her sons suffering make her seem vulnerable in a way that other goddesses are not. In comparison to Thetis's anguish, an episode like the wounding of Aphrodite in Book 5 (334ff.) is a parodic one, which serves to illustrate that the Olympians are beyond anything more than the most transient pain. There is nothing anywhere in the *Iliad*'s immortal realm comparable to the sorrowful isolation of Thetis.

Her inferiority to the Olympian hierarchy is spelled out in Book 20. When Aeneas is reluctant to meet Achilles in battle, Apollo (in the guise of Lykaon) reassures him that he is entitled to challenge Achilles because his mother, Aphrodite, "outranks" Thetis:

> ἥρως, ἀλλ' ἄγε καὶ σὺ θεοῖς αἰειγενέτῃσιν
> εὔχεο· καὶ δὲ σέ φασι Διὸς κούρης Ἀφροδίτης
> ἐκγεγάμεν, κεῖνος δὲ χερείονος ἐκ θεοῦ ἐστίν·
>
> (20.104–6)

> Hero, come now and pray, you also, to the gods who live forever;
> they say you were born from Aphrodite, the daughter of Zeus,
> while he is the son of a lesser goddess.

It is this reminder with which Aeneas then responds to Achilles' taunts. He matches the account of Achilles' demonstrated superiority, Achilles' pursuit and near-capture of him, and his own flight, simply with the claim of his own genealogy, at 20.206–9.[27]

If we want to square the inferior place in the ranks to which the speeches of Apollo and Aeneas appear to relegate Thetis with the rest of her history as we have seen it, we may consider the suggestion in Erwin Rohde's *Psyche* (although Rohde does not address himself to this particular problem) that an explanation for such disparity is to be found in the prevailing influence of pan-Hellenism, through which the Homeric view of the gods was shaped. The impetus of this unifying perspective, of which the Homeric

---

[27] For a thorough refutation of the view that this episode (and Aeneas's role in Book 20) must have been motivated by the patronage of a historical clan of Aeneidai, as well as an interpretation that reads it in particular relation to the confrontation between Achilles and Hektor in Book 22, that is, as integral to its context, see P. M. Smith, "Aeneidai as Patrons of *Iliad* XX and the *Homeric Hymn to Aphrodite*," *HSCP* 85 (1981): 17–58, esp. (on this speech) 50.

poems themselves are a monumental and influential example, is evident in the Homeric poems'

> conception...and consistent execution of the picture of a single and unified world of gods, confined to a select company of sharply characterized heavenly beings, grouped together in certain well-recognized ways and dwelling together in a single place of residence above the earth. If we listened to Homer alone we should suppose that the innumerable local cults of Greece, with their gods closely bound to the soil, hardly existed. Homer ignores them almost entirely. His gods are pan-Hellenic, Olympian.[28]

While the deities whose cult-worship was most widespread throughout the city-states are elevated to the superior status of Olympians, those divinities with a more restricted range of influence are treated as lesser in importance and authority, however significant they may have been in local belief. In this way local traditions remain intact but are de-emphasized, while the resulting generalized pan-Hellenic conception is acceptable throughout the city-states. The assembly of the gods before the theomachy in which they all compete makes explicit the subsidiary position of the locally powerful "gods of the countryside." As Rohde points out,

> even the river-gods and Nymphs who are usually confined to their own homes are called to the *agora* of all the gods in Olympos, Y 4ff. These deities who remain fixed in the locality of their worship are weaker than the Olympians just because they are not elevated to the ideal summit of Olympos. Kalypso resignedly admits this, ε 169f....They have sunk to the second rank of deities.[29]

Thus the Homeric poems, subordinating realities of religious practice to pan-Hellenic goals, systematically demote such potent figures as the Nymphs—who, as a group, in the *Theogony* occupy a lofty position appropriate to their tremendous stature and antiquity, being the daughters of Gaia and consanguineous siblings of the Erinyes and the Giants.[30] Hesiod also recognizes the Nereids as occupying an elevated position in the divine

---

[28] Rohde, *Psyche*, vol. 1, trans. W. B. Hillis (New York, 1925), 25; see also especially 94.
[29] Ibid., 50.
[30] See M. L. West's discussion of the Nymphs in his edition of the *Theogony*, pp. 154 n.7, 161 n.25, 199 n. 130, 221 n.187.

scheme, and we know of their importance in popular religion from a variety of other sources.[31] Prestige is denied them by Homeric epic, which either assigns these non-Olympian deities inconsequential roles in the narrative or demonstrates their subordinate status through a decisive confrontation with the Olympians. Such is the case of Kalypso in *Odyssey* 5. In the *Iliad*, a highly dramatic example is the battle between Hephaistos and Skamandros (Kalypso's brother in the *Theogony*), in which Skamandros is forced, improbably, to capitulate to the Olympian's superior might (21. 342ff.). At the same time, the poem acknowledges the river god's intrinsic stature by calling him θεὸς μέγας (21.248), a title otherwise reserved for Olympian gods.

It may be the case that Thetis's stature in a local context is a factor in the *Iliad*'s reticence or indirectness of reference with respect to her power and prestige. Pausanias (3.14.4–6) tells us that she was worshiped with great reverence in cult in Laconia; this may be reflected in local poetic traditions, if Alcman's poem (frag. 5 Page) featuring her is a clue.[32]

---

[31] E.g., Hdt. 7.191; Paus. 2.1.8 and 3.26.7. A related group are the daughters of Tethys and Okeanos, who, however, number three thousand and are not all named. See West, *Theogony*, 260 n.337, on the *kourotrophos* function of the Nymphs. Hesiod stresses their local nature by saying of their equally numerous brothers, the rivers:

τόσσοι δ' αὖθ' ἕτεροι ποταμοὶ καναχηδὰ ῥέοντες

. . . .

τῶν ὄνομ' ἀργαλέον πάντων βροτὸν ἄνδρα ἐνισπεῖν,
οἳ δὲ ἕκαστοι ἴσασιν, ὅσοι περιναιετάουσι.

(*Theog.* 367, 369–70)

So many other noisily flowing rivers are there...
It is difficult for a mortal man to say all their names
But the men who live near them know them.

[32] Edited by E. Lobel in *POxy.* 24 (London, 1957), no. 2390, frag. 2; published as Alcman frag. 5 in D. L. Page, ed., *Poetae Melici Graecae* (Oxford, 1962); more recently as frag. 81 in C. Calame, ed., *Alcman* (Rome, 1983). Known to us only through a tantalizing commentary, Alcman's poem has been assumed by modern scholars to be an early cosmogony and has been interpreted as such, following the reading of its ancient commentator, according to whom the poem envisaged a sequence of creation in which at first only undifferentiated matter existed; then Thetis, the *genesis pantōn*, appeared and generated *Poros*, "the way," and *Tekmōr*, "the sign." Darkness existed as a third feature, later followed by day, moon, and stars. With Thetis the creatrix as demiurge, this cosmogonic process involved not so much the bringing into being of matter as the discrimination of objects, the ordering of space, the illumination of darkness with light: an intellectual rather than a physical creation. In the commentator's reading, Alcman presented Thetis as the primal, divine creative force—the generative principle of the universe. This aspect of Alcman's poem has been discussed by M. Detienne and J.-P. Vernant, who argue for a close connection between Thetis and Mêtis. See Detienne and Vernant's *Les ruses de l intelligence: La Métis des grecs* (Paris, 1974), 127–64, which develops a number of ideas first presented in Vernant's "Thétis et le poème cosmogonique d'Alcman,"

Thetis in the *Iliad*, however, is neither merely ineffectual, like Kalypso, nor insignificant, like Leukothea; the epic shows her to us as at once weak *and* powerful: subsidiary, helpless, but able to accomplish what the greatest of the heroes cannot and what the greatest of the gods cannot.[33] The poem's explicitly and emphatically contradictory presentation of her leads to an explanation that addresses the interpretive process inherent in the *Iliad*'s treatment of the mythology it builds on, rendered more readily accessible to us through comparative evidence. The central element in the structure of Thetis's mythology, common to its representations in both *Isthmian 8* and *Prometheus Bound*, is the covertness of her power; it is a secret weapon, a concealed promise, a hidden agenda requiring discovery, revelation. It is precisely this covert, latent aspect of Thetis's potential in cosmic relations to which the *Iliad* draws attention as well, both exploiting and reinforcing it *as allusion*.

The *Iliad*'s acknowledgment of Thetis's cosmic power, known to these traditions, locates it in a past to which she herself does not refer.[34] Her

---

in *Hommages à Marie Delcourt*, Collection Latomus 114 (Brussels, 1970), 219–33. In various versions of their mythology, Thetis and Mêtis have associations with bonds and binding; both are sea powers; both shape-shifters; both loved by Zeus; both destined to bear a son greater than his father. Some scholars, like M. L. West, have seen the name of Thetis as defining her role in Alcman's poem; see West's "Three Presocratic Cosmologies," *CQ* 57 (1963): 154–57; "Alcman and Pythagoras," *CQ* 61 (1967): 1–7; and *Early Greek Philosophy and the Orient* (Oxford, 1971), 206–8. Detienne and Vernant, *Métis des grecs*, suggest that it is the power of metamorphosis as an attribute that disposes these goddesses of the sea to a crucial cosmological role: they "contain" the potential shapes of everything created and creatable. More recently, G. Most, "Alcman's 'Cosmogonic' Fragment (Fr. 5 Page, 81 Calame)," *CQ* 37, no. 1 (1987): 1–19, has argued that although the extant commentary is cosmogonic, Alcman's poem was not. According to Most, Alcman's poem was a *partheneion*, whose mythic section contained—appropriately for its genre—an account of Thetis's metamorphoses when Peleus attempted to ravish her; it was her transformations that were allegorized by the ancient commentator as a cosmogony. If, as Most suggests, the partheneion context required some erotic narrative element—such as the "erotic rivalry" between the Tyndarids and the Hippocoontids in the fragmentary opening lines of the Louvre Partheneion—then it seems to me conceivable that Alcman may have used the framework of the Thetis-Peleus story as *Isthmian 8* gives it to us: including not only the episode of the metamorphoses but the background rivalry of Zeus and Poseidon that necessitated assigning Thetis to a mortal mate.

[33] In Book 24, Zeus must appeal to Thetis for the release of Hector's body by Achilles, admitting that the gods are powerless to rescue the corpse without her intervention.

[34] It is important to stress that we cannot assume a single common bearing on Thetis's mythology in Pindar, Alcman, Aeschylus, and Apollodorus (or, for example, Herodotus, who records at 6.1.191 that the Persians sacrificed to Thetis at Cape Sepias); but at the same time we may usefully draw attention to these authors' identification of Thetis as invested with vast cosmic power—an identification that clearly stems from elsewhere than the *Iliad*'s *overt* presentation of her. Thetis's silence on the subject of her own power is all the more striking

grief is her preeminent attribute in the poem. Her references to herself, as mentioned above, are uniquely to her sorrow over her son. In contexts where we might expect reminders of her former potency—like that in Achilles' speech in Book 1—she claims for herself only suffering beyond that of all other Olympians. What lies tacitly behind the surpassing grief of Thetis, linking her past and her present in the *Iliad*, remains privileged knowledge, signaled by allusive references that are oblique, but sufficient. As we shall see in the following chapter, the *Iliad* makes her very grief a signifier of her former power, now suppressed or redefined. At the same time, by focusing on her sorrow as preeminent—while her power remains an allusion, displaced at the level of narrative—the poem locates its subject matter decisively in the human realm.

---

in view of Achilles' description at 1.396–97 of her boasting about it.

CHAPTER 3
The Wrath of Thetis

An inconsolable mother, unable to save her only child—Thetis is the paradigm for the image of bereavement conjured up with the fall of each young warrior for whom the poem reports that the moment of his death leaves his anguished parents forlorn. Shaped by allusion to her mythology, however—its resonance augmented, as we shall see, through various forms of reference—the *Iliad*'s rendering of Thetis makes hers a grief with a history; while in the poem's unfolding action Thetis's sorrow is conflated with that of Achilles: she laments not only for her son, but with him:

> ὄφρα δέ μοι ζώει καὶ ὁρᾷ φάος ἠελίοιο
> ἄχνυται, οὐδέ τί οἱ δύναμαι χραισμῆσαι ἰοῦσα.
> ἀλλ᾽ εἶμ᾽, ὄφρα ἴδωμι φίλον τέκος, ἠδ᾽ ἐπακούσω
> ὅττι μιν ἵκετο πένθος ἀπὸ πτολέμοιο μένοντα.

(18.61–64)

> Still, while he lives and looks on the sunlight
> he grieves, and I, going to him, am all unable to help him.
> But I shall go, so that I may see my dear child, and may hear
> what grief has come to him as he waits out the battle.

Grief is never static, never passive, in the *Iliad*. Often it is what motivates warriors to plunge into the thick of harrowing battle, renewing their murderous efforts.[1] For Achilles in particular, ἄχος (*achos*, "grief") is a constant; and because it is linked to his wrath, his continuous grief involves shifting consequences for other people.[2] Achilles' capacity, as G. Nagy has shown, to effect a *transfert du mal* through which his ἄχος is passed on to the Achaeans and finally to the Trojans engages the dynamic of his μῆνις (*mênis,*

---

[1] See Fenik, *Typical Battle Scenes;* "Les amis mortels," this volume, pp120-138.
[2] See Nagy, *Best of the Achaeans,* 60-83, esp. 82.

"wrath"): "the ἄχος of Achilles leads to the μῆνις of Achilles leads to the ἄχος of the Achaeans."[3]

The *Iliad* marks the wrath of its hero with a special denotation. Achilles is the only mortal of whom the substantive μῆνις is used in Homer. In a study of the semantics of μῆνις, C. Watkins has demonstrated that "μῆνις is on a wholly different level from the other Homeric words for 'wrath.' The ominous, baneful character of μῆνις is plain. It is a dangerous notion, which one must fear; a sacral, 'numinous' (θεῶν) notion, to be sure, but one of which even the gods are concerned with ridding themselves." Therefore "the association of divine wrath with a mortal by this very fact elevates that mortal outside the normal ambience of the human condition toward the sphere of the divine."[4]

Μῆνις thus not only designates Achilles' power—divine in scope—to exact vengeance by transforming events according to his will, but it specifically associates Achilles with Apollo and Zeus, the two gods whose μῆνις is, in the case of each, explicitly identified and isolated as propelling and controlling the events of the poem.[5] Significantly, in addition, Zeus, Apollo, and—uniquely among mortals—Achilles are able both to generate and to remove ἄχος.

When Apollo and Achilles are involved in removing ἄχος from the Achaeans, they are said to ward off λοιγός (*loigos*, "destruction"). Apollo is appealed to by Chryses to remove the λοιγός with which the god has afflicted the Greek army (1.456). Achilles is requested to λοιγὸν ἀμύνειν ("ward off destruction") where, as in the case of Apollo, λοιγός denotes the plight into which he himself has cast the Achaeans: it is the term used at 16.32 and 21.134 to denote the Battle at the Ships. In fact, the successful capacity to λοιγὸν ἀμύνειν (or ἀμῦναι) *within the framework* of the *Iliad* is restricted to the two figures of μῆνις—Apollo and Achilles—who, like the third, Zeus, can both ward off devastation for the Greeks and bring it on them as well.

The single other possessor of the ability to λοιγὸν ἀμῦναι successfully is Thetis. We have examined the passage in Book 1 that identifies her as the rescuer of the divine regime; she alone was able to λοιγὸν ἀμῦναι for Zeus, to protect him from destruction. But if the power to λοιγὸν ἀμῦναι is bivalent—if

---

[3] Ibid., 80.

[4] C. Watkins, "On ΜΗΝΙΣ," *Indo-European Studies* 3 (1977): 694–95 and 690, respectively.

[5] Zeus's *mênis* is referred to at 5.34, 13.624, and 15.122. On the *mênis* of Apollo, see 1.75, 5.444, 16.711.

the one who wields it can not only avert destruction but also bring it on—then the threat posed by Thetis, who could λοιγὸν ἀμῦναι on a cosmic level, is potentially the greatest of all; for Thetis's ἄχος is supreme among the gods of the *Iliad*: the *transfert du mal* she might effect would be on an equal scale. Remembering that for Achilles ἄχος leads to μῆνις leads to the ἄχος of others, we may ask the question, why does the *Iliad* not predicate a μῆνις of Thetis? The answer, I think, is that it does—integrating into its own narrative by means of allusion and digression mythology that does not belong to the *kleos* of warriors.

If we consider the grief that Thetis endures because of the imminent loss of her son (whose prospective death she already mourns in her γόος [*goos*, "lament"] at 18.52-64), and her power to respond on a cosmic scale, we recognize elements that combine elsewhere in a context in which it is appropriate to show full-fledged divine μῆνις in action, namely in the *Homeric Hymn to Demeter*. The hymn is precisely about the consequences of the μῆνις that ensues from Demeter's grief over the loss of Korê.

Much as Thetis's grief is evoked instantly when she hears Achilles' lament for Patroklos in Book 18, prefiguring his own death,

> σμερδαλέον δ' ᾤμωξεν· ἄκουσε δὲ πότνια μήτηρ
> ἡμένη ἐν βένθεσσιν ἁλὸς παρὰ πατρὶ γέροντι,
> κώκυσέν τ' ἄρ' ἔπειτα·
>
> (18.35-37)

> He cried out piercingly, and his regal mother heard him
> as she sat in the depths of the sea beside her aged father,
> and she cried in lament in turn,

so ἄχος seizes Demeter at the moment that she hears her daughter's cry as she is abducted into the underworld by Hades:

> ἤχησαν δ' ὀρέων κορυφαὶ καὶ βένθεα πόντου
> φωνῇ ὑπ' ἀθανάτῃ, τῆς δ' ἔκλυε πότνια μήτηρ.
> ὀξὺ δέ μιν κραδίην ἄχος ἔλλαβεν...
>
> (*Hymn. Hom. Dem.* 38-40)

> The crests of the mountains and the depths of the sea echoed
> with her immortal voice, and her regal mother heard her.
> Instantly grief seized her heart...

What follows is Demeter's wrath at the gods' complicity in the irrevocable violation of Persephone, and through that wrath both Olympians and mortals are bound to suffer disastrously. Demeter isolates herself from the gods, prepares full-scale devastation, and finally brings the Olympians to their knees. Zeus is compelled to dissuade her, sending Iris with his appeal:

ἵκετο δὲ πτολίεθρον Ἐλευσῖνος θυοέσσης,
εὗρεν δ' ἐν νηῷ Δημήτερα κυανόπεπλον,
καί μιν φωνήσασ' ἔπεα πτερόεντα προσηύδα·
Δήμητερ καλέει σε πατὴρ Ζεὺς ἄφθιτα εἰδώς
ἐλθέμεναι μετὰ φῦλα θεῶν αἰειγενετάων.
ἀλλ' ἴθι, μηδ' ἀτέλεστον ἐμὸν ἔπος ἐκ Διὸς ἔστω.

(*Hymn. Hom. Dem.* 318–23)

She arrived at the town of fragrant Eleusis
and found dark-robed Demeter in the temple
and addressed her, speaking winged words:
Demeter, Zeus the father, whose wisdom is
        unfailing, summons you
to come among the tribes of the immortal gods.
Come then, do not let my message from Zeus be unaccomplished.

But Demeter's *mênis* is too great: she does not comply, and Hermes must be sent to Hades so that Demeter may see her daughter. Hermes reports:

Ἅιδη κυανοχαῖτα καταφθιμένοισιν ἀνάσσων
Ζεύς σε πατὴρ ἤνωγεν ἀγαυὴν Περσεφόνειαν
ἐξαγαγεῖν Ἐρέβευσφι μετὰ σφέας, ὄφρα ἑ μήτηρ
ὀφθαλμοῖσιν ἰδοῦσα χόλου καὶ μήνιος αἰνῆς
ἀθανάτοις παύσειεν·

(*Hymn. Hom. Dem.* 347–51)

Hades, dark-haired ruler of the perished,
Zeus the father bids you to bring illustrious Persephone
out of Erebos to be among the gods, so that her mother,
looking upon her, may cease from anger and dire wrath
against the immortals.

Among a number of striking correspondences between Demeter and Thetis, there is an especially telling parallel in the κάλυμμα κυάνεον (*kalumma kuaneon*, "black cloak") Demeter puts on as she rushes out in search of Kore, which is subsequently reflected in her epithet κυανόπεπλος (*kuano-peplos*, "dark-garbed"). κυανόπεπλος is used to describe Demeter four times in the course of the hymn, within a space of only slightly over one hundred

75

lines, characterizing her at the height of her ominous wrath, in the course of the gods' efforts to appease her.[6] The final instance of the epithet occurs after the joyful reunion of Demeter and Korê, but *before* Zeus has appeased Demeter's wrath, promising her *timai* and the return of her daughter for two-thirds of the year. Once Demeter has agreed to renounce her wrath, the epithet is not used again.

Demeter's dark aspect originates with the onset of her ἄχος:

ἤχησαν δ' ὀρέων κορυφαὶ καὶ βένθεα πόντου
φωνῇ ὑπ' ἀθανάτῃ, τῆς δ' ἔκλυε πότνια μήτηρ.
ὀξὺ δέ μιν κραδίην ἄχος ἔλλαβεν, ἀμφὶ δὲ χαίταις
ἀμβροσίαις κρήδεμνα δαΐζετο χερσὶ φίλῃσι,
κυάνεον δὲ κάλυμμα κατ' ἀμφοτέρων βάλετ' ὤμων,
σεύατο δ' ὥς τ' οἰωνὸς ἐπὶ τραφερήν τε καὶ ὑγρὴν
μαιομένη·

(*Hymn. Hom. Dem.* 38–44)

The crests of the mountains and the depths of the sea echoed
with her immortal voice, and her regal mother heard her.
Instantly grief seized her heart, and she ripped
the covering on her fragrant hair with her own hands,
and around both shoulders she threw a black cloak,
and sped like a bird over land and sea,
searching.

This gesture of Demeter covering herself with a dark shawl has been shown to signify her transformation from a passive state of grief to an active state of anger.[7] In contrast to the image of the black cloud that surrounds a

---

[6] The epithet occurs at 319, 360, 373, and 442. κυανόπεπλος is glossed by a fuller description of the goddess at 181–83, when she has separated herself from the gods specifically out of wrath:

ἡ δ' ἄρ' ὄπισθε φίλον τετιημένη ἦτορ
στεῖχε κατὰ κρῆθεν κεκαλυμμένη, ἀμφὶ δὲ πέπλος
κυάνεος ῥαδινοῖσι θεᾶς ἐλελίζετο ποσσίν.

Disturbed in her dear heart, she walked behind,
with her head veiled, and her dark cloak
waved around the lithe feet of the goddess.

[7] Full argumentation is given by D. Petegorsky in "Demeter and the Black Robe of Grief" (unpublished paper), who clarifies the distinction between the dying warrior being covered by a dark cloud, expressed by such phrases as νεφέλη δέ μιν ἀμφεκάλυψε / κυανέη (*Il.* 20.417–18) and μέλαν νέφος ἀμφεκάλυψεν (16.350), and Demeter's assertive action in cloaking herself with her black garment. Petegorsky compares Simonides (frag. 121 Diehl) on

dying warrior or a mourner, here the goddess's deliberate assumption of the dark garment betokens her dire spirit of retaliation, the realization of her immanent wrath.

In this connection, the cult of Demeter Melaina at Phigalia in Arcadia deserves attention. Pausanias reports (8.42) that the Phigalians, by their own account, have given Demeter the *epiklêsis Melaina* because of her black clothing, which she put on for two reasons: first, out of anger at Poseidon for his intercourse with her, and second, out of grief over the abduction of Persephone. Two reasons—but her anger is the first. The Phigalians further explain that Zeus, having learned about Demeter's appearance (σχήματος…ὡς εἶχε) and her *clothing* (ἐσθῆτα ἐνεδέδυτο ποίαν), sent the Moirai to persuade the goddess to put aside her anger (first) and to abate her grief (second). Moreover, in their worship of Demeter Melaina the Phigalians are said—by way of introduction to their cult—to agree with the Thelpusian account of Demeter's rape by Poseidon. This account, which the Phigalia passage begins by referring to, Pausanias records at 8.25.4–5 in order to explain why the goddess is worshiped by the Thelpusians as Demeter Erinus. After Poseidon forced himself on her as she was searching for her daughter, Demeter was enraged at what had happened and was therefore given the *epiklêsis Erinus* because of her wrath (τοῦ μηνίματος μὲν ἕνεκα Ἐρινύς, 8.25.6). Demeter Melaina and Demeter Erinus are congruent references to the same story: the black-garbed goddess is a metonym of the wrathful, avenging goddess.

There is only one other dark κάλυμμα in Homeric epic, and it belongs to Thetis. She wraps herself in it when in Book 24 Iris announces Zeus's

---

the death of the heroes who perished at Thermopylae:
ἄσβεστον κλέος οἵδε φίλῃ περὶ πατρίδι θέντες
κυάνεον θανάτου ἀμφεβάλοντο νέφος·
οὐδὲ τεθνᾶσι θανόντες, ἐπεί σφ' ἀρετὴ καθύπερθεν
κυδαίνουσ' ἀνάγει δώματος ἐξ Ἀΐδεω.

To quote from Petegorsky's analysis, "what is crucial in the poem is the change from a situation in which the cloud of death, as a force beyond their control, consumes the warriors, to one in which they have appropriated death by turning it into a willful act—they are not passively slain, rather they choose actively to die. The grammar reflects this change. The familiar dark covering phrase is transformed from one in which the dark agent is the subject of the verb of covering and the person who is to die is the object, into one in which the heroes have become the subjects and the cloud the object of the verb ἀμφιβάλλομαι. This is especially interesting in that the verb which is used of Demeter putting on the dark shawl is βάλλομαι, and it is said that she puts it on both (ἀμφοτέρων) shoulders" (23). As the hymn proceeds to show, Demeter is not passively overcome with grief; she is grief-stricken indeed, but actively enraged as well.

request that she come to Olympos. Here the context is again, as in the *Hymn to Demeter*, one of *achos*. Thetis replies to Iris:

ἔχω δ' ἄχε' ἄκριτα θυμῷ.

(24.91)

I have endless grief in my heart.

Because of her *achos* Thetis all but refuses to join the other gods. Unlike Demeter in the hymn, she does respond to the summons; and yet the dark cloak she then puts on expresses—as with Demeter—the active principle that her grief presupposes:

Ὣς ἄρα φωνήσασα κάλυμμ' ἕλε δῖα θεάων
κυάνεον, τοῦ δ' οὔ τι μελάντερον ἔπλετο ἔσθος.
βῆ δ' ἰέναι, πρόσθεν δὲ ποδήνεμος ὠκέα Ἶρις
ἡγεῖτ'·

(24.93–96)

So she spoke and, radiant among goddesses, she took up
her dark cloak, and there is no blacker garment than this.
She set out, and before her swift wind-stepping Iris
led the way.

The very request from Zeus acknowledges that Thetis and Achilles together have, like Demeter, brought Olympos to submission. Thetis's potential for retaliation is signaled explicitly: Zeus says, as she takes her place next to him:

Οὔλυμπόνδε, θεὰ Θέτι, κηδομένη περ,
πένθος ἄλαστον ἔχουσα μετὰ φρεσίν· οἶδα καὶ αὐτός·

(24.104–5)

You have come to Olympos, divine Thetis, although sorrowing
with a grief beyond forgetting in your heart. And I
myself know it.

Ἄλαστον (*alaston*), derived from λανθάνομαι (*lanthanomai*), means "unforgettable." The semantics of ἀλάστωρ (*alastôr*) in tragedy, however, as well as the morphological parallel with ἄφθιτον (*aphthiton*), indicate that ἄλαστον can also mean "unforgetting."[8] In this sense the πένθος of Thetis has

---

[8] Among other examples from tragedy, see Aesch. *Ag.* 1500–1504. In *Comparative Studies of Greek*

the same ominous character as that of her son, whose final πένθος over the death of Patroklos drives him to his devastating vengeance.

The image of the goddess taking up her κάλυμμα κυάνεον may be seen, I suggest, as alluding to the implicit threat of μῆνις.[9] That Thetis wears a dark cloak than which "there is no blacker garment" accords with her having a cosmic potential for revenge—bivalent as we have seen λοιγὸν ἀμῦναι to be— that is greater than any other.

Why then does the *Iliad* not refer overtly to the wrath of Thetis? Thetis, as observed earlier, never refers to her own power, in contexts where we would expect it, but to her grief. That grief, however, is twofold. When she accounts for it most fully, to Hephaistos in Book 18, she separates its two aspects:

> Ἥφαιστ', ἦ ἄρα δή τις, ὅσαι θεαί εἰσ' ἐν Ὀλύμπῳ,
> τοσσάδ' ἐνὶ φρεσὶν ᾗσιν ἀνέσχετο κήδεα λυγρά,
> ὅσσ' ἐμοὶ ἐκ πασέων Κρονίδης Ζεὺς ἄλγε' ἔδωκεν;
> ἐκ μέν μ' ἀλλάων ἁλιάων ἀνδρὶ δάμασσεν,
> Αἰακίδῃ Πηλῆϊ, καὶ ἔτλην ἀνέρος εὐνὴν
> πολλὰ μάλ' οὐκ ἐθέλουσα. ὁ μὲν δὴ γήραϊ λυγρῷ
> κεῖται ἐνὶ μεγάροις ἀρημένος, ἄλλα δέ μοι νῦν·
> υἱὸν ἐπεί μοι δῶκε γενέσθαι τε τραφέμεν τε,
> ἔξοχον ἡρώων· ὁ δ' ἀνέδραμεν ἔρνεϊ ἶσος·
>
> (18.429–37)

Hephaistos, is there anyone, of all the goddesses on Olympos,
who has endured so many baneful sorrows in her heart,
as many as the griefs Zeus the son of Kronos has
  given me beyond all others?
Of all the daughters of the sea he forced on me a mortal man
Aiakos' son Peleus, and I endured the bed of a mortal man,
utterly unwilling though I was. And that one lies in
his halls, shattered by baneful old age. But now for
  me there are other sorrows:

---

and Indic Meter (Cambridge, Mass., 1974), 256–61, G. Nagy discusses the traditional complementarity of the themes of κλέος and πένθος and the morphology of their epithets. See as
well the analysis in Chantraine, *Dictionnaire étymologique*, 54; also the discussion of line 911 in
volume 3 of Wilamowitz's edition of Euripides' *Herakles* (1895; reprint, Bad Homburg, 1959),
202.

9 Nagler, *Spontaneity and Tradition*, 27–63, has demonstrated the symbolic signification of
clothing and gestures related to it in his discussion of Homeric *krēdemnon*. See also S.
Lowenstam, *The Death of Patroklos: A Study in Typology*, Beiträge zur klassischen Philologie 133
(Königstein, 1981), on the symbolic force of gesture in the *Iliad*.

since he gave me a son to bear and to raise,
preeminent among heroes, and he grew like a young shoot.

The primary cause of her suffering was being forced by Zeus, the son of Kronos, to submit against her will to marriage to a mortal. Thus the *Iliad* returns us to the crucial feature of Thetis's mythology, her role in the succession myth. She was forced to marry a mortal because her potential for bearing a son greater than his father meant that marriage to Zeus or Poseidon would begin the entire world order over again.

Here once more there is a striking parallel with the *Hymn to Demeter*, which stresses Demeter's anger not so much against Hades as against Zeus, who ordained the rape of Persephone by his brother. The poem is explicit on this point. Helios identifies Zeus as exclusively *aitios* ("responsible") in the abduction of Persephone (75–79), upon hearing which Demeter is said to feel a "more terrible" ἄχος and to withdraw from the company of the gods out of rage at Zeus:

τὴν δ' ἄχος αἰνότερον καὶ κύντερον ἵκετο θυμόν.
χωσαμένη δ' ἤπειτα κελαινεφέϊ Κρονίωνι
νοσφισθεῖσα θεῶν ἀγορὴν καὶ μακρὸν Ὄλυμπον
ᾤχετ' ἐπ' ἀνθρώπων πόλιας καὶ πίονα ἔργα
εἶδος ἀμαλδύνουσα πολὺν χρόνον·

(*Hymn. Hom. Dem.* 90–94)

And grief more terrible and savage entered her heart.
Thereupon in anger at the son of Kronos of the black clouds,
shunning the assembly of the gods and high Olympos
she went to the cities and fertile fields of men,
long disfiguring her appearance.

In the context of her wrathful isolation from the gods, as noted above, elaborate mention is made of her black garment.[10]

---

[10] See *Hom. Hymn. Dem.* 181–83, quoted in note 6. It is perhaps worth adding that in Homer the formula τετιημένος ἦτορ ("disturbed at heart") when it is used to describe the gods always means "angry." When Hera and Athena sit apart from Zeus and refuse to speak to him for preventing them from assisting the Achaeans, they are said to be φίλον τετιημέναι ἦτορ (*Il.* 8.437); and when Hephaistos discovers the adultery of Aphrodite and Ares, he is described as follows:
βῆ δ' ἴμεναι πρὸς δῶμα, φίλον τετιημένος ἦτορ·
ἔστη δ' ἐν προθύροισι, χόλος δέ μιν ἄγριος ᾔρει·
(*Od.* 8.303–4)
He set out for his house, disturbed in his dear heart;

The implicit wrath of Thetis has an analogous source. Given that the tripartite division of the universe is shared by the three brothers, Zeus and Poseidon on the one hand, Hades on the other, we see that these two myths share in the first place a preoccupation with the imposition and preservation of the existing hierarchy of divine power. Both the *Hymn to Demeter* and Pindar's *Isthmian* 8, in its treatment of Thetis's mythology, are equipped by the nature of their genres to emphasize this concern. Their other common element, namely grief over the confrontation with mortality, is what heroic epic uniquely elaborates.

The *Iliad* is about the condition of being human and about heroic endeavor as its most encompassing expression. The *Iliad* insists at every opportunity on the irreducible fact of human mortality, and in order to do so it reworks traditional motifs, such as the protection motif, as described in Chapter 1. The values it asserts, its definition of heroism, emerge in the human, not the divine, sphere.

For this reason it is more useful to ask not why the *Iliad* omits specific mention of a *mênis* of Thetis, but why it gives us so much evidence for one; and why at crucial points in the narrative it reminds its audience, by allusion, of the theogonic mythology of Thetis as cosmic force. Questions of this kind may be said to motivate an inquiry like the present one, whose goal is to reinforce our awareness of how and for what purposes Homeric epic integrates diverse mythological material into its narrative, and how such material serves a coherent thematic imperative.

Thetis provides an intriguing example of the convergence of these dynamic processes, in that the way in which her mythology is resonant but subordinated corresponds to the Homeric insight that it literally underlies or forms the substratum of the heroism of Achilles. The intrinsic relation of parent to child, in which the parent's story becomes the child's story, is not banal here, but has special significance. The reality of Thetis's generative power has as its issue the fact of Achilles' mortality. In this sense *Isthmian* 8 describes where the *Iliad* should begin.

It has been argued by Watkins that whereas the *Iliad* demands the resolution of a wrath (whose religious stature is established by its very diction) in

---

and he stood in the doorway, and savage anger seized him.

For a psychoanalytic perspective on the hymn's representation of Demeter's resistance to the patriarchal order, see M. Arthur, "Politics and Pomegranates: An Interpretation of the *Homeric Hymn to Demeter*," *Arethusa* 10.1 (Spring 1977): 7–47.

its initial thematic statement, the formula that would express such a resolution is rigorously suppressed. Suffice it here to quote his conclusion:

> We have shown on the one hand the equivalence of μῆνις and χόλος in the mouth of the one who says "I," and the equivalence of μῆνις and μηνιθμός, for which the latter is the tabu substitute precisely in μηνιθμὸν καταπαυσέμεν 16 62. We have shown on the other hand that μῆνις in the sense of "anger, wrath" is an echo, a phonetic icon of the forbidden word μῆνις. Everything then would indicate that the dramatic resolution of the *Iliad* as a whole, whose theme "wrath" is announced from its very first word, is expressed by a formula "put an end to one's wrath," *whose real verbal expression* παύειν + μῆνιν *never surfaces*. It is a formula whose workings take place always beyond our view, a formula hidden behind the vocabulary tabu, a particular condition on the plane of the parole, of the message, of the one who is speaking and the one who is addressed.[11]

Similarly, what informs the human stature of Achilles is Thetis's cosmic, theogonic power—her role in the succession myth; and although the *Iliad* never reverts to it explicitly, it returns us to it repeatedly. If Themis had not intervened, Thetis would have borne to Zeus or Poseidon the son greater than his father, and the entire chain of succession in heaven would have continued: Achilles would have been not the greatest of the heroes, but the ruler of the universe. The price of Zeus's hegemony is Achilles' death. This is the definitive instance of the potency of myths in Homeric epic that exert their influence on the subject matter of the poems yet do not "surface" (using Watkins's term), because of the constraints of the genre. Nevertheless, the poem reveals them, through evocative diction, oblique reference, even conspicuous omission.

It is in this sense that we can understand what appears to be a revision of the prayer formula by Achilles through Thetis to Zeus in Book 1. The typical arrangement of prayers as represented in archaic poetry, we remember, consists of the invocation of the god or goddess, the claim that the person praying is entitled to a favor on the basis of favors granted in the past, and the specific request for a favor in return—based on the premise that this constitutes a formal communication of reciprocal obligations between god and hero.[12]

---

[11] Watkins, "On ΜΗΝΙΣ," 703–4.
[12] See Muellner, *Meaning of Homeric EYXOMAI*, 27–28.

In directing his request for a favor from Zeus to Thetis, Achilles has translated his reminder of a past favor granted into *her* past aid to Zeus. But he prefaces his request, and invokes his mother, by saying:

μῆτερ, ἐπεί μ' ἔτεκές γε μινυνθάδιόν περ ἐόντα
τιμήν πέρ μοι ὄφελλεν Ὀλύμπιος ἐγγυαλίξαι
Ζεὺς ὑψιβρεμέτης.

(1.352–54)

Mother, since you did bear me to be short-lived,
surely high-thundering Olympian Zeus ought to
grant me honor.

In other words, Achilles' favor to Zeus consists in his being *minunthadios*, whereby Zeus's sovereignty is guaranteed.

To reiterate, the *Iliad* reminds us of Thetis's mythology, through allusions to her power and through emphasis on the reciprocity of *achos* that she and Achilles share—his Iliadic and hers meta-Iliadic—in order to assert the meaning of human life in relation to the entire cosmic structure: in order to show that cosmic equilibrium is bought at the cost of human mortality. The alternative would mean perpetual evolution, perpetual violent succession, perpetual disorder.

The tradition of Thetis's power, the eventual issue of which is in the figure of Achilles, both enhances his stature and is subsumed in it. It thus represents the ultimate example of thematic integration. Heroic epic is concerned with the *erga andrôn* rather than the *erga theôn*. Thus with Achilles the mortal hero, the wrath of Thetis—potent in another framework—becomes absorbed in the actual wrath of her son. Achilles' invocation, in Book 1, of Thetis's cosmic power that once rescued Zeus must also invoke the power that once threatened to supplant Zeus; and once again, as in *Isthmian 8*, its corollary is the death of Achilles in battle.

That Thetis's power to persuade Zeus to favor Achilles has a source that the poem sees as located in an anterior (or extra-Iliadic) tradition is expressed not only in Achilles' speech in Book 1, but in a telling passage in Book 15. The result of Thetis's persuading Zeus to favor Achilles is the Trojans' success in bringing fire to the Achaean ships. In Book 15, at the final stage of the Trojans' advantage from the favor granted to Achilles before the death of Patroklos commits him to reenter the fighting, the situation is described as follows:

Τρῶες δὲ λείουσιν ἐοικότες ὠμοφάγοισι
νηυσὶν ἐπεσσεύοντο, Διὸς δὲ τέλειον ἐφετμάς,

ὅ σφισιν αἰὲν ἔγειρε μένος μέγα, θέλγε δὲ θυμὸν
Ἀργείων καὶ κῦδος ἀπαίνυτο, τοὺς δ' ὀρόθυνεν.
Ἕκτορι γάρ οἱ θυμὸς ἐβούλετο κῦδος ὀρέξαι
Πριαμίδῃ, ἵνα νηυσὶ κορωνίσι θεσπιδαὲς πῦρ
ἐμβάλοι ἀκάματον, Θέτιδος δ' ἐξαίσιον ἀρὴν
πᾶσαν ἐπικρήνειε·

(15.592–99)

But the Trojans like ravening lions
charged at the ships, and were fulfilling the bidding of Zeus
who continually roused great strength in them, and beguiled the
    spirit of the Argives
and denied them victory, but urged on the others.
For Zeus's intention was to give victory to Hektor,
Priam's son, so that he might hurl on the curved ships
blazing, unwearying fire, and accomplish entirely
the extraordinary prayer of Thetis.

Significantly, Thetis's prayer is qualified by the Iliadic *hapax* ἐξαίσιον (*exaision*). It has been shown that the phrases ὑπὲρ μοῖραν (*huper moiran*) and κατὰ μοῖραν (*kata moiran*), and by extension the equivalent phrases ὑπὲρ αἶσαν (*huper aisan*) and κατὰ αἶσαν (*kata aisan*), are used in Homeric epic self-referentially, to signify adherence to or contravention of the compositions own traditions.[13] We may therefore observe that the exercise of Thetis's power, with its massive consequences for inverting the course of the Trojan War, is ἐξαίσιον—neither according to nor opposed to Iliadic tradition, but *outside* it and requiring integration into it.

The *Hymn to Demeter* demands a sacral resolution in terms appropriate to Demeter's wrath. Heroic epic demands a human one, and the *Iliad* presents it in Book 24. Thetis must accept the mortal condition of Achilles, of which, as *Isthmian* 8 explains, she is the cause. This acceptance means the defusing of μῆνις, leaving only ἄχος. It is thus comprehensible thematically that Thetis should be the agent of Achilles' returning the body of Hektor, of his acceptance not only of his own mortality but of the universality of the conditions of human existence as he expounds them to Priam in Book 24.

---

[13] Nagy, *Best of the Achaeans*, 40: "Within the conventions of epic composition, an incident that is untraditional would be ὑπὲρ μοῖραν 'beyond destiny.' For example, it would violate tradition to let Achilles kill Aeneas in *Iliad* XX, although the immediate situation in the narrative seems to make it inevitable; accordingly, Poseidon intervenes and saves Aeneas, telling him that his death at this point would be 'beyond destiny' (ὑπὲρ μοῖραν: XX 336)."

As such, Thetis is the instrument of Achilles' renunciation of μῆνις in the poem. In a sense the submerged formula παύειν + μῆνιν is enacted twice—not only on the human and divine levels, but twice in time: in the "long-time" eternality of the succession myth and in the time span of the Iliadic plot. The intersection is the life span of Achilles. With this perspective we can come to apprehend the *Iliad's* concern with the individual's experience of his mortal limitations and the existential choices they demand, and equally its concern with their metaphysical consequences in relation to the entire cosmic structure.

CHAPTER 4
Allusion and Interpretation

To the *Iliad*'s modern audiences, compelled by the urgent momentum of the poem's action and absorbed in the inexorability of its progress and the frontal intensity of its character portrayals, the epic's digressions from the imperative of its plot can seem to be a perplexing distraction, and its texture of oblique allusion and elliptical reference, of glancing, arcane hint and obscure, indirect suggestion can seem to be interlayered against the grain of its densely compact dramatic core. Where the *Iliad* has been described as subtly symmetrical in its formal construction, these features would appear to overbalance or re-center its inner patterning.[1] They have been accounted quirks of style: hallmarks of ancient epic, to be sure, but peripheral narrative features whose appearances have been justified as compositional "devices," serving the exigencies of the bard's technique.[2] Thus an exemplary school text designed to introduce students of Greek to selections from the *Iliad* will, for instance, bracket Nestor's speeches and will propose that, if short of time, the reader may omit the Meleager episode; it will itself forgo including the entire story of Bellerophon.[3] The *Iliad*, in other words, may be satisfactorily introduced without such passages.

Our example of Thetis suggests that allusions, both abbreviated and extended in lengthy digressions, are highly charged and repay scrutiny for the myths whose resonance or "reverberation" they carry into the narrative as a whole, signaling a constellation of themes that establish bearings for the poem as it unfolds and linking it continually to other traditions and

---

[1] On the structure of the *Iliad*, see, for example, J. T. Sheppard, *The Pattern of the Iliad* (London, 1922); and especially Whitman, *Homer and the Heroic Tradition*, chap. 11.

[2] See, for instance, G. Murray, *The Rise of the Greek Epic*, 4th ed. (Oxford, 1934; reprint, 1961), chap. 7, esp. 173ff.; C. M. Bowra, *Tradition and Design in the Iliad* (Oxford, 1930; reprint, 1963), chap. 4, esp. 84–86; also his *Homer* (New York, 1972), chap. 4; J. B. Hainsworth, *Homer* (Oxford, 1969), 31.

[3] The otherwise extremely sound A. R. Benner, *Selections From Homer's Iliad* (New York, 1903) serves as an example.

paradigms and to a wider mythological terrain.[4] We might say that allusions provide the coordinates that locate the poem's action within a multidimensional mythological realm.

Evocations of the succession myth through allusions to Thetis's role in it ground the Iliadic theme of mortality in a complex set of divine-human relations. The *Iliad* presupposes an established hierarchy on Olympos, but behind the static resolution that hierarchy represents lies a history of contention and struggle, as the gods themselves obliquely but forcefully remind each other. Zeus's authority is firmly in place. Claiming a preeminence that cannot be subverted, Zeus asserts that not all the other gods combined can dislodge him from his position of superiority. References to their past efforts to do so—or suggestions of possible attempts in the future—are reminiscent of such combats as are described in the Hesiodic version of divine competition for supremacy. Specific elements recognizable from the Hesiodic account are present in the *Iliad*, as in the passing mention of the monstrous Typhoeus at 2.782. But competition among the gods for power—and indeed reconciliation among them—is now, as it were, managed symbolically, through the partisan efforts of the gods on behalf of the mortal adversaries they favor. The gods' very participation in the war on behalf of competing human interests becomes an allusion to their own history: when they take sides against each other in the war, that is, in aid of Greeks or Trojans, their actions rehearse the older, larger conflict that digressions about divine strife have recalled.

There are, therefore, more layers of allusion than one, and in this sense the term "reverberation" is particularly expressive. Digressions about divine disorder echo another clash; they refer us to the ultimate contest for cosmic rule. Allusions form a system of evocation in which each reference produces not a single meaning but a sequence of overlapping significations—as with echoes, in which it is not the original sound but each subsequent iteration that is picked up and relayed. The direction of allusion may be reversed, proleptic: as when (for example) Hera refuses to renounce her intention to destroy the Trojans and their city, and Zeus resignedly accepts her intransigence but promises that in the future he will in return unhesitatingly sack whichever of her favorite cities he chooses—remembering her savagery toward his beloved Troy (4.30ff.). Here Zeus sets in motion a prospective

---

[4] "Reverberation" is M. Lang's effective term; see her article "Reverberation and Mythology," in *Approaches to Homer*, ed. Rubino and Shelmerdine.

allusion, anticipating an episode in the future that will allude to his present accommodation over Troy, and thus to their history of conflict.[5]

Such allusions as this, intertwining divine and human interests, bind past and future in a continuum whose effect is to blur the boundaries between digression and the narrative proper and to show the poem reasserting those boundaries by taking stock of, or reflecting on, its own plot. In the *Dios apatê* in Book 14, Hera's purpose is, literally, to create a digression, a countervailing movement against the narrative's momentum. Her seduction of Zeus is filled with innuendos of every kind, including suggestive hints about cosmogonic disharmony, as she enlists the services of Aphrodite and Sleep, and as she inveigles Zeus into thinking that the idea of their going to bed together is his.[6] Zeus appropriates the making of allusions, cataloging his former lovers (14.313ff.); and it is these erotic references that are resonant, more than Hera's staged reminiscence of Okeanos and Tethus, because they remind us of what we know from Thetis's mythology: Zeus's omniscience fails in the face of his own desire. Invincible and all-knowing, he is nevertheless baffled by eros. In the *Dios apatê* he is unable to see beyond his desire for Hera: the digression *becomes* the action; and the consequence is that the plot of the *Iliad* is temporarily out of his control. Thus when he awakens to find what has happened, his response has less to do with punishing Hera than with reclaiming control over the narrative: he declares what the plot of the rest of the poem will be, and goes beyond:

Ἕκτορα δ' ὀτρύνῃσι μάχην ἐς Φοῖβος Ἀπόλλων,
αὖτις δ' ἐμπνεύσῃσι μένος, λελάθῃ δ' ὀδυνάων
αἵ νῦν μιν τείρουσι κατὰ φρένας, αὐτὰρ Ἀχαιοὺς
αὖτις ἀποστρέψῃσιν ἀνάλκιδα φύζαν ἐνόρσας,
φεύγοντες δ' ἐν νηυσὶ πολυκλήϊσι πέσωσι
Πηλεΐδεω Ἀχιλῆος· ὁ δ' ἀνστήσει ὃν ἑταῖρον
Πάτροκλον· τὸν δὲ κτενεῖ ἔγχεϊ φαίδιμος Ἕκτωρ
Ἰλίου προπάροιθε πολέας ὀλέσαντ' αἰζηοὺς
τοὺς ἄλλους, μετὰ δ' υἱὸν ἐμὸν Σαρπηδόνα δῖον.
τοῦ δὲ χολωσάμενος κτενεῖ Ἕκτορα δῖος Ἀχιλλεύς.
ἐκ τοῦ δ' ἄν τοι ἔπειτα παλίωξιν παρὰ νηῶν

---

[5] Similarly, Hektor at 7.81–91 anticipates subsequent retrospection over the death of the hero he expects to kill in the duel to which he challenges the Achaean chiefs.

[6] See Janko 1992, ad loc.

αἰὲν ἐγὼ τεύχοιμι διαμπερές, εἰς ὅ κ' Ἀχαιοὶ
Ἴλιον αἰπὺ ἕλοιεν Ἀθηναίης διὰ βουλάς.

(15.59–71)

Let Phoibos Apollo rouse Hektor into battle
and again breathe strength into him, and make him
     forget the pains
that now wear down his spirit; let him meanwhile
     turn the Achaeans
back again, urging them to unresisting panic,
and let them, fleeing, fall among the benched ships
of Achilles, son of Peleus. And he shall send out his companion
Patroklos; but him shining Hektor shall kill with the spear
before Ilion, once Patroklos has killed many other
young men, among them my son, radiant Sarpedon.
And angered because of Patroklos, brilliant Achilles
     shall kill Hektor.
From that point I shall contrive a continuous, steady
retreat from the ships, until the Achaeans
capture steep Ilion through the plans of Athena.

But if the divine battlefield has become the human battlefield, it is not that the *Iliad* represents the suffering of its characters merely as a function— or as a reenactment at one remove—of divine dissatisfactions. Allusions to Thetis's mythology in particular, continually retrojecting into a pre-Iliadic past the process of resolving divine discord, help to evoke stages in an evolution of cosmic order in which men have had a part—in which there is a place for the human condition. In the Hesiodic version of the achievement of hegemony on Olympos in the *Theogony*, Zeus averts the predicted challenge of a child who will overmaster him by swallowing one goddess and giving birth to another; men are not in the picture.[7] The solution implicit in the mythology of Thetis, by contrast, posits a relationship between the achieved stability of the divine order and the mutability of the human order, where each generation must yield to the next. Allusions recalling hostility and competition among the gods, then—far from serving either to burlesque the drama at Troy or to emphasize the gods' role as vicarious spectators—link divine and human in a profoundly reciprocal connection, pointing to an intersection between the two that accounts for the gods' stake in the war as other than that of detached, if sentimental, onlookers.

---

[7] The mysterious threat of a son, at *Theogony* 897–98, never materializes.

Viewed from the vantage point of the mythology they recover, the digressions that encase these evocative allusions—in some instances at length—take on a different aspect from that assigned them in many recent studies of the subject, among them Erich Auerbach's memorable opening essay in *Mimesis*.[8] Citing correspondence between Goethe and Schiller on the digressive mode of epic, Auerbach affirms his own sense that Homeric style is not impelled by "any tensional and suspensive striving toward a goal." Yet he proposes that the origins of the digressive style must be accounted for not so much in terms of its peculiar effect on the movement of the plot, but more as a consequence of a characteristic Homeric phenomenology: an object (or character, or action) is constituted by whatever can be expressed about it on the surface. Auerbach explains: "The basic impulse of the Homeric style...[is] to represent phenomena in fully externalized form, visible and palpable in all their parts." Observing that the long passage in *Odyssey* 19 that describes how Odysseus acquired his distinguishing scar might easily have been recounted not as part of the "externalizing" descriptive narrative but as a recollection voiced by Odysseus himself, Auerbach elaborates: "But any such subjectivist-perspectivist procedure, creating a foreground and background, resulting in the present lying open to the depths of the past, is entirely foreign to the Homeric style; Homeric style knows only a foreground, only a uniformly illuminated, uniformly objective present."[9]

As our understanding of the distinctive properties of oral traditional poetry has grown over the past several decades, however, we have come increasingly to see that—as the present study aims to demonstrate—fundamental to the poetics of compositions like the *Iliad* and *Odyssey* is a process of selection, combination, and adaptation that draws out the full resonance and evocative power of the mythological material the poems incorporate. To an audience familiar with the mythological corpus available to the poet, the digressions create a topography the recesses of which reveal a rich and dense foundation beneath the evenly illuminated surface Auerbach describes. The more we are able to perceive the range and coherence of the references themselves, the more we can see how they serve to provide a context and a perspective in which to account for—to make sense of—character, action, and theme.

For all that he may underestimate the background they constitute and the shadows cast by the very obliqueness of their allusive representation,

---

[8] E. Auerbach, *Mimesis* (Princeton, 1953), chap. 1, 1–20.
[9] Ibid., 3, 4, and 5, respectively.

Auerbach himself clearly perceives that the continuous integration of mythological passages supplementing (although they appear to delay) the poem's narrative progress must be appreciated as the reflection, on the level of style, of a distinctive way of seeing and comprehending epic personages and events in their totality. This mode, which Auerbach takes to be characteristically Homeric, we may recognize, in all its cognitive dimensions, as intrinsic to traditional literature of the archaic period, including the poetry of Hesiod, the Homeric hymns, and Pindar.

More recent discussion has concentrated on the relationship of digressions to the exigencies of their immediate narrative situation.[10] Students of the subject have focused in particular on the function of digressions as *paradeigmata* exploited in a rhetorical strategy designed to persuade an addressee toward or away from a particular action. Attention has been fixed so determinedly on this point that it has led some scholars to the conclusion that the mythological allusions employed in hortatory situations were "ad hoc" inventions, improvised by the poet to offer his characters greater rhetorical power.[11] It is certainly true that our sources for identifying and piecing together the mythology underlying any number of epic allusions are limited and that the subtlety and virtuosity with which fragmentary references are worked into the poem may make it difficult to know even where to look for the appropriate sources, especially because the more familiar a reference was to the Homeric audience, the more abbreviated or schematic its presentation is likely to be. Yet to infer that allusions for which we have no other corroborating text are inventions devised for the sake of the immediate context is only one—and perhaps not the most far-reaching—approach to the workings of traditional narrative. Indeed, the logic of an argument that puts emphasis

---

[10] So, for example, Willcock, "Mythological Paradeigma," followed by B. K. Braswell, "Mythological Innovation in the *Iliad*," *CQ* 21 (1971): 16–26. In a subsequent article, "Ad Hoc Invention," 43, Willcock describes his earlier study as "endeavor[ing] to show that Homer has a genial habit of inventing mythology for the purpose of adducing it as a parallel to the situation in his story." In this article, which supports the original thesis by explaining "invention" as an inevitable consequence of "formulaic composition," Willcock concludes that "the oral poet concentrates on the particular scene which he is describing. He does his best to make it acceptable, producing corroborative evidence and circumstantial details as he requires them to that end" (45). N. Austin's perceptive study "The Function of Digressions in the *Iliad*," *GRBS* 7, no. 4 (1966): 295–312, emphasizes the role of digressions in "concentrat[ing] tension" at "high points in the drama," so as to create "dramatic urgency" (311–12). A. Köhnken, in his thoughtful discussion of Auerbach's essay in "Die Narbe des Odysseus: Ein Beitrag zur homerisch-epischen Erzähltechnik," *AuA* 22.2 (1976): 101–14, also assigns priority to the narrative circumstances as giving significance to the digressions; see esp. pp. 107–8.

[11] See especially Willcock, "Ad Hoc Invention."

on the hortatory context for mythological allusions would seem to require that in such contexts the most familiar, recognizable exemplars would be cited as instruments of persuasion; presumably a speaker would most effectively advert to a paradigm that had obvious meaning for his audience, in order to compel assent.[12]

As analyses of such digressions as the Meleager episode have shown, details may be suppressed, highlighted, or significantly rearranged; and as we see from the multiple versions of the Oresteia story within the *Odyssey*, the speaker's point of view may be shown by the poet to be a factor in the shading of details of a well-known model.[13] Beyond their utility for the speaker, however, is their meaning for the narrative as a whole; much as the Oresteia story has meaning that includes, but does not end with, what any individual speaker intends, its themes of seduction, betrayal, and the disintegration of the *oikos* are resonant beyond the persuasive or dissuasive goals of a particular narrator. Rather than assuming, then, that mythological precedents are invented "ad hoc" to suit the speaker's particular hortatory injunction, it would be equally possible to suppose that the rhetorical situation is created as a vehicle to introduce and frame mythological material valuable for its thematic impact.

The *Iliad*'s fundamental narrative mode of evocation elicits from its audience a particular kind of recognition that retrieves as full a context as possible for each fragmentary reference: a process of continuous recollection operating simultaneously with the audience's anticipation and apprehension of the developments of the poem's plot. As this study has aimed to illustrate, allusions remind the audience of other enriching traditions and serve to alert us to instances not of invention but of selection and adaptation. The *Dios boulê*, with which the poem opens, itself alludes, it has been convincingly argued, to a tradition explicit outside the *Iliad* with which its audience would have been well acquainted.[14] Proclus's summary of the *Cypria*, at the beginning of the Epic Cycle, mentions Zeus's taking counsel to arrange the Trojan War.[15] More specifically, a scholion at 1.5 gives a *historia* ascribing to

---

[12] Thus the address of Nestor to Agamemnon and Achilles at 1.254ff. would have seemed an effective place to interpolate a reference to Theseus. On 1.265 as a later, Athenian addition, see Kirk, *The Iliad: A Commentary* ad loc.

[13] See the discussion in Kakridis, *Homeric Researches*, chap. 1; N. Felson-Rubin, "Penelope's Perspectives: Character from Plot," in *Beyond Oral Poetry*, ed. J. M. Bremer, I. J. F. de Jong, J. Kalff (Amsterdam, 1987), 61–83.

[14] See W. Kullmann, "Ein vorhomerisches Motiv im Iliasproömium," *Philologus* 99 (1955): 167–92, as well as "Zur ΔΙΟΣ ΒΟΥΛΗ des Iliasproömiums," *Philologus* 100 (1956): 132–33.

[15] With Themis or Thetis? See A. Severyns, "Sur le début des chants cypriens," *Mededelingen*

the *Cypria* the account of a grand plan devised by Zeus to lessen the oppression suffered by Earth because of overpopulation and to punish men for their lack of piety. War is to be the remedy, war generated by Thetis's marriage to a mortal.[16] The scholion proceeds to quote seven lines from the *Cypria* as illustration, in which Zeus's solution for relieving Earth's burden is specified: it is the Trojan War; the heroes will perish at Troy.

The encompassing implications of this reference may be echoed in two proleptic digressions later in the poem. It has been shown that the passages in Books 7 and 12 about the obliteration of the Achaean wall by Poseidon and Apollo evoke nothing less than the conjoined themes of mankind's destruction and of heroic glory, by alluding to a mythological complex linking the plan of Zeus, the separation of men from gods, the demise of the demigods, the end of the Golden Age, and the threat of a universal deluge.[17]

With the image of divinely orchestrated devastation prefigured in the passage at 12.3–33, "the poem places its events far away in a past which becomes remote and fated not only to end, but to vanish."[18] The passage concludes as follows:

ὄφρα μὲν Ἕκτωρ ζωὸς ἔην καὶ μήνι' Ἀχιλλεὺς
καὶ Πριάμοιο ἄνακτος ἀπόρθητος πόλις ἔπλεν,
τόφρα δὲ καὶ μέγα τεῖχος Ἀχαιῶν ἔμπεδον ἦεν.
αὐτὰρ ἐπεὶ κατὰ μὲν Τρώων θάνον ὅσσοι ἄριστοι,
πολλοὶ δ' Ἀργείων οἱ μὲν δάμεν, οἱ δὲ λίποντο,
πέρθετο δὲ Πριάμοιο πόλις δεκάτῳ ἐνιαυτῷ,
Ἀργεῖοι δ' ἐν νηυσὶ φίλην ἐς πατρίδ' ἔβησαν,
δὴ τότε μητιόωντο Ποσειδάων καὶ Ἀπόλλων
τεῖχος ἀμαλδῦναι, ποταμῶν μένος εἰσαγαγόντες.
ὅσσοι ἀπ' Ἰδαίων ὀρέων ἅλαδε προρέουσι,
Ῥῆσός θ' Ἑπτάπορός τε Κάρησός τε Ῥοδίος τε
Γρήνικός τε καὶ Αἴσηπος δῖός τε Σκάμανδρος
καὶ Σιμόεις, ὅθι πολλὰ βοάγρια καὶ τρυφάλειαι
κάππεσον ἐν κονίῃσι καὶ ἡμιθέων γένος ἀνδρῶν·
τῶν πάντων ὁμόσε στόματ' ἔτραπε Φοῖβος Ἀπόλλων,

---

der *Koninklijke Nederlandse Akademie van Wetenschappen, afd. Letterkunde* n.s. 28, no. 5 (1965): 285–89.
[16] See schol. AD ad A 5–6. Thetis's marriage is called *Thetidos thnētogamian*; for the text, see A. Ludwich, *Textkritische Untersuchungen über die mythologischen Scholien zu Homers Ilias*, vol. 1 (Königsberg, 1900), 10–11.
[17] I refer to Scodel's important article "The Achaean Wall and the Myth of Destruction."
[18] Scodel, "Achaean Wall and Myth of Destruction," 48.

ἐννῆμαρ δ' ἐς τεῖχος ἵει ῥόον· ὗε δ' ἄρα Ζεὺς
συνεχές, ὄφρα κε θᾶσσον ἁλίπλοα τείχεα θείη.

(12.10–26)

As long as Hektor was still alive and Achilles still wrathful
and the city of lord Priam remained unsacked,
for so long did the great wall of the Achaeans also remain
  steadfast.
But when all the best of the Trojans had died,
and many of the Argives were crushed, and some were left,
and the city of Priam was sacked in the tenth year,
and the Argives returned in their ships to their dear homeland,
then finally Poseidon and Apollo contrived to destroy
the wall, sending the strength of rivers against it:
as many as flow from the mountains of Ida to the sea,
Rhesos and Heptaporos and Karesos and Rhodios
and Grenikos and Aisepos and brilliant Skamandros
and Simoeis, where many ox-hide shields and helmets
fell in the dust, and the race of the demigods.
Of all these rivers Phoibos Apollo turned the mouths together,
and for nine days he hurled their stream against the wall,
and Zeus rained unceasingly, to dissolve the wall
    more quickly into the sea.

The *Iliad* echoes here a myth of destruction that is reflected in both
the *Cypria* and the Hesiodic *Ehoeae*—in which Zeus is said to have planned
the Trojan War in order to destroy the demigods, so as to widen the breach
between gods and men; it is prominent as well in Near Eastern traditions that
make the Flood the means of destroying mankind.[19]

Yet the Homeric poems, as this study began by observing, are interpreters of their mythological resources at every step; and "destruction"
as understood by the traditions represented by Hesiod, the Cycle, and

---

[19] R. Scodel, "Achaean Wall and Myth of Destruction," provides a convincing demonstration
of the *Iliad*'s evocation of the myth. See frag. 204 Merkelbach-West for the Hesiodic reflection of the myth. For the Babylonian epic of Atra-ḫasīs, see W. G. Lambert and A. R. Millard,
Atra-hasis: The Babylonian Story of the Flood (Oxford, 1969); also J. B. Pritchard, ed., *Ancient Near
Eastern Texts*, 2d ed. (Princeton, 1955). Among the increasingly rich and valuable studies of
the interconnections between Near Eastern and Greek mythology and literature, see now
especially W. Burkert, *Die orientalisierende Epoche in der griechischen Religion und Literatur*
(Heidelberg, 1984), in particular 85ff.

Mesopotamian literature has been reinterpreted by the *Iliad* and translated into its own terms. The *Iliad* evokes these traditions, through passages that retrieve the theme of destruction, to place them ultimately in a perspective that, much as it rejects immortality, rejects utter annihilation as well.

Components of the mythological complex of the end of the race survive in Iliadic allusions, and reverberate, but are transformed. Thetis's marriage to a mortal is central to the *Iliad*, not as it is to the *Cypria*, as an instrument in the wholesale eradication of heroes—not to efface human beings from a crowded landscape—but as a paradigmatic explanation of why human beings, in order not to threaten to be greater than their divine parents, must die. The themes of separation of men and gods, of human calamity, are not—in G. S. Kirk's phrase—"watered down" by the *Iliad*, but are distilled.[20] The plan of Zeus is there, but it is the plan agreed upon by Zeus and Thetis to honor her short-lived son, the demigod, before he dies. Earth's complaint requesting that her load be lightened is rendered by the *Iliad* in Achilles' anguished self-reproach that he is an ἄχθος ἀρούρης (*achthos arourês*, 18.104)—a burden to the earth. Destruction means not the decimation of humanity, but the shattering loss and sorrow that inescapably define the life of every individual.

---

[20] G. S. Kirk, "Greek Mythology: Some New Perspectives," *JHS* 92 (1972): 79. Kirk writes: "The 'plan of Zeus' at the beginning of the *Iliad* was probably in origin a reflexion of the Mesopotamian or Egyptian gods' recurrent itch to destroy mankind; the *Cypria* preserved the idea, but in the *Iliad* this un-Hellenic conception is in process of being watered down into Zeus's more limited intention of gratifying Thetis by avenging Achilles."

Part II
Essays

Theban Traces at Troy[1]

OUR UNDERSTANDING OF THE SUBTLETY AND SCOPE of allusion as a feature of the poetics of early Greek epic has been greatly augmented in recent years by a number of valuable studies on the intricate narrative relationship between the *Iliad* and *Odyssey*, and more generally among hexameter poems of the Archaic period.[2] Thanks to their insights we are better able to recognize that the Homeric poems not only allude to a wide range of myths (including those apparently peripheral to the personages and events of the Trojan War), but also make reference to other poetic narratives, including those from other traditions.[3] The most persuasive account of how the *Iliad* and *Odyssey* may have evolved, offered to us by the pioneering work of Parry and Lord,[4] helps us to hypothesize an awareness on the part of the oral poet not of a fixed text[5] but of a narrative shape and thematic opportunities within it.[6]

Although myths or mythic motifs are frequently adapted and incorporated from other poetic traditions without particular emphasis on their participation in any other narrative[7]—that is, without any special reference

---

[1] This paper was delivered at the Ohio State University conference "The *Iliad* and its Contexts," October 1994. My thanks to Liz Irwin for her careful comments.

[2] Signal contributions include Edwards 1985, Ford 1992, Nagy 1979, Pucci 1987, Sacks 1987, Segal 1994; more recently: Burgess 2001, Danek 1998, Dué 2002, Irwin 2005, Mayer 1996, and especially Muellner 1996.

[3] See the discussion by Nagy 1979 on the sophistication of the *Odyssey*'s reference to the *Iliad* while avoiding duplicating Iliadic scenes (a restriction noted by D. Monro in his edition of the *Odyssey*). Nagy writes: "Perhaps it was part of the Odyssean tradition to veer away from the Iliadic" (21).

[4] Milman Parry's papers are collected in A. Parry 1971; the indispensable study by A. B. Lord is *The Singer of Tales*.

[5] See the discussion in Edwards 1971:189, Lord 1960, and Nagy 1996a and 1996b.

[6] So the *Odyssey* may hint at other endings for Odysseus, including that familiar from the *Telegony*. See S. West 1981:169–75 and Sacks, "Ending the *Odyssey*: Odysseus Traditions and the Homeric *Odyssey*" (forthcoming).

[7] We might think, among countless examples, of the mythological material in the *Dios apatê*, on which see Janko 1992:168ff.

to their part in the telling of another story—there are, at the same time, intriguing instances in which both the *Iliad* and *Odyssey* draw attention to myths precisely for their value as the subject matter of narrative. Thus the *Odyssey* recounts the myth of Orestes—which it invokes for a variety of reasons[8]—in such a way as to draw specific attention to its meaning as a story to be told and retold. The myth's significance for the *Odyssey* may be multiple, but the *Odyssey* itself explicitly highlights it as an exemplary *plot*, a satisfying and instructive *narrative* sequence of episodes.[9] At the same time, the poem's presentation of the varying accounts of the myth by different speakers, who suppress and bring to the fore different features, provides an effective illustration of the dynamics of adaptation in oral storytelling.

The developments of the Oresteia myth are framed in the *Odyssey*, not only as a set of events to be appreciated by its hearers within the poem, but *as a story* to be compared to their own. Thus Nestor advises Telemachus to do what is necessary to emulate the *kleos* of Orestes—to attain equal narrative renown. The present story—the one that is unfolding—of a son's vengeance on behalf of his father must be as impressive and memorable a narrative as its antecedent; ultimately, it must transcend it. What is told about Orestes, then, is underscored for its value as a paradigm in a number of parallel situations in the *Odyssey*,[10] but especially forcefully for its stature as narrative.

The *Iliad*, similarly, if less programmatically and explicitly, acknowledges other narratives, the statures of which it recognizes and locates in relation to its own. One of these is brought to prominence, as with the Oresteia story in the *Odyssey*, through the structuring of the poem around the absence of its hero. With the removal of Achilles from the action of the war in Book I, the poet creates a vacuum in the narrative that allows for the emergence of an alternate hero and for the possibility of a direction for the story other than the familiar one.[11] The potential transition to an unprecedented narrative path, from the point of view of the *Iliad*'s external audience, mirrors the uncertainty of the audience within the poem in the face of Achilles' withdrawal.

It is at this stage in the plot that the epic's audience is reminded of another poetic tradition, through allusions that are concentrated around the character who is given the role of preeminent warrior in Achilles' absence:

[8] As M. A. Katz has demonstrated (1990).
[9] Indeed, its status as an exemplary plot to be recapitulated by Telemachus is specifically given divine authorization by Athene at *Odyssey* i 45–50; see "Composition by Theme" (this volume) 144.
[10] For a thorough analysis, see again Katz, 1990.
[11] For a consideration of this strategy in the *Odyssey*, see again "Composition by Theme" (this volume).

Diomedes, son of Tydeus.[12] To refer to him by his patronymic is to follow the poem's own example; more frequently than any other single character in the poem, Diomedes is named with a patronymic, either with the patronymic alone or as an epithet in combination with his own name. The patronymic Atreides occurs slightly more frequently, but it is doing double duty for both Agamemnon and Menelaos. Only Achilles receives the patronymic roughly as often as Diomedes, but what is perhaps more striking is that, unlike the case of Achilles, Diomedes is referred to as son of Tydeus more often than he is referred to by his own name. Formulas for "son of Tydeus"—not only the patronymic but phrases such as Τυδέος υἱός, Τυδέος ἄλκιμον υἱόν, Τυδέος ἱπποδάμου υἱός, Τυδέος ἔκγονος (ἔκγονος, it should be noted, is used only twice in the poem: once to specify the lineage of Diomedes and once, at *Iliad* XX 206, that of Achilles)—occur in every position in the verse, indicating that they have been developed for great utility.

The reiterated, one might say relentless, designation of Diomedes as son of Tydeus cumulatively creates the effect of an inextricable identification of son with father. This effect, moreover, is reinforced by the additional phenomenon that in every episode in which he figures, either Diomedes himself includes an explicit reference to his father or an interlocutor addresses him with a reminder of Tydeus and his accomplishments.

One such reference occurs in a suggestive passage in which Diomedes produces the equation between himself and his father in the context of a prayer to Athene:

'κλῦθί μευ, αἰγιόχοιο Διὸς τέκος, Ἀτρυτώνη,
εἴ ποτέ μοι καὶ πατρὶ φίλα φρονέουσα παρέστης
δηΐῳ ἐν πολέμῳ, νῦν αὖτ' ἐμὲ φῖλαι, Ἀθήνη·'

Iliad V 115–117

'Hear me, Atrytone, child of aegis-bearing Zeus:
if ever before you stood devotedly by my father
in the dire fighting, be my friend now also, Athene.'

an equation he repeats in the same context in Book X:

Δεύτερος αὖτ' ἠρᾶτο βοὴν ἀγαθὸς Διομήδης·
'κέκλυθι νῦν καὶ ἐμεῖο, Διὸς τέκος, Ἀτρυτώνη·

---

[12] See Anderson 1978 for a discussion of the coherence of Diomedes' function in relation to Achilles. For an analysis of the poem's treatment of the parallels between Diomedes and Achilles, see Whitman 1958, esp. 154–180 and 264–266.

σπεῖό μοι ὡς ὅτε πατρὶ ἅμ' ἕσπεο Τυδέϊ δίῳ
ἐς Θήβας, ὅτε τε πρὸ Ἀχαιῶν ἄγγελος ᾔει.'

Iliad X 283—286

After him, Diomedes of the great war spoke a prayer:
'Hear me also, child of Zeus, Atrytone.
Accompany me now as you accompanied my father, brilliant
    Tydeus,
into Thebes, when he went as a messenger before the Achaians...'

As Leonard Muellner has shown in detail,[13] the typical structure for prayer involves appealing to a god or goddess on the basis either of a favor the petitioner has done for the divinity in the past or of one previously performed for the petitioner by the god or goddess in the past, which presupposes an ongoing, or renewable, contract. Thus we may think of the opening prayer of Chryses to Apollo in Book I, or, to take an example more relevant to the present one, the prayer of Odysseus to Athene in Book X, directly preceding that of Diomedes:

'κλῦθί μευ, αἰγιόχοιο Διὸς τέκος, ἥ τέ μοι αἰεὶ
ἐν πάντεσσι πόνοισι παρίστασαι, οὐδέ σε λήθω
κινύμενος· νῦν αὖτε μάλιστά με φῖλαι, Ἀθήνη,
δὸς δὲ πάλιν ἐπὶ νῆας ἐϋκλεῖας ἀφικέσθαι,
ῥέξαντας μέγα ἔργον, ὅ κε Τρώεσσι μελήσῃ.'

Iliad X 278—282

'Hear me, child of aegis-bearing Zeus, you who always
stand beside me in all ordeals, and do not overlook me
as I make my way: cherish me, indeed, above all, Athene,
and grant that we come back in glory to the strong-benched
    vessels
having accomplished a great task that the Trojans will regret.'

In Diomedes' prayer, then, we observe an anomaly: he appeals to Athene on the basis of her past affection for and favor to his father, rather than himself. Yet, given that Diomedes has apparently already had his own epic success, we might well wonder about what the poem refers us to here, and how it matters to the audience of the *Iliad's* brilliant presentness what happened to

---

[13] Muellner 1976:27–28; see Norden 1913:143–176 and the survey in Lateiner 1997:241–272. For a discussion of the other Iliadic instance of this anomaly (and its possible allusions) in Achilles' prayer to Zeus in Book I, see Slatkin, *The Power of Thetis* (this volume, pp. 77–78).

Tydeus in a time and place far removed from Troy. Is Tydeus' history inserted in order to make Diomedes more prepossessing as he takes center stage by producing a well-connected genealogy for him?

To Diomedes' request in Book V Athene assents without hesitation, and in just the terms that Diomedes proposes:

> Ὣς ἔφατ' εὐχόμενος· τοῦ δ' ἔκλυε Παλλὰς Ἀθήνη,
> γυῖα δ' ἔθηκεν ἐλαφρά, πόδας καὶ χεῖρας ὕπερθεν·
> ἀγχοῦ δ' ἱσταμένη ἔπεα πτερόεντα προσηύδα·
> 'θαρσῶν νῦν, Διόμηδες, ἐπὶ Τρώεσσι μάχεσθαι·
> ἐν γάρ τοι στήθεσσι μένος πατρώϊον ἧκα
> ἄτρομον, οἷον ἔχεσκε σακέσπαλος ἱππότα Τυδεύς·'
>
> *Iliad* V 121–126

So he spoke praying, and Pallas Athene heard him.
She made his limbs agile, and his feet, and his hands above them,
and standing beside him she uttered winged words:
'Take courage now, Diomedes, to fight with the Trojans,
for in your chest I have placed your father's strength
intrepid, the sort the horseman Tydeus of the great shield used
     to have...'

Thereupon begins the first *aristeia* of the poem, and the most extensive and exceptional after that of Achilles—so much so that it leads the Trojans to assert that they did not fear even Achilles as much as they do Diomedes.[14]

Remarkable as well is that Diomedes' prayer to Athene initiates a partnership between god and hero more sustained and continuous than any other in the poem—to think of their combined efforts not only in the *aristeia* but in the *Doloneia* and in the funeral games, when, thanks to Athene's help, Diomedes is victorious in the chariot race. Athene's aid to Diomedes throughout is comparable to (although of course without the climactic finality of) her crucial assistance to Achilles in his *monomachia* with Hector in Book XXII. There Athene indeed returns Achilles' spear to him, but when she and Diomedes together attack Ares, Athene shoves in the spear herself! To no other hero—including, in this poem, Odysseus—does Athene appear with such constant solicitous attention. And when she does appear to Diomedes, it is in the context of a reminiscence of his father.

---

[14] *Iliad* VI 96–101. On a comparison of the *aristeiai* of Diomedes and Achilles, see Whitman 1958:167–168.

At the opening line of Book V, the scholiast expresses surprise and perturbation at what is to follow: why should Diomedes have the first *aristeia* and not Ajax?[15] In reflecting on the scholiast's question, we may ask whether the emphasis on Tydeus has any role to play in the answer. Diomedes's first appearance in the poem[16] provides the occasion for the initial narration of the story that includes, as an evidently well-known feature, the demonstration of Athene's affection for Tydeus. Agamemnon, who tells it, reminds his listeners that he never knew Diomedes' father—but he knows the story. It is, he makes clear, a well-established one, the various dramatic episodes of which are familiar from numerous tellings:

'οὐ μὲν Τυδέϊ γ' ὧδε φίλον πτωσκαζέμεν ἦεν,
ἀλλὰ πολὺ πρὸ φίλων ἑτάρων δηΐοισι μάχεσθαι,
ὡς φάσαν οἵ μιν ἴδοντο πονεύμενον· οὐ γὰρ ἔγωγε
ἤντησ' οὐδὲ ἴδον· περὶ δ' ἄλλων φασὶ γενέσθαι.'

Iliad IV 372-375

'Tydeus was never fond of cowering like this
but of fighting the enemy far ahead of his own companions.
So *they said* who had seen him at work; for I never saw nor
encountered him ever; but *they say* he surpassed all the others.'

The fame of Tydeus' exploits has survived him, to be reanimated on another battlefield. The episode is recounted no less than three times in the *Iliad*, its repetition providing an ideal demonstration of the capacity of oral storytelling for expansion and compression, elaboration and selective emphasis.

Agamemnon gives the fullest account of Tydeus' adventure as an advance man among the Kadmeians:[17]

ἤτοι μὲν γὰρ ἄτερ πολέμου εἰσῆλθε Μυκήνας
ξεῖνος ἅμ' ἀντιθέῳ Πολυνείκεϊ, λαὸν ἀγείρων·
οἱ δὲ τότ' ἐστρατόωνθ' ἱερὰ πρὸς τείχεα Θήβης,
καί ῥα μάλα λίσσοντο δόμεν κλειτοὺς ἐπικούρους·
οἱ δ' ἔθελον δόμεναι καὶ ἐπήνεον ὡς ἐκέλευον·
ἀλλὰ Ζεὺς ἔτρεψε παραίσια σήματα φαίνων.
οἱ δ' ἐπεὶ οὖν ᾤχοντο ἰδὲ πρὸ ὁδοῦ ἐγένοντο,

---

[15] Schol. AbT *ad loc.*; see the discussion in Van der Valk 1952:269ff.

[16] Apart from his inclusion in the Catalogue at Book II 563.

[17] Although Agamemnon's recollection is intended to compare Diomedes unfavorably to his father, it also invites an unfavorable comparison of Agamemnon's leadership with the fearless Tydeus.

Ἀσωπὸν δ' ἵκοντο βαθύσχοινον λεχεποίην,
ἔνθ' αὖτ' ἀγγελίην ἐπὶ Τυδῆ στεῖλαν Ἀχαιοί.
αὐτὰρ ὁ βῆ, πολέας δὲ κιχήσατο Καδμεΐωνας
δαινυμένους κατὰ δῶμα βίης Ἐτεοκληείης.
ἔνθ' οὐδὲ ξεῖνός περ ἐὼν ἱππηλάτα Τυδεὺς
τάρβει, μοῦνος ἐὼν πολέσιν μετὰ Καδμείοισιν,
ἀλλ' ὅ γ' ἀεθλεύειν προκαλίζετο, πάντα δ' ἐνίκα
ῥηϊδίως· τοίη οἱ ἐπίρροθος ἦεν Ἀθήνη.
οἱ δὲ χολωσάμενοι Καδμεῖοι κέντορες ἵππων
ἂψ ἄρ' ἀνερχομένῳ πυκινὸν λόχον εἶσαν ἄγοντες,
κούρους πεντήκοντα· δύω δ' ἡγήτορες ἦσαν,
Μαίων Αἱμονίδης, ἐπιείκελος ἀθανάτοισιν,
υἱός τ' Αὐτοφόνοιο, μενεπτόλεμος Πολυφόντης.
Τυδεὺς μὲν καὶ τοῖσιν ἀεικέα πότμον ἐφῆκε·
πάντας ἔπεφν', ἕνα δ' οἶον ἵει οἶκόνδε νέεσθαι·
Μαίον' ἄρα προέηκε, θεῶν τεράεσσι πιθήσας.
τοῖος ἔην Τυδεὺς Αἰτώλιος· ἀλλὰ τὸν υἱὸν
γείνατο εἷο χέρεια μάχῃ, ἀγορῇ δέ τ' ἀμείνω.'

Iliad IV 376–400

'For once, not in war, he came to Mykenai as a guest and friend,
with godlike Polyneikes, gathering a fighting host,
since they were laying siege to the sacred walls of Thebes,
and they begged us indeed to provide illustrious companions.
And our men were willing to give them and assented to what
        they urged;
but Zeus turned them back, showing ill-omened signs.
Now as these proceeded and were well on their way, and reached
the river Asopos, and the meadows of grass and the deep rushes,
from there the Achaians sent Tydeus ahead with a message.
He went then and came upon numerous Kadmeians
feasting throughout the house of the mighty Eteokles.
There, stranger though he was, the driver of horses, Tydeus,
was not frightened, alone among so many Kadmeians,
but dared them to compete with him, and defeated them all
easily, such a helper was Pallas Athene to him.
But the Kadmeians who lash their horses, being angered
laid a dense ambush on his way home, assembling together
fifty fighting men, and their leaders were two,

Maion, Haimon's son, like the immortals,
and the son of Autophonos, Polyphontes steadfast in battle.
Upon these men Tydeus let loose a fate that was shameful.
He killed them all, but one he let reach home again.
He let Maion go in obedience to the god's portents.
Such was Tydeus, the Aitolian; yet he fathered
a son worse than himself in battle, better in the assembly.'

Athene follows with a more condensed version, to which the audience may
fill in particulars supplied earlier by Agamemnon:

'ἦ ὀλίγον οἷ παῖδα ἐοικότα γείνατο Τυδεύς.
Τυδεύς τοι μικρὸς μὲν ἔην δέμας, ἀλλὰ μαχητής·
καί ῥ' ὅτε πέρ μιν ἐγὼ πολεμίζειν οὐκ εἴασκον
οὐδ' ἐκπαιφάσσειν, ὅτε τ' ἤλυθε νόσφιν Ἀχαιῶν
ἄγγελος ἐς Θήβας πολέας μετὰ Καδμείωνας·
δαίνυσθαί μιν ἄνωγον ἐνὶ μεγάροισιν ἔκηλον·
αὐτὰρ ὁ θυμὸν ἔχων ὃν καρτερόν, ὡς τὸ πάρος περ,
κούρους Καδμείων προκαλίζετο, πάντα δ' ἐνίκα
ῥηϊδίως· τοίη οἱ ἐγὼν ἐπιτάρροθος ἦα.'

Iliad V 800–808

'Tydeus fathered a son scarcely like himself.
Tydeus was a small man in stature, yes, but he was a fighter.
Even that time when I would not permit him to fight
nor rush into the fray, when he went by himself without the
        Achaians
as a messenger to Thebes among the many Kadmeians,
then I urged him to feast at his ease in their great halls;
even so, keeping his spirit strong as before,
he challenged the young men of the Kadmeians, and bested
        them all
easily; such a helper was I who stood beside him.'

Finally, at *Iliad* X 285, Diomedes himself repeats it, allusively, in an abbreviated
version in which a phrase like μάλα μέρμερα μήσατο ἔργα 'he planned grim
deeds' assumes not only his listener's privileged knowledge but the poem's
audience's familiarity with a much-told story:[18]

---

[18] Of this episode, Vermeule 1987, citing Ruijgh 1985, esp. 149–152, writes: "By linguistic criteria
the Theban ambush should not only be Bronze Age but deep within it" (142). This partic-

'κέκλυθι νῦν καὶ ἐμεῖο, Διὸς τέκος, Ἀτρυτώνη·
σπεῖό μοι ὡς ὅτε πατρὶ ἅμ' ἕσπεο Τυδέϊ δίῳ
ἐς Θήβας, ὅτε τε πρὸ Ἀχαιῶν ἄγγελος ἦει.
τοὺς δ' ἄρ' ἐπ' Ἀσωπῷ λίπε χαλκοχίτωνας Ἀχαιούς,
αὐτὰρ ὁ μειλίχιον μῦθον φέρε Καδμείοισι
κεῖσ'· ἀτὰρ ἂψ ἀπιὼν μάλα μέρμερα μήσατο ἔργα
σὺν σοί, δῖα θεά, ὅτε οἱ πρόφρασσα παρέστης.
ὣς νῦν μοι ἐθέλουσα παρίστασο καί με φύλασσε.'

Iliad X 284–291

'Hear me also, Atrytone, child of Zeus.
Accompany me now as you accompanied my father, brilliant
    Tydeus,
into Thebes, when he went as a messenger before the Achaians,
and left the bronze-armoured Achaians beside Asopos
while he bore friendly words to the Kadmeians
in that place; but on his way back he planned grim deeds
with your aid, divine goddess, since you stood beside him in
    support.
So now again be willing to stand by me, and watch over me.'

Diomedes' appropriation in this way of what Agamemnon has narrated represents the mode by which the story's continuity into another generation is ensured.

Tydeus' story thus takes its audience—and the poem's audience—to Thebes, to an earlier and spectacular assault on a walled city, an event widely celebrated. From the perspective of archaic poetry, as we learn from Hesiod in the *Works and Days*, first the Theban War and later on the Trojan War define the *genos* of heroes. The race of heroes is said to consist precisely of those who died fighting at seven-gated Thebes, and those who, subsequently, perished at Troy fighting over Helen:

---

ular incident from Theban mythology is known to us otherwise only from late sources, e.g., Diodorus 4.65.4 and Apollodorus *Bibliotheca* 3.6.5, where it is amplified with further details. If it formed part of an early epic about the Theban War, it may have had a place as a preparation in a narrative of the attack on the city, much as Books III and IV of the *Iliad* recount an attempt at a negotiated settlement to the war before proceeding to the hostilities proper. An *aristeia* of Tydeus among the Cadmeians may have followed, prior to the body of the poem about the attack on the city. This can only be speculation about narrative possibilities, given the fragmentary nature of our evidence for early epic poetry about Thebes.

αὖτις ἔτ' ἄλλο τέταρτον ἐπὶ χθονὶ πουλυβοτείρῃ
Ζεὺς Κρονίδης ποίησε, δικαιότερον καὶ ἄρειον,
ἀνδρῶν ἡρώων θεῖον γένος, οἳ καλέονται
ἡμίθεοι, προτέρῃ γενεῇ κατ' ἀπείρονα γαῖαν.
καὶ τοὺς μὲν πόλεμός τε κακὸς καὶ φύλοπις αἰνὴ
τοὺς μὲν ὑφ' ἑπταπύλῳ Θήβῃ, Καδμηίδι γαίῃ,
ὤλεσε μαρναμένους μήλων ἕνεκ' Οἰδιπόδαο,
τοὺς δὲ καὶ ἐν νήεσσιν ὑπὲρ μέγα λαῖτμα θαλάσσης
ἐς Τροίην ἀγαγὼν Ἑλένης ἕνεκ' ἠυκόμοιο.

Works and Days 157–165

Zeus the son of Kronos created another generation, the fourth
on the fertile earth, who were superior and more just:
a godly race of heroic men, who were called
demigods, the generation before our own on the boundless earth.
Some of them cruel war with its dread battle cry
destroyed under seven-gated Thebes in the land of Kadmos
as they contended with each other over the flocks of Oedipus,
others brought across the vast gulf of the sea in
ships to Troy for the sake of lovely-haired Helen.

From the standpoint of a narrative about warrior-heroes such as the one in which Agamemnon, Achilles, and Diomedes are prominent actors, the Theban expedition is *the other*—and *prior*—celebrated story. Perhaps it is the song Achilles is singing when the Embassy arrives at his tent. Will the present heroes achieve similar renown—will the present narrative, that is, achieve comparable, enduring stature? The unmatched primacy of the Theban story poses a problem for the stories that come after it.[19]

Just how that Theban story might have been narrated we cannot determine; the few lines we possess of the poem called the *Thebais* offer at best a limited basis for reconstruction[20] (and for a secure appraisal of its date). Compelling arguments have been advanced, however, from several perspe-

---

[19] B. King, in *The End of Adventure* (forthcoming), discusses the *Iliad*'s acknowledgement of its ambiguous status as commemorative of the closing of the heroic story, the passing of epic itself.

[20] Cf. E. Bethe 1891:76ff. on the *Thebais* and 109ff. on the *Epigonoi*. Pausanias's version of the events (9.9.3–5) ends with his appraisal of the *Thebais*: ἐποιήθη δὲ ἐς τὸν πόλεμον τοῦτον καὶ ἔπη Θηβαΐς· τὰ δὲ ἔπη ταῦτα Καλλῖνος ἀφικόμενος αὐτῶν ἐς μνήμην ἔφησεν Ὅμηρον τὸν ποιήσαντα εἶναι, Καλλίνῳ δὲ πολλοί τε καὶ ἄξιοι λόγου κατὰ ταὐτὰ ἔγνωσαν· ἐγὼ δὲ τὴν ποίησιν ταύτην μετά γε Ἰλιάδα καὶ τὰ ἔπη τὰ ἐς Ὀδυσσέα ἐπαινῶ μάλιστα.

tives, including those of archaeology, linguistics, and the history of religion, to substantiate the view that (regardless of the dating of the *Thebais* from which our fragments come, or that of any of the Epic Cycle poems on the subject) the constellation of myths having to do with the Theban War are of Mycenaean provenance and were in circulation in a narrative form from a period as early as that of the Trojan myths.[21] Thus Walter Burkert concludes that "a Theban tale in oral poetry [existed], besides and sometimes interfering with the Trojan tales."[22]

The two poetic traditions intersect in Diomedes. The *Iliad* first introduces him, with a long passage about Tydeus, at the actual inception of warfare, when the talking stops and the killing begins. This is, in a sense, another beginning for the poem: the point at which it settles into its presumed subject, the war against Troy—and yet it does so in the absence of its presumed hero, though very much in the presence of the son of Tydeus. From a narrative standpoint, it is Diomedes who enables the war—and the poem—to proceed after the withdrawal of Achilles; but will he undermine its principal focus? Might he, with the heritage he represents—of another poetic tradition of city-sacking—come to dominate the *Iliad*'s plot? What we see at work in the poem's allusions, through Diomedes, to Theban myths and their narrative prestige, is, I suggest, the way in which the *Iliad* controls Theban "interference"—with the result that eventually, as Emily Vermeule writes, "the *Iliad* partly drove the *Thebaid* out of circulation, and epic shaped itself around Troy rather than Thebes or Argos."[23]

When the *Iliad* reminds us repeatedly of Athene's extraordinary affection for Tydeus, as in Diomedes' prayer in Book V (phrased in general terms as it is: εἴ ποτέ μοι καὶ πατρὶ φίλα φρονέουσα παρέστης / δηΐῳ ἐν πολέμῳ), it may evoke not only the incident related by Agamemnon in Book IV, but also a macabre and haunting episode in the last stage of the attack on Thebes,[24] told, according to the scholia, by "the Cyclic poets."[25] In this episode, Tydeus

---

[21] See the presentation of evidence for Bronze Age dactylic poetry in Horrocks 1980 as well as the argument for Bronze Age elements in the *Thebais* and for its contemporaneity with the Homeric poems in Vermeule 1987; also Burkert's article in Brillante et al. 1981:29–48 and responses to Burkert by commentators, esp. B. Hainsworth (49–51).

[22] Burkert 1981:32.

[23] Vermeule 1987:130. For the *Iliad*'s competition with the tradition of Heracles as sacker of Troy (and its treatment of Heracles's heroism more generally), see the insights of Haubold 2005, esp. 95; the deification of Heracles, however, puts him *hors concours* from the standpoint of competing heroes, as Liz Irwin points out to me.

[24] Bernabé, *Thebais* fr.9.

[25] AbT *ad* 5.126; it was said as well to have been narrated by Pherecydes (Gen *ad* 5.126). On

was mortally wounded by Melanippos, who was then himself killed by the Argive seer Amphiaraus. Amphiaraus cut off Melanippos' head and gave it to the dying Tydeus; who thereupon—"like a wild animal," in the words of the scholiast—broke open the head and gnawed (ῥοφᾶν) on the brains. Athene arrived at just this moment in order to bring immortality to Tydeus, but upon seeing her favorite eating the brains of his enemy she turned away from him in disgust.[26] The dying Tydeus then begged Athene to bestow on his son the immortality intended for himself. This is the tradition known to Pindar, who says that Athene made Diomedes immortal:

> Διομήδεα δ' ἄμβροτον ξαν-
>   θά ποτε Γλαυκῶπις ἔθηκε θεόν·
> γαῖα δ' ἐν Θήβαις ὑπέδεκτο κεραυνω-
>   θεῖσα Διὸς βέλεσιν
> μάντιν Οἰκλείδαν, πολέμοιο νέφος·

Nemean Odes 10.7–9

> And Diomedes golden bright-eyed Athene
>   once made an immortal god.
> But the earth at Thebes, stricken
>   by Zeus' thunderbolts, received
> the son of Oikles,
> seer and cloud of battle.

In *Iliad* V, in response to Diomedes' request that Athene replicate her help to his father, Athene endows him not simply with strength or accurate aim or stamina, but with invincibility, and with what none of the other heroes is explicitly granted: the ability to share immortal vision—quite literally, to see with the eyes of a god:[27]

> ἐν γάρ τοι στήθεσσι μένος πατρώϊον ἧκα
> ἄτρομον, οἷον ἔχεσκε σακέσπαλος ἱππότα Τυδεύς·
> ἀχλὺν δ' αὖ τοι ἀπ' ὀφθαλμῶν ἕλον, ἣ πρὶν ἐπῆεν,
> ὄφρ' εὖ γιγνώσκῃς ἠμὲν θεὸν ἠδὲ καὶ ἄνδρα.'

Iliad V 125–128

Pherecydes' knowledge of the *Thebais*: Severyns 1928:218ff. Apollodorus recounts the episode in detail at 3.6.8.

[26] A red-figured bell-crater in the Metropolitan Museum (12.229.14) is painted with Athena leading *Athanasia* ('Immortality', named as such) away from Tydeus. See Schefold and Jung 1989:80, fig. 61. For other representations of this scene, see Brommer 1973:488–489.

[27] On Achilles' native ability to recognize the gods, see Slatkin 2006:21–22.

'...for in your chest I have placed your father's strength
intrepid, the sort the horseman Tydeus of the great shield
used to have; and I have removed the mist from your eyes that
    formerly
was there, so that you may surely recognize both god and the
    mortal.'

In the poems of the Epic Cycle, immortality is an option for the heroes; in this, as many have noted, the Cycle differs from the *Iliad*, which (as is now commonplace to observe) is emphatic in its avoidance of the possibility.[28] But the *Iliad* brings immortality tantalizingly close, only to remove it, pointedly and definitively, in a number of representative instances—most vividly when Zeus declines to obtain immortality for Sarpedon.

What Diomedes is granted is as close to immortality as the *Iliad* allows anyone. Not only does he fight with the immortals (and wound them), but he also resembles them; the Trojans think he may be one. Like Ares, who fights on both sides, Diomedes is everywhere, so that it is said to be impossible to tell which side he is on. So close does he come to the condition of the immortals, that Apollo is obliged to rebuke him with a reminder:

ἀλλ' ὅτε δὴ τὸ τέταρτον ἐπέσσυτο δαίμονι ἶσος,
δεινὰ δ' ὁμοκλήσας προσέφη ἑκάεργος Ἀπόλλων·
'φράζεο, Τυδεΐδη, καὶ χάζεο, μηδὲ θεοῖσιν
ἶσ' ἔθελε φρονέειν, ἐπεὶ οὔ ποτε φῦλον ὁμοῖον
ἀθανάτων τε θεῶν χαμαὶ ἐρχομένων τ' ἀνθρώπων.'

Iliad V 438–442

...but when for the fourth time he charged, the equal of a god,
then, threatening terribly, far-worker Apollo addressed him:
'Watch out and back away, son of Tydeus, and do not try
to understand as gods do, since never the same are the race
of immortal gods and that of men who walk on the earth.'

Even after the poem's focus, and the advantage in battle, have shifted to Hector, Zeus has to intervene to make Diomedes retreat, and he does so by hurling a thunderbolt at Diomedes' feet. It is an action unparalleled in the *Iliad*—but there is a parallel in the Theban myth: Sthenelos' father, the Argive chief Kapaneus, who brings his ladder to Thebes, attempts to scale the wall,

---

[28] On immortality in the Cycle poems, see Nagy 1979:151–175, and now Burgess 2001:167. See discussions of the *Iliad*'s treatment in Schein 1985:67–88 and Griffin 1977:39–53.

and is killed by a thunderbolt from Zeus. Perhaps in the *Iliad* Zeus is sending an evocative warning to the son of Tydeus—Tydeus, who stood at the next gate to Kapaneus.

But in addition to its absorption of Theban mythic motifs into its own narrative, the *Iliad* uses the *epigonoi* to integrate the Theban paradigm and relegate it to the position of a respected, but subsidiary, precedent. E. T. Owen writes, "the whole matter of the *epipolesis* is designed as a setting for Agamemnon's rebuke of Diomedes";[29] similarly, we might suggest that the rebuke, and its *paradeigma*, are designed to enable the response that alludes to the last phase of Thebes: the triumph of the subsequent generation of Argive warriors. Sthenelos replies to Agamemnon's reproach by reminding him that the sons outdid their fathers and took Thebes—an implicit challenge that the *epigonoi* may outdo the Achaean contingent at Troy:[30]

ὣς φάτο, τὸν δ' οὔ τι προσέφη κρατερὸς Διομήδης,
αἰδεσθεὶς βασιλῆος ἐνιπὴν αἰδοίοιο·
τὸν δ' υἱὸς Καπανῆος ἀμείψατο κυδαλίμοιο·
"Ἀτρεΐδη, μὴ ψεύδε' ἐπιστάμενος σάφα εἰπεῖν·
ἡμεῖς τοι πατέρων μέγ' ἀμείνονες εὐχόμεθ' εἶναι·
ἡμεῖς καὶ Θήβης ἕδος εἵλομεν ἑπταπύλοιο,
παυρότερον λαὸν ἀγαγόνθ' ὑπὸ τεῖχος ἄρειον,
πειθόμενοι τεράεσσι θεῶν καὶ Ζηνὸς ἀρωγῇ·
κεῖνοι δὲ σφετέρῃσιν ἀτασθαλίῃσιν ὄλοντο·
τῶ μή μοι πατέρας ποθ' ὁμοίῃ ἔνθεο τιμῇ.'

Iliad IV 401–410

So he spoke, and powerful Diomedes did not answer him,
awed by the reproach of the august king.
But the son of renowned Kapaneus replied, saying:
'Son of Atreus, do not speak falsely, since you are surely aware:
we two claim that we are far better than our fathers;
we captured the foundation of seven-gated Thebes,
though we led fewer people beneath a wall that was stronger,
trusting in the portents of the gods and Zeus' help,
while they perished through their own folly.
Therefore, never compare our fathers to us in honor.'

---

[29] Owen 1947:47.

[30] For a discussion of Sthenelos' claim/threat and the implications of its specific diction, see Nagy 1979:162–163; see also the consideration of this passage in Huxley 1969:47.

But the *Iliad* uses Diomedes to silence Sthenelos and that challenge and to represent a more complex role for the heirs of the Theban story—one not bound to the past, as Sthenelos is, but instead, we might say, transitional:

> τὸν δ' ἄρ' ὑπόδρα ἰδὼν προσέφη κρατερὸς Διομήδης·
> 'τέττα, σιωπῇ ἧσο, ἐμῷ δ' ἐπιπείθεο μύθῳ·
> οὐ γὰρ ἐγὼ νεμεσῶ Ἀγαμέμνονι, ποιμένι λαῶν,
> ὀτρύνοντι μάχεσθαι ἐϋκνήμιδας Ἀχαιούς·
> τούτῳ μὲν γὰρ κῦδος ἅμ' ἔψεται, εἴ κεν Ἀχαιοὶ
> Τρῶας δῃώσωσιν ἕλωσί τε Ἴλιον ἱρήν,
> τούτῳ δ' αὖ μέγα πένθος Ἀχαιῶν δῃωθέντων.
> ἀλλ' ἄγε δὴ καὶ νῶϊ μεδώμεθα θούριδος ἀλκῆς.'

Iliad IV 411–418

> Then looking at him darkly strong Diomedes spoke to him:
> 'Friend, stay quiet rather and do as I tell you; I will
> find no fault with Agamemnon, shepherd of the people,
> for stirring thus into battle the strong-greaved Achaians;
> this will be his glory to come, if ever the Achaians
> cut down the men of Troy and capture sacred Ilion.
> If the Achaians are slain, then his will be the great sorrow.
> Come, let you and me remember our fighting courage.'

Diomedes proposes that the story of Troy is the story of its leader and does not, for good or ill, belong to the *epigonoi*—neither its eventual triumph nor its sorrow, which, in Diomedes' formulation, are the only alternative outcomes. He reminds his companion that this story is still incomplete, and the reputation of Agamemnon still in the making;[31] the unfinished narrative he and Sthenelos now inhabit—one not dominated by their fathers—will record other, unprecedented *timai* and, with their participation, establish its own standard of *kûdos* and *penthos*.

His more extensive speech in Book IX, much praised by Nestor, suggests the *Iliad*'s subtle negotiation of its Theban antecedent; although his address to Agamemnon echoes Sthenelos' tacitly competitive claim on behalf of the *epigonoi* to be capable of taking Troy (*Iliad* IV 401ff.),[32] it places Diomedes and his companion firmly within the Achaean cohort:

---

[31] As Telemachus declares to his mother (*Odyssey* i 351–352): τὴν γὰρ ἀοιδὴν μᾶλλον ἐπικλείουσ' / ἄνθρωποι, / ἥ τις ἀκουόντεσσι νεωτάτη ἀμφιπέληται.

[32] Like Sthenelos, Diomedes alludes to the oracle favoring their expedition, included in Apollodorus' account at 3.7.3.

"Ατρεΐδη, σοὶ πρῶτα μαχήσομαι ἀφραδέοντι,
ἦ θέμις ἐστίν, ἄναξ, ἀγορῇ· σὺ δὲ μή τι χολωθῇς.
ἀλκὴν μέν μοι πρῶτον ὀνείδισας ἐν Δαναοῖσι,
φὰς ἔμεν ἀπτόλεμον καὶ ἀνάλκιδα· ταῦτα δὲ πάντα
ἴσασ' Ἀργείων ἡμὲν νέοι ἠδὲ γέροντες.
σοὶ δὲ διάνδιχα δῶκε Κρόνου πάϊς ἀγκυλομήτεω·
σκήπτρῳ μέν τοι δῶκε τετιμῆσθαι περὶ πάντων,
ἀλκὴν δ' οὔ τοι δῶκεν, ὅ τε κράτος ἐστὶ μέγιστον.
δαιμόνι', οὕτω που μάλα ἔλπεαι υἷας Ἀχαιῶν
ἀπτολέμους τ' ἔμεναι καὶ ἀνάλκιδας, ὡς ἀγορεύεις;
εἰ δέ τοι αὐτῷ θυμὸς ἐπέσσυται ὥς τε νέεσθαι,
ἔρχεο· πάρ τοι ὁδός, νῆες δέ τοι ἄγχι θαλάσσης
ἑστᾶσ', αἵ τοι ἕποντο Μυκήνηθεν μάλα πολλαί.
ἀλλ' ἄλλοι μενέουσι κάρη κομόωντες Ἀχαιοὶ
εἰς ὅ κέ περ Τροίην διαπέρσομεν. εἰ δὲ καὶ αὐτοὶ
φευγόντων σὺν νηυσὶ φίλην ἐς πατρίδα γαῖαν·
νῶϊ δ', ἐγὼ Σθένελός τε, μαχησόμεθ' εἰς ὅ κε τέκμωρ
Ἰλίου εὕρωμεν· σὺν γὰρ θεῷ εἰλήλουθμεν.'

Iliad IX 32–49

'Son of Atreus: I will be first to fight with your nonsense,
which is my right, lord, in the assembly; but do not be angry,
since I was the first of the Danaans whose valor you slighted,
calling me unwarlike and timid. All these things the Argive
young men know, and the elders as well.
The son of crooked-minded Kronos has given you
disparate gifts: with the scepter he granted you honor beyond all,
but he did not give you courage, which is much the greatest power.
Strange man, do you really believe the sons of the Achaians
are so unwarlike and cowardly as you call them?
But if your own heart is so set upon returning,
go. There is the way, and next to the water your ships
are standing, those many, many that came with you from
　　　Mykenai.
But the rest of the flowing-haired Achaians will stay here
until we have sacked the city of Troy. Or let these too
flee with their ships to the beloved land of their fathers,
still we two, Sthenelos and I, will fight till we witness
the end of Ilion; for it was with God that we came here.'

By emphasizing Diomedes' assent to Agamemnon's leadership and his enthusiasm for the enterprise, expressed as the promise that he and Sthenelos will fight its last stand, the *Iliad* (as in Book IV) keeps alive the memory of the Theban siege, but subordinates it to present events.[33] Diomedes acknowledges Agamemnon's preeminence and mirrors Agamemnon's own earlier *parainesis*; here, as elsewhere, his speech both evokes the success of the Theban victors and displaces it, as it accentuates the resolute valor of the Achaean forces and the arduousness of their undertaking. The implied battle cry of the *epigonoi*—Sthenelos' assertion that they are better than their fathers (ἡμεῖς τοι πατέρων μέγ' ἀμείνονες εὐχόμεθ' εἶναι, *Iliad* IV 405), uttered as the *Iliad*'s fighting begins—is at first suppressed by Diomedes' rejoinder (*Iliad* IV 412) and ultimately revised in his last invocation of Tydeus in Book XIV, which is in fact Diomedes' final speech in the poem:

τοῖσι δὲ καὶ μετέειπε βοὴν ἀγαθὸς Διομήδης·
ἐγγὺς ἀνήρ, οὐ δηθὰ ματεύσομεν, αἴ κ' ἐθέλητε
πείθεσθαι, καὶ μή τι κότῳ ἀγάσησθε ἕκαστος
οὕνεκα δὴ γενεῆφι νεώτατός εἰμι μεθ' ὑμῖν·
πατρὸς δ' ἐξ ἀγαθοῦ καὶ ἐγὼ γένος εὔχομαι εἶναι,
Τυδέος, ὃν Θήβῃσι χυτὴ κατὰ γαῖα καλύπτει.
πορθεῖ γὰρ τρεῖς παῖδες ἀμύμονες ἐξεγένοντο,
οἴκεον δ' ἐν Πλευρῶνι καὶ αἰπεινῇ Καλυδῶνι,
Ἄγριος ἠδὲ Μέλας, τρίτατος δ' ἦν ἱππότα Οἰνεύς,
πατρὸς ἐμοῖο πατήρ· ἀρετῇ δ' ἦν ἔξοχος αὐτῶν.
ἀλλ' ὁ μὲν αὐτόθι μεῖνε, πατὴρ δ' ἐμὸς Ἄργεϊ νάσθη
πλαγχθείς· ὣς γάρ που Ζεὺς ἤθελε καὶ θεοὶ ἄλλοι.
Ἀδρήστοιο δ' ἔγημε θυγατρῶν, ναῖε δὲ δῶμα
ἀφνειὸν βιότοιο, ἅλις δέ οἱ ἦσαν ἄρουραι
πυροφόροι, πολλοὶ δὲ φυτῶν ἔσαν ὄρχατοι ἀμφίς,
πολλὰ δέ οἱ πρόβατ' ἔσκε· κέκαστο δὲ πάντας Ἀχαιοὺς
ἐγχείῃ· τὰ δὲ μέλλετ' ἀκουέμεν, εἰ ἐτεόν περ.
τῶ οὐκ ἄν με γένος γε κακὸν καὶ ἀνάλκιδα φάντες
μῦθον ἀτιμήσαιτε πεφασμένον, ὅν κ' ἐῢ εἴπω.

Iliad XIV 109–127

Now among them spoke Diomedes of the great war cry:
'That man is nearby, we shall not search far for him, if you are willing
to be persuaded, and not be amazed and angry at me, each of you,

[33] Here Diomedes is not recalled by his patronymic.

because by birth I am the youngest among you. I
claim that my generation is of a noble father,
Tydeus, whom now the piled earth covers over in Thebes.
For three blameless sons were born to Portheus,
and they dwelled in Pleuron and lofty Kalydon: Agrios
and Melas, and the third was the horseman Oineus,
my father's father, preeminent in valour beyond the others.
While Oineus remained in that place, my father wandered and settled
in Argos; for so I suppose Zeus and the other immortals wanted it.
He married one of the daughters of Adrestos, and inhabited
a house rich in substance, and had plenty of wheat-bearing fields,
and many orchards of fruit trees circled about him,
and he kept many herds. And he surpassed all other Achaians
with the spear. You must have heard of this, if it is true.
So you could not, calling me base and cowardly
by birth, dishonor my speech, if I speak well.'

As the poem moves toward its climax, Diomedes' reference to his father recalls and implicitly inverts Sthenelos' claim on behalf of the sons' superiority to their fathers; he reintroduces Tydeus here as bearer of a distinguished genealogy and as the greatest of all Achaean spearmen, to be the guarantor of *timê* for his son, establishing his place as strategist and *promachos* within Agamemnon's army. Yet Thebes is not absent even from this recollection—if only present as the place where Tydeus is buried.

The *Iliad* keeps the Theban narrative in play, even as it defuses its power—keeps it in play up to a point. The possibility that the earlier achievement of the heroes at Thebes—a victory accomplished by a smaller force, against a stronger fortification—may in fact surpass that of the present expedition offers a continuous challenge to the narrative, the aim of which is to commemorate the latter. Thus it is the *Iliad*'s ongoing poetic triumph that it continuously displaces and replaces the asserted primacy of that earlier tradition. For the narrative of battle and eventual conquest, shadowed by the Theban precedent, frames but does not constitute this poem's core. The *Iliad* highlights the exploits of Diomedes and brings him and his father to prominence in the absence of Achilles; yet what matters about the figure on whom this poem turns is not who his father is, but who he is not: Zeus.[34]

---

[34] This suggestion is developed in *The Power of Thetis* (this volume); I owe the formulation here to Liz Irwin.

And as it aligns not with the earlier war but with this one, the *Iliad* also separates the son of Tydeus from its central drama and its culmination. Diomedes' suggestion in Book IX that he and Sthenelos alone will take Troy because god is on their side—"still we two, Sthenelos and I, will fight till we witness the end of Ilion" (νῶϊ δ', ἐγὼ Σθένελός τε, μαχησόμεθ' εἰς ὅ κε τέκμωρ / Ἰλίου εὕρωμεν, *Iliad* IX 48–49)—anticipates that most poignant of appeals for divine acquiescence:

αἲ γάρ, Ζεῦ τε πάτερ καὶ Ἀθηναίη καὶ Ἄπολλον,
μήτε τις οὖν Τρώων θάνατον φύγοι, ὅσσοι ἔασι,
μήτε τις Ἀργείων, νῶϊν δ ἐκδῦμεν ὄλεθρον,
ὄφρ' οἶοι Τροίης ἱερὰ κρήδεμνα λύωμεν.

Iliad XVI 97–100

Father Zeus, Athene and Apollo, if only
not one of the Trojans, however many there are, could flee
destruction,
not one of the Argives, but we two could emerge from the slaughter
so that we alone could break the holy crown of Troy.

Diomedes may begin as a foil to Achilles and perform remarkable feats, but he is not part of the *Dios boulê*, the stamp of which is on this narrative: his exploits take place while it is in abeyance, and once Achilles returns to battle—indeed, once that distinctively Iliadic figure Patroclus rises up—Diomedes disappears, and with him the traces of Thebes.

Works Cited

Anderson, Ø. 1978. *Die Diomedesgestalt in der Ilias*. Symbolae Osloenses, vol. suppl. 25. Oslo.

Bernabé, A., ed. 1987–2007. *Poetarum Epicorum Graecorum: Testimonia et Fragmenta*. 2 vols. Leipzig.

Bethe, E. 1891. *Thebanische Heldenlieder: Untersuchungen über die Epen des thebanisch-argivischen Sagenkreises*. Leipzig.

Brillante, C., Cantilena, M., and Pavese, C. O., eds. 1981. *I poemi rapsodici non Omerici e la tradizione orale*. Università di Venezia, Facoltà di lettere e filosofia 3. Padova.

Brommer, F. 1973. *Vasenlisten zur griechischen Heldensage*. 3rd ed. Marburg.

Burgess, J. 2001. *The Tradition of the Trojan War in Homer and the Epic Cycle*. Baltimore.

Burkert, W. 1981. "Seven Against Thebes: An Oral Tradition Between Babylonian Magic and Greek Literature." In Brillante, Cantilena, and Pavese 1981:29–48.

Danek, G. 1998. *Epos und Zitat: Studien zu den Quellen der Odyssee.* Wiener Studien. Beiheft 22. Vienna.

Dué, C. 2002. *Homeric Variations on a Lament by Briseis.* Lanham, MD.

Edwards, A. 1985. *Achilles in the Odyssey.* Beträge zur klassischen Philologie. Heft 171. Königstein.

Edwards, G. P. 1971. *The Language of Hesiod in its Traditional Context.* Publications of the Philological Society 22. Oxford.

Ford, A. 1992. *Homer: The Poetry of the Past.* Ithaca.

Griffin, J. 1977. "The Epic Cycle and the Uniqueness of Homer." *Journal of Hellenic Studies* 97:39–53.

Hainsworth, J. B., ed. 1985. *The Iliad: A Commentary. Vol. 3: Books 9–12.* Cambridge.

Haubold, J. 2005. "Heracles in the Hesiodic Catalogue of Women." *The Hesiodic Catalogue of Women: Constructions and Reconstructions* (ed. R. Hunter) 85–99. Cambridge.

Horrocks, G. 1980. "The Antiquity of the Greek Epic Tradition: Some New Evidence." *Proceedings of the Cambridge Philological Society* 206:1–10.

Huxley, G. L. 1969. *Greek Epic Poetry from Eumelos to Panyassis.* Cambridge, MA.

Irwin, E. 2005. *Solon and Early Greek Poetry: The Politics of Exhortation.* Cambridge.

Janko, R., ed. 1992. *The Iliad: A Commentary. Vol. 4: Books 13–16.* Cambridge.

Katz, M. A. 1990. *Penelope's Renown: Meaning and Indeterminacy in the Odyssey.* Princeton.

King, B. Forthcoming. *The End of Adventure.*

Lateiner, D. 1997. "Homeric Prayer." *Arethusa* 30:241–272.

Lord, A. B. 1960. *The Singer of Tales.* 2nd ed. 2000 by S. Mitchell and G. Nagy. Cambridge, MA.

Mayer, K. 1996. "Helen and the *Dios Boulē.*" *American Journal of Philology* 117:1–15.

Monro, D., ed. 1901. *Odyssey. Books 13–24.* Oxford.

Muellner, L. 1976. *The Meaning of Homeric EYXOMAI through its Formulas.* Innsbrucker Beiträge zur Sprachwissenschaft 13. Innsbruck.

———. 1996. *The Anger of Achilles: Mênis in Greek Epic.* Ithaca, NY.

Nagy, G. 1979. *The Best of the Achaeans*. Baltimore.

———. 1996a. *Homeric Questions*. Austin.

———. 1996b. *Poetry as Performance: Homer and Beyond*. Cambridge.

Norden, E. 1913. *Agnostos Theos: Untersuchungen zur Formengeschichte religiöser Rede*. Leipzig.

Owen, E. T. 1947. *The Story of the Iliad, As Told in the Iliad*. Oxford.

Parry, A., ed. 1971. *The Making of Homeric Verse: The Collected Papers of Milman Parry*. Oxford.

Pucci, P. 1987. *Odysseus Polytropos: Intertextual Readings in the Odyssey and the Iliad*. Cornell Studies in Classical Philology 46. Ithaca, NY.

Ruijgh, C. 1985. "Problèmes de philologie." *Minos* 19:149–152.

Sacks, R. 1987. *The Traditional Phrase in Homer*. Columbia Studies in the Classical Tradition 14. Leiden.

———. Forthcoming. "Ending the Odyssey: Odysseus Traditions and the Homeric Odyssey."

Schefold, K., and Jung, F. 1989. *Die Sagen von den Argonauten, von Theben und Troia in der klassischen und hellenistischen Kunst*. Munich.

Schein, S. 1985. *The Mortal Hero: An Introduction to Homer's Iliad*. Berkeley.

Segal, C. 1994. *Singers, Heroes, and Gods in the Odyssey*. Cambridge, MA.

Severyns, A. 1928. *L'école d'Aristarque et le cycle épique*. Bibliothèque de la Faculté de philosophie et lettres de l'Unversité de Liège, fasc. 40. Liège.

Slatkin, L. 2006. "Notes on Tragic Visualizing in the *Iliad*." *Visualizing the Tragic: Drama, Myth, and Ritual in Greek Art and Literature. Essays in Honour of Froma Zeitlin*. (eds. C. Kraus et al.) 19–34. Oxford.

———. 2011. "Composition by Theme and the *Mêtis* of the *Odyssey*." This volume, 139-156.

———. 2011. *The Power of Thetis*. This volume, 19-95.

Van der Valk, M. H. 1952. "Ajax and Diomede in the *Iliad*." *Mnemosyne* 5:269–286.

Vermeule, E. 1987. "Baby Aigisthos and the Bronze Age." *Proceedings of the Cambridge Philological Society* n.s. 33:122–147.

West, S. 1981. "An Alternative Nostos for Odysseus." *Liverpool Classical Monthly* 6/7:169–175.

Whitman, C. 1958. *Homer and the Heroic Tradition*. Cambridge, MA.

Les Amis Mortels[1]

ATTLE IN THE *ILIAD* IS FAR FROM WORDLESS CARNAGE, resonating only with the sound of armor clashing. The general description of the poem's first military encounter begins strikingly by contrasting the eerie silence of the Greek troops with the heteroglossia of the Trojans. But once the battle is joined:

> ἔνθα δ' ἅμ' οἰμωγή τε καὶ εὐχωλὴ πέλεν ἀνδρῶν
> ὀλλύντων τε καὶ ὀλλυμένων, ῥέε δ' αἵματι γαῖα.

Iliad VIII 64–65

There the screaming and the shouts of triumph rose up together
of men killing and men killed, and the ground ran blood.

This paper is about how Homeric warriors talk to each other in battle. The *Iliad*, as has often been observed, repeatedly emphasizes a distinction between the requirements of warfare and those of debate (*agorê*) or council (*boulê*). Achilles, for example, in Book XVIII, claims unparalleled ability in the former, while yielding to others' superiority in the latter.[2] My concern, however, is with an intersecting category, namely with what warriors say to each other not in an assembly, passing around the scepter, but in the setting of battle—just the place where we would expect speech to be at most a vehicle for conveying a blueprint of the battle plan: "Advance!" "Retreat!" and so forth. But on the contrary, as every reader of the *Iliad* comes to appreciate, verbal exchanges between warriors in combat are extensive and often elaborate. What function and value does the *Iliad* assign to speech in this setting?

---

[1] This paper was given in the seminar of Nicole Loraux under the auspices of the Centre de Recherches Comparées sur les Sociétés Anciennes, May 1988. It was published in French, under the same title, in *L'Écrit du Temps* 19, 1988, translated by Nicole Loraux.

[2] *Iliad* XVIII 105–106. See also *Iliad* IV 400, I 258, and II 202, among other examples.

In recent Homeric studies, much important work has been done on *kleos* as a theme and as an epic value—that is, on what will be said about warriors by those generations of men who come after them. My focus here is on what is said to them, or rather, what they say to each other. If the fair division of prizes and the distribution of food are an issue in the *Iliad*, if there is a calculus and a weighing of everything heroes get, is there an implicit measure for language as well—is there language that is fitting, language that gives too little, language that says too much? In the Homeric world of formally marked exchanges—oaths, prayers, vows, laments—that confirm a range of socio-religious ties, virtually all belong to other arenas, from which they are imported into the world of war. My subject here will be the exchanges that are fundamentally shaped by the condition of battle, those exchanges not adapted but indigenous to it.

Early in Book XIII of the *Iliad*, at a perilous moment for the Greeks, with the fighting growing increasingly brutal and with many of their chief fighters wounded, as Hector and the Trojans advance on the ships, the Cretan leader Idomeneus encounters Thoas, son of Andraimon (or so he believes; in fact it's Poseidon in disguise); brief conversation ensues. Questioned by "Thoas," Idomeneus attributes the Achaeans' disadvantage in the war to Zeus' ill-will, and (as though to explain why this turn in their military fortunes cannot be blamed on inadequate Achaean fighting) he pauses to praise Thoas, speci-fying not his strength or his speed, but his practice of rousing up other warriors—of inciting them to battle:

ἀλλά, Θόαν, καὶ γὰρ τὸ πάρος μενεδήϊος ἦσθα,
ὀτρύνεις δὲ καὶ ἄλλον, ὅθι μεθιέντα ἴδηαι·
τῶ νῦν μήτ᾽ ἀπόληγε κέλευέ τε φωτὶ ἑκάστῳ.

Iliad XIII 228–230

'Since you, Thoas, have been before this a man stubborn in battle
and stirred up another whenever you saw one hang back, so now
also do not give up, and urge on each man as you find him.'

Idomeneus here draws attention to an essential aspect of the warrior func-tion, one that is as crucial in epic action as wielding a spear or planning battle strategy. To incite men to combat (*otrunai*) is a demonstration of vital authority on the part of any warrior and a critical—in some ways the most critical—contribution to the war effort. It is principally what the gods have to offer when they enter the fray with partisan intent, either in their own guise or in someone else's. Poseidon in Book XIV (367ff.) asserts that the Greeks "will feel the absence of Achilles less if we spur each other on (*otrunometha*)." Diomedes, at XIV 131ff., urges the other heroes, wounded though they are, to *otrunai* the men. Nestor, in Book X, blames Menelaos for what he thinks may be his failure to rouse up the other heroes.[3] Sarpedon's dying words to Glaukos are:

> ἀλλ' ἔχεο κρατερῶς, ὄτρυνε δὲ λαὸν ἄπαντα.
> ὡς ἄρα μιν εἰπόντα τέλος θανάτοιο κάλυψεν
>
> *Iliad* XVI 501–502

> 'But hold strongly on and stir up all the rest of our people.'
> He spoke, and as he spoke death's end closed over his nostrils.

To rouse the *laos* 'fighting host', to succeed at inciting (*otrunai*) them, urging them as a group and individually to risk their lives, is a complicated proposition because it is done not simply by example but through words—and by words that must invoke and underscore fundamental assumptions about reciprocal relations between *philoi* in the context of battle, or, to put it another way, how the context of battle defines what it means to be *philoi*.

In a general sense, and (it would seem) paradoxically, it is the military event—just the thing one would expect to render talking superfluous—that draws attention to the power of words in the *Iliad*. What invites Idomeneus' commentary on the dire situation for the Greeks, and his praise of his interlocutor as one who rouses the troops, is a single, telling question. "Thoas" demands:

> Ἰδομενεῦ, Κρητῶν βουληφόρε ποῦ τοι ἀπειλαὶ
> οἴχονται, τὰς Τρωσὶν ἀπείλεον υἷες Ἀχαιῶν;
>
> *Iliad* XIII 219–220

> 'Idomeneus, lord of the Kretans' councils, where are those
>   threats you gave
> now, that the sons of the Achaians uttered against the Trojans?'

This question, I suggest, has not only an ironic, metonymic, rhetorical value— "Where are the actions you promised? Where are the goods you said you'd deliver?"—but also an important literal meaning: what has become of that indispensable instrument of aggression, the *threat* that heartens one's allies and alarms the enemy? "Where have the threats gone?" is a question that is posed elsewhere in the *Iliad*—for example, by Apollo to Aeneas in Book XX:

---

[3] *Iliad* X 114–130.

Αἰνεία, Τρώων βουληφόρε, ποῦ τοι ἀπειλαὶ
ἃς Τρώων βασιλεῦσιν ὑπίσχεο οἰνοποτάζων
Πηλεΐδεω Ἀχιλῆος ἐναντίβιον πολεμίξειν;

Iliad XX 83–85

'Aineias, lord of the Trojans' counsels, where are those threats
   gone
which as you drank your wine you made before Troy's kings,
   solemnly,
that you would match your battle strength with Peleian
   Achilleus?'

Achilles, as he sends the Myrmidons with Patroklos out to terrify the Trojans, reminds them not to forget their *apeilai*, the boasting threats they uttered while waiting by the ships.[4] When Hera in Book VIII (219ff.) puts it into Agamemnon's mind to *otrunai* his troops, he asks where the hostile words against the Trojans have gone that the men had uttered at Lemnos. Threats have two audiences: one's comrades, on the one hand, and the enemy on the other. The reference to threats constitutes in itself a form of encouragement, and as such draws attention to the double-edged quality of words as weapons in the *Iliad*.[5]

Addressed to either audience, hostile words may be potent, but they must be justified; otherwise they become a testimony to cowardice, pusillanimity. Threats that are empty are like an ineffective spear cast or sword thrust that leaves the initiator more vulnerable, or like armor that does not protect its wearer. Thus Aeneas challenges Pandaros (at *Iliad* V 171):

Πάνδαρε, ποῦ τοι τόξον ἰδὲ πτερόεντες ὀϊστοί....

'Pandaros, where now are your bow and your feathered arrows...'

To which Pandaros, having failed at mortally wounding Diomedes, replies in disgust that his bow is *anemôlia* 'useless, futile'—a term that occurs formulaically in the phrase *anemôlia badzein* 'to speak idly'.[6]

---

[4] *Iliad* XVI 200–202.

[5] See the suggestive remarks of Dunkel 1979:250–251, who points out that the representation of the relation between talking and fighting in Homer offers a contradiction: at times they are contrasted as "diametric opposites," while at other times "prowess (or the lack of it) at one implies prowess (etc.) at the other." Dunkel argues that "this opposition is mediated by the phenomenon of verbal conflict, which can take the shape of quarrel, council, or poetic competition."

[6] *Anemôlia badzeis*, *Iliad* IV 355; *anemôlia badzein*, *Odyssey* iv 837, xi 464.

Menelaos in Book VII, when he wants to move the reluctant Greek chiefs to accept Hektor's challenge to a duel, simultaneously stirs and reproaches them in a speech that begins by addressing them as *apeilêteres* 'threateners'.[7] In Menelaos' words, if none of the Danaans had stood forth to face Hector, it would have been a *lôbê* 'disgrace', an affront for the 'threateners'—one they would have inflicted upon themselves: every threat is potentially a boomerang that may rebound against the speaker, and the speaker may be exposed, or expose himself, by having spoken. But champions do stand forth, and Ajax, who presents himself to meet the challenges from Hektor (and from Menelaos and Nestor), and who wins the lottery among the *aristoi Achaiôn*, is then indeed described as advancing against Hektor with threats (*apeilêsas prosêuda*). Hektor replies to Ajax' speech by saying *mê meu peirêtidze* (*Iliad* VII 235), which is a term used otherwise only for military action (*Iliad* XII 47, 257; XV 615)—it denotes 'breaking through enemy lines'.[8]

Addresses to one's enemy, this suggests, are military actions in themselves—not an adjunct to combat but a form of combat. Thus Apollo instructs Aeneas in Book XX on how to face Achilles in battle with the following remarkable advice:

ἀλλ' ἰθὺς φέρε χαλκὸν ἀτειρέα, μηδέ σε πάμπαν
λευγαλέοις ἐπέεσσιν ἀποτρεπέτω καὶ ἀρειῇ.

Iliad XX 108-109

'Carry your weariless bronze straight against him, let him by no
means
turn you back by blustering words and his threats of terror.'

He warns Aeneas to defend himself not against Achilles' spear, but against his *words*. The Ajaxes similarly instruct their followers:

μή τις ὀπίσσω
τετράφθω ποτὶ νῆας ὁμοκλητῆρος ἀκούσας,
ἀλλὰ πρόσω ἵεσθε καὶ ἀλλήλοισι κέλεσθε...

Iliad XII 272–274

'...Now let no man let himself
be turned back upon the ships for the sound of their blustering
but keep forever forward calling out courage to each other.'

---

[7] *Iliad* VII 94–102.
[8] See Dunkel 1979:251–252 on *makhomai* and other military terms for speech in Homer.

In their final duel, Hektor equates Achilles' faulty spearcast with his speech—the inaccuracy of the one necessarily implies the falseness of the other:

ἤμβροτες, οὐδ' ἄρα πώ τι, θεοῖς ἐπιείκελ' Ἀχιλλεῦ
ἐκ Διὸς ἠείδης τὸν ἐμὸν μόρον, ἦ τοι ἔφης γε·
ἀλλά τις ἀρτιεπὴς καὶ ἐπίκλοπος ἔπλεο μύθων,
ὄφρά σ' ὑποδείσας μένεος ἀλκῆς τε λάθωμαι.

Iliad XXII 279–282

'You missed; and it was not, o Achilleus like the immortals,
from Zeus that you knew my destiny; but you thought so; or
    rather
you are someone clever in speech and spoke to swindle me,
to make me afraid of you and forget my valour and war strength.'

We learn, moreover, from a dialogue between Sarpedon and Tlepolemos, that there is a heroic precedent (perhaps in an epic tradition) for the catastrophic effects of hostile language: Herakles sacked Troy, we are told, because of a 'rebuke' (*enipê*) by Laomedon.[9] There are of course passages in which speech is explicitly devalued, but it is worth bearing in mind that these occur in contexts that at the same time emphasize and highlight the efficacy of hostile words—so that such passages appear to acknowledge the power of words by attempting to deflect or minimize it.[10]

The heroes themselves, then, acknowledge a special aggressive impact of language, which returns us to the warrior's function of inciting (*otrunai*) his comrades. As Idomeneus' statement to "Thoas" makes clear, combative words spoken to encourage those on one's own side are judged by the heroes themselves to have equally powerful force.

What language, then, is used to rouse warriors to lay down their lives? In the most frequent form of collective address, which can serve as the unmarked model for such exhortations, they are specifically invoked as *philoi*:

Ἀργείους δ' ὄτρυνε μέγας Τελαμώνιος Αἴας·
ὦ φίλοι ἀνέρες ἔστε, καὶ αἰδῶ θέσθ' ἐνὶ θυμῷ...

Iliad XV 560–561

---

[9] *Iliad* V 648ff.
[10] See, for example, the response of Aeneas to Achilles at *Iliad* XX 200ff.

But huge Telamonian Aias stirred on the Argives:
'Dear friends, be men; let shame be in your hearts, and discipline...'

Nestor, at XV 661, begins with: "Dear friends, be men" (ὦ φίλοι ἀνέρες ἔστε), and the passage concludes: "So he spoke, and stirred the spirit and heart in each man" (ὣς εἰπὼν ὄτρυνε μένος καὶ θυμὸν ἑκάστου, *Iliad* XV 667).

A related form of this, occurring seven times in the poem, spoken by both Greeks and Trojans, is:

ἀνέρες ἔστε φίλοι, μνήσασθε δὲ θούριδος ἀλκῆς

Be men now, dear friends, remember your furious valour.

It occurs, for example, at VI 112, VIII 147, XI 287, and Hektor delivers it at XV 487. "Be men"; "remember your valour"—these iterations encourage by implying that the *philoi* are adequate to their task intrinsically, by virtue of being the men that they are; they need only be reminded of it. Hektor continues:

ἀλλὰ μάχεσθ' ἐπὶ νηυσὶν ἀολλέες· ὃς δέ κεν ὑμέων
βλήμενος ἠὲ τυπεὶς θάνατον καὶ πότμον ἐπίσπῃ
τεθνάτω· οὔ οἱ ἀεικὲς ἀμυνομένῳ περὶ πάτρης
τεθνάμεν· ἀλλ' ἄλοχός τε σόη καὶ παῖδες ὀπίσσω,
καὶ οἶκος καὶ κλῆρος ἀκήρατος, εἴ κεν Ἀχαιοὶ
οἴχωνται σὺν νηυσὶ φίλην ἐς πατρίδα γαῖαν.
ὣς εἰπὼν ὄτρυνε μένος καὶ θυμὸν ἑκάστου.

Iliad XV 494–500

'Fight on then by the ships together. He who among you
finds by spear thrown or spear thrust his death and destiny,
let him die. He has no dishonour when he dies defending
his country, for then his wife shall be saved and his children
    afterwards,
and his house and property shall not be damaged, if the Achaians
must go away with their ships to the beloved land of their
    fathers.'
So he spoke, and stirred the spirit and strength in each man.

Menelaos' speech and the words of "Thoas," however, show us a significant transformation of this model. Menelaos challenges his fellow Achaeans as Ἀχαιΐδες οὐκέτ' Ἀχαιοί (*Iliad* VII 96)—they are not men; they may not even be human, but inert "water and earth" (ὕδωρ καὶ γαῖα). In contrast to the reassurance Hektor offers to the warriors about to die, moreover, "Thoas" demonstrates his ability, praised by Idomeneus, to urge on—*otrunai*—his comrades with the lines:

Ἰδομενεῦ, μὴ κεῖνος ἀνὴρ ἔτι νοστήσειεν
ἐκ Τροίης, ἀλλ' αὖθι κυνῶν μέλπηθρα γένοιτο,
ὅς τις ἐπ' ἤματι τῷδε ἑκὼν μεθίῃσι μάχεσθαι.

Iliad XIII 232–234

'Idomeneus, may that man who this day willfully hangs back
from the fighting never win home again out of Troy land,
but stay here and be made dogs' delight for their feasting.'

Agamemnon, as well, predicts this frightful future:

ὃν δέ κ' ἐγὼν ἀπάνευθε μάχης ἐθέλοντα νοήσω
μιμνάζειν παρὰ νηυσὶ κορωνίσιν, οὔ οἱ ἔπειτα
ἄρκιον ἐσσεῖται φυγέειν κύνας ἠδ' οἰωνούς.

Iliad II 391–393

'But any man whom I find trying, apart from the battle,
to hang back by the curved ships, for him no longer
will there be any means to escape the dogs and the vultures.'

To add simply one other example of this kind of revision, one might point to the passage in Book VI, where Nestor urges on the fighters with:

ὦ φίλοι ἥρωες Δαναοί, θεράποντες Ἄρηος
μή τις νῦν ἐνάρων ἐπιβαλλόμενος μετόπισθε
μιμνέτω, ὥς κε πλεῖστα φέρων ἐπὶ νῆας ἵκηται,
ἀλλ' ἄνδρας κτείνωμεν· ἔπειτα δὲ καὶ τὰ ἕκηλοι
νεκροὺς ἂμ πεδίον συλήσετε τεθνηῶτας.

Iliad VI 67–71

'O beloved Danaan fighters, henchmen of Ares,
let no man any more hang back with his eye on the plunder
designing to take all the spoil he can gather back to the vessels;
let us kill the men now, and afterwards at your leisure
all along the plain you can plunder the perished corpses.'

He calls on them not to hang back in order to plunder their Trojan victims, but to kill more men (ἀλλ' ἄνδρας κτείνωμεν) with the reassurance that they will soon plunder them unhindered, and his speech concludes with "speaking

127

thus, he spurred on the strength and spirit of each one" (ὡς εἰπὼν ὄτρυνε μένος καὶ θυμὸν ἑκάστου). How important spoils are to every warrior we know from the *Iliad* as a whole: that they are an emblem of valor is illustrated by the dialogue between Meriones and Idomeneus in Book XXIII; how much their value is endorsed by Hektor in particular we know from Book VI, where his ideal for his son is that Astyanax shall one day bring back the ἔναρα βροτόεντα from a warrior he has slain (*Iliad* VI 480–481).

Consider then Hektor's speech at *Iliad* XV:

> νηυσὶν ἐπισσεύεσθαι, ἐὰν δ᾽ ἔναρα βροτόεντα·
> ὃν δ᾽ ἂν ἐγὼν ἀπάνευθε νεῶν ἑτέρωθι νοήσω,
> αὐτοῦ οἱ θάνατον μητίσομαι, οὐδέ νυ τόν γε
> γνωτοί τε γνωταί τε πυρὸς λελάχωσι θανόντα,
> ἀλλὰ κύνες ἐρύουσι πρὸ ἄστεος ἡμετέροιο.

> *Iliad* XV 347–351

> 'Make hard for the ships, let the bloody spoils be. That man
> I see in the other direction apart from the vessels,
> I will take care that he gets his death, and that man's relations
> neither men nor women shall give his dead body the rite of
>   burning.
> In the space before our city the dogs shall tear him to pieces.'

In other words, side by side with the sort of *otrunai* rallying cry, cited earlier (ἀνέρες ἔστε, etc.), that we might imagine would be offered to inspire fighters—the kind that guarantees warriors the security of their heroic expectations as to their masculinity and as to their entitlement to a warrior's prizes, a warrior's funeral, and a warrior's renown—there exists another verbal strategy that evidently undermines that security and inverts the image of the warrior as given by warriors themselves (as by Hektor of Astyanax in Book VI), and these messages are offered as a form of inciting to battle as well.

In a famous scene in Book IV,[11] Agamemnon rebukes Diomedes, one of his most reliable champions, reproaching him for lurking in the background rather than fighting in the forefront (the verb used here, *ptôssein* 'to cower like an animal', recurs regularly in such speeches). It is an accusation of cowardice cast in terms that attest to the glorious reputation of Tydeus while denigrating his son by comparison. Not only has Diomedes failed in

---

[11] *Iliad* IV 368–395.

the heroic ideal of surpassing one's father, but Agamemnon's harangue also implies that Diomedes will not earn the *kleos* that his father deservedly attained. Diomedes' friend and fellow *epigonos*, Sthenelos, objects—"we are better than our fathers!"—but Diomedes silences him:

τὸν δ' ἄρ' ὑπόδρα ἰδὼν προσέφη κρατερὸς Διομήδης·
τέττα, σιωπῇ ἧσο, ἐμῷ δ' ἐπιπείθεο μύθῳ·
οὐ γὰρ ἐγὼ νεμεσῶ Ἀγαμέμνονι, ποιμένι λαῶν,
ὀτρύνοντι μάχεσθαι ἐϋκνήμιδας Ἀχαιούς·

Iliad IV 411–414

Then looking at him darkly strong Diomedes spoke to him:
'Friend, stay quiet rather and do as I tell you; I will
find no fault with Agamemnon, shepherd of the people,
for stirring thus into battle the strong-greaved Achaians.'

Agamemnon's insults, which would deny Diomedes heroic stature, are justified by virtue of constituting a gesture of encouragement.

Not only the hero himself but his family as well—his whole collection of male relatives—are the object of Sarpedon's abuse of Hektor at *Iliad* V 471ff. By way of exhorting Hektor, Sarpedon asks him where his former *menos* has gone, proceeding to demean Hektor's brothers and brothers-in-law, whom he describes as cowering (*kataptôssousi*) like frightened dogs. His words "bite" Hektor and send him back into the fray.

Immediately prior to Agamemnon's attack on Diomedes, the Greek leader treats Odysseus and Menestheus to an equally vitriolic rebuke, charging that although they eat as much as they can at the feast (*dais*), they do not take their share of the fighting, an accusation that implies a breach of the *isê dais*.[12] Agamemnon calls Odysseus a string of abusive terms, including *kerdaleophron*—an insult otherwise used only by an enraged Achilles to Agamemnon in their quarrel in Book I. Odysseus responds furiously in his own defense, lashing out verbally at Agamemnon, whereupon Agamemnon responds happily that "what you think is just what I think" (τὰ γὰρ φρονέεις ἅ τ' ἐγώ περ).[13] This exchange of insults is evidently an expression of *homophrosunê* 'like-mindedness'—which, as we know from the *Odyssey*, is the definition of a happy marriage![14]

---

[12] *Iliad* IV 338–348.
[13] *Iliad* IV 358–361.
[14] *Odyssey* vi 180–185.

The warriors implicitly acknowledge the message underlying this rhetorical code, and later, when Agamemnon proposes that they return home, Diomedes himself explicitly questions whether Agamemnon has confused code and message. At the opening of Book IX, he reprimands Agamemnon, asking, "You don't think that we *really* are as unwarlike and cowardly as you *said* we were, do you?"[15]

But the possibility of that confusion is allowed for by the verb *neikeô*, which here designates Agamemnon and Sarpedon's verbal action (e.g., καὶ τὸν μὲν νείκεσσεν ἰδὼν κρείων Ἀγαμέμνων, *Iliad* IV 368), as well as Menelaos' *acte de langage* in Book VII (νείκει ὀνειδίζων, μέγα δὲ στεναχίζετο θυμῷ, *Iliad* VII 95) and, also in Book VII, Nestor's long reproach designed to rouse the fighting spirit in the chiefs (ὣς νείκεσσ᾽ ὃ γέρων, οἳ δ᾽ ἐννέα πάντες ἀνέσταν, *Iliad* VII 161), to cite only a few examples. *Neikos* is the term that designates (for the characters themselves) the entire conflict between the Greeks and the Trojans (*Iliad* III 87; VII 374 = *Iliad* VII 388), as well as the literal battle in progress (δὴ γὰρ μέγα νεῖκος ὄρωρεν, *Iliad* XII 361, XIII 122, XV 400, etc.). If we remember that Paris *neikesse* (*Iliad* XXIV 29) the goddesses in his courtyard, we know that denigration can have far-reaching consequences. The example of Achilles, who withdraws even before Agamemnon takes Briseis because of his *threat* to do so, is close at hand.

So these are violent, hostile, trouble-making speeches intended to promote solidarity and consensus—speeches that at the same time verge on being conflicts (*neikea*), utterances whose charged content has explosive potential; they are, as it were, one side, or half, of a *neikos*. The language used to enforce collective bonds, to promote active participation in the collective enterprise, is in fact the same language used to challenge and intimidate the enemy, to dominate him; it is the language of the verbal *aristeia*.[16]

To represent your opponent as a woman, a helpless child, as a frightened animal, to question his lineage, to promise him mutilation, to predict the misery of his parents, the anguish of his bereft wife and infant: these are enemy artillery, so to speak—the enemy's destructive blows against a hero's integrity.[17]

Characteristic is the insult that Herakles' son Tlepolemos hurls at Sarpedon when they confront each other on the battlefield (*Iliad* V 628ff.):

---

[15] δαιμόνι᾽ οὕτω που μάλα ἔλπεαι υἷας Ἀχαιῶν / ἀπτολέμους τ᾽ ἔμεναι καὶ ἀνάλκιδας ὡς ἀγορεύεις, *Iliad* IX 40–41.

[16] We may note as well that Hektor threatens violence against Poulydamas (*Iliad* XII 250) in the same language that he and Achilles use of each other (*Iliad* XVI 861, XVIII 92).

[17] To adduce simply some representative instances, e.g., *Iliad* VIII 161ff., XI 384ff., XIII 620ff.

Sarpedon is a coward incapable of the exploits of his forebears—so much so that Tlepolemos doubts his genealogy. Reminiscent of Agamemnon's denigration of Diomedes, this is, however, the initial move in a deadly duel:

> Σαρπῆδον, Λυκίων βουληφόρε, τίς τοι ἀνάγκη
> πτώσσειν ἐνθάδ᾽ ἐόντι μάχης ἀδαήμονι φωτί;
> ψευδόμενοι δέ σέ φασι Διὸς γόνον αἰγιόχοιο
> εἶναι, ἐπεὶ πολλὸν κείνων ἐπιδεύεαι ἀνδρῶν
> οἳ Διὸς ἐξεγένοντο ἐπὶ προτέρων ἀνθρώπων·
>
> *Iliad* V 633–637

'Man of counsel of the Lykians, Sarpedon, why must you
be skulking here, you who are a man unskilled in the fighting?
They are liars who call you issue of Zeus, the holder
of the aegis, since you fall far short in truth of the others
who were begotten of Zeus in the generations before us.'

These are the last words Tlepolemos utters; he and Sarpedon match rebukes and exchange spears simultaneously. But both Tlepolemos' taunt and his spear cast miss their mark; they are vitiated, both of them, by the fact that Zeus truly is Sarpedon's father, and he brushes the spear away from his son.

What, then, are we to make of this pronounced replication of the language and thematics of verbal assault and domination, designed for one's mortal enemy, appropriated in the service of enhancing allegiance to one's own side?

One explanation that must be excluded is formulaic rigidity, because despite the formal typological consistency of these exchanges[18] there is in fact extensive formulaic repetition only in the *positive* (so to speak) exhortations (ἀνέρες ἔστε, φίλοι, etc.) and not in the negative ones. At the same time there is careful formula restriction, so that, for example, although the verb *neikeô* occurs several times in conjunction with the phrases *oneideiois epeessi* and *cholotoisin epeessi* of different speakers to different addressees, *neikeô* with the phrase *aischrois epeessi* occurs three times, used only of Hektor addressing Paris.[19] It has been fully demonstrated[20] that such precise formula distribution is a traditional compositional technique and could clearly be brought to bear on these passages as well.

---

[18] This has been well analyzed in Latacz 1977.
[19] *Iliad* III 38 = *Iliad* VI 325, XIII 768.
[20] See, for example, Muellner 1976, Nagy 1979, Sacks 1987.

Are these exchanges that serve to establish a hierarchy of heroes so that an order of authority, a chain of command, can be determined?[21] Evidently not, as the previously cited passages indicate, in that the prominent fighters on both sides rebuke and are rebuked in turn. One might, on the contrary, suggest that there is a leveling, equalizing effect to these reciprocal, vituperative utterances. Pierre Bourdieu has proposed that such insults and rebukes actually dignify the receiver—that they put the insulter and the insulted on an equal footing.[22] There may be some element of this in the Iliadic exchanges.

Many passages in the *Iliad* attest to the fine line, or unstable complementarity, between competitive and cooperative behavior among the heroes. The tension this generates plays a decisive role in the events of the poem at every level, and clearly at its turning points, among them the opening quarrel and Achilles' sending Patroklos into battle with instructions not to storm the walls of Troy. Equilibrium *is* possible, though fleeting, because it occurs most often on the field of battle, as lives end, yet it is again disrupted in the brief space between deadly encounters on that field.

One can see the shifting balance on a verbal level in the scene in Book XIII, where Idomeneus, returning to the battlefield, meets his friend Meriones on his way back to pick up a spear at Idomeneus' tent.[23] The ensuing dialogue can be read as an implicit rebuke and response on the pattern of other speeches of encouragement that question why the addressee is somewhere other than the front line of battle or on his way to it.

Idomeneus makes no explicit reproach, but elaborately asserts his own prowess, measured in war plunder that attests to his courage in close fighting; if Meriones needs a spear, he, Idomeneus, has more than he needs—Meriones should help himself. Meriones replies to the suppressed reproach. As though Idomeneus had enjoined him, on the *otrunai* pattern, to remember his valor (*alkê*), he responds that he has not forgotten it (*Iliad* XIII 269), that he stands in the forefront of the fighting, and, significantly, that Idomeneus, of all people, should know it.

Idomeneus agrees, and inverts the kind of rebuke Diomedes delivers to Odysseus (to *epotrunai* him):

---

[21] On challenges between warriors on opposing sides as confirming a heroic hierarchy, see Létoublon 1983:27–48.

[22] Bourdieu 1972.

[23] *Iliad* XIII 240ff.

διογενὲς Λαερτιάδη, πολυμήχαν' Ὀδυσσεῦ,
πῇ φεύγεις μετὰ νῶτα βαλὼν κακὸς ὣς ἐν ὁμίλῳ;
μή τίς τοι φεύγοντι μεταφρένῳ ἐν δόρυ πήξῃ

Iliad VIII 93–95

'Son of Laertes and seed of Zeus, resourceful Odysseus,
where are you running, turning your back in battle like a coward?
Do not let them strike the spear in your back as you run for it.'

No one, Idomeneus now says, could disparage the courage of Meriones; Meriones will never be killed by a spear in his back: he will go face forward into the προμάχων ὀαριστύν (*Iliad* XIII 291). The competitive potential of this exchange, negotiated into agreement, is reintegrated into a cooperative effort in which the two warriors join forces in battle. They abandon their cooperative conversation in order to avoid words of reproach from another man.[24]

Who should know Meriones better than Idomeneus? Who should know you better than your comrade-in-arms? Nothing is more evident in the *Iliad* than the absolute dependence of the *philoi* on each other for their lives. Although this is obviously true of the phalanx as a whole, it is given clearest expression through the representation of warriors joined in closely linked pairs. The warriors themselves articulate this bond primarily in relation to military aggression (e.g., Thoas/Poseidon-Idomeneus, *Iliad* XIII 235–238). Diomedes claims, prefiguring Achilles in Book XVI, that he and Sthenelos alone could take the city of Troy (*Iliad* IX 46–49).[25] But from the first marshaling of the troops, the poem's emphasis is on the mutual efforts of the *philoi* to protect each other (*Iliad* III 8–9).

The battle books are composed for the most part of the actions (aggressive and defensive) of warriors in pairs. A vivid example of a pair of warriors at work might be Teucer and Ajax at Book VIII:

Τεῦκρος δ' εἴνατος ἦλθε, παλίντονα τόξα τιταίνων,
στῆ δ' ἄρ' ὑπ' Αἴαντος σάκεϊ Τελαμωνιάδαο.
ἔνθ' Αἴας μὲν ὑπεξέφερεν σάκος· αὐτὰρ ὅ γ' ἥρως
παπτήνας, ἐπεὶ ἄρ τιν' ὀϊστεύσας ἐν ὁμίλῳ
βεβλήκοι, ὃ μὲν αὖθι πεσὼν ἀπὸ θυμὸν ὄλεσσεν,

---

[24] *Iliad* XIII 293.
[25] Among other explicit examples, see *Iliad* X 222–226.

αὐτὰρ ὁ αὖτις ἰὼν πάϊς ὡς ὑπὸ μητέρα δύσκεν
εἰς Αἴανθ᾽· ὁ δέ μιν σάκεϊ κρύπτασκε φαεινῷ.

Iliad VIII 266–272

...and ninth came Teukros, bending into position the curved bow,
and took his place in the shelter of Telamonian Aias'
shield, as Aias lifted the shield to take him. The hero
would watch, whenever in the throng he had struck some man
    with an arrow,
and as the man dropped and died where he was stricken, the
    archer
would run back again, like a child to the arms of his mother,
to Aias, who would hide him in the glittering shield's protection.

The fraternal bond is a model for the countless pairings of which the larger collective is composed, and of which Achilles and Patroklos are only one fully elaborated instance.[26] It is a bond indissoluble in death—indeed, it is especially activated by the death of one of the pair. Studies of the narrative structure of the battle scenes have detailed the range of the fighters' interdependence,[27] and one may add that they are dependent on each other for the motivation to fight—the immediate motivation; for one of the most common narrative patterns describing entry into combat is that a warrior is wounded or (more likely) killed, a friend or close relative sees, is stricken with pity or grief, and plunges more deeply into the fray.[28] Countless examples illustrate the reality, underlying the ideology of the *philotês* of the *Männerbund*,[29] that in battle your life is as fully in the hands of your friend as of your enemy; the former is as dangerous to you, as potentially fatal, as the latter.

    Sarpedon, gravely wounded, pleads with Hektor not to let him become a spoil of battle (*helôr*) for the Danaans. He beseeches Hektor, as one would supplicate an enemy, not to deprive him of his return to fatherland, wife, and child (*Iliad* V 684–688). Earlier (*Iliad* V 488–492), he warns Hektor that, lest the Trojans become the prey and plunder (*helôr kai kurma*) of the Greeks, Hektor must supplicate the leaders of his allies to stand fast.

---

[26] On this subject, see Loraux 1989 (= 1997).

[27] See especially Fenik's thorough analysis (1968).

[28] E.g. *Iliad* V 561ff., 608ff., XI 248ff., XIII 463ff., 580, XV 422, XVI 508ff., 581ff., XVII 344–355 (a chain of such sequences), and XX 419ff. (where Hektor is described as witnessing the death of his brother Polydoros at Achilles' hands and as consequently feeling impelled to face Achilles directly).

[29] On this subject, see Sinos 1980.

It is those on your own side who have it in their power to ensure that you do not become a spoil of war—or die in obscurity, unavenged. The Trojan Akamas kills the warrior attempting to drag off the body of Akamas' brother, crying out that he has not left his brother's death unrepaid for long; "thus a man prays to leave behind someone close to him as an avenger in battle" (*Iliad* XIV 484–485).

What your enemy speaks as a threat, that intolerable prospect that you will end as carrion for dogs and vultures, is a truer threat in the mouth of your friend. For warrior allies to speak to each other in the language of the enemy, to collude with the enemy in words, is to reinforce their reciprocal obligations as *philoi* by reference to that devastating potential. The life-and-death import of *philotês* is underscored by the appropriation of the enemy's diction. In this sense, the speeches of rebuke recapitulate in themselves the nature of the *philos* bond—not only functionally, by subsuming competition into cooperation and turning *neikos* against the enemy, but symbolically, by representing one's ally as the enemy he *could* be, in order to enhance his value as the friend that he *is*.

In this connection it is worth pointing out that in the human sphere of the *Iliad*, *echthros*, *echthos*, *echthairô* and their derivatives are applied only to those on one's own side. Greeks do not use it of Trojans, nor do Trojans of Greeks. You must be *philos* in order to be *echthros*.[30]

There is, of course, another side to this paradox. Who knows you better than your comrade-in-arms? No one, perhaps; but there is someone who knows you equally well: your enemy. The common vocabulary of sexual relations and military combat has been fruitfully investigated,[31] and it represents an important aspect of the way in which the *Iliad* develops the theme of the intimate enemy. The individual who appraises your body most carefully in every detail (e.g., Achilles scrutinizing Hektor in Book XXII), who knows the particulars of your strengths and weaknesses, who apprehends your courage and deepest fear, who is with you at the moment of truth—that person is your enemy. But this knowledge is not solely corporal.[32]

Your friends pity you, grieve for you, avenge you, but it is your killer who speaks your disappointed hopes. Idomeneus addresses the corpse of Othryoneus, whom he has just slain; he tells Othryoneus' story: the promises,

---

[30] See, among other examples, *Iliad* IX 614, III 413–417: Helen may be *echthros* 'enemy' to both sides because she has been *philos* to both.
[31] See Vermeule 1981:97ff. and Monsacré 1984:53–77.
[32] On the "paradoxical community" of enemy warriors in Homer and of political adversaries in later Greek thought, see Loraux 1987.

now never to be fulfilled, by which Othryoneus was to have received Priam's daughter in marriage in return for beating the Greeks back from the city:

Ὀθρυονεῦ, περὶ δή σε βροτῶν αἰνίζομ' ἁπάντων
εἰ ἐτεὸν δὴ πάντα τελευτήσεις ὅς' ὑπέστης
Δαρδανίδῃ Πριάμῳ· ὁ δ' ὑπέσχετο θυγατέρα ἥν.
καί κέ τοι ἡμεῖς ταῦτά γ' ὑποσχόμενοι τελέσαιμεν,
δοῖμεν δ' Ἀτρεΐδαο θυγατρῶν εἶδος ἀρίστην
Ἄργεος ἐξαγαγόντες ὀπυιέμεν, εἴ κε σὺν ἄμμιν
Ἰλίου ἐκπέρσῃς εὖ ναιόμενον πτολίεθρον.
ἀλλ' ἕπε', ὄφρ' ἐπὶ νηυσὶ συνώμεθα ποντοπόροισιν
ἀμφὶ γάμῳ, ἐπεὶ οὔ τοι ἐεδνωταὶ κακοί εἰμεν.

Iliad XIII 374–382

'Othryoneus, I congratulate you beyond all others
if it is here that you will bring to pass what you promised
to Dardanian Priam, who in turn promised you his daughter.
See now, we also would make you a promise, and we would fulfill it;
we would give you the loveliest of Atreides' daughters,
and bring her here from Argos to be your wife, if you joined us
and helped us storm the strong-founded city of Ilion.
Come then with me, so we can meet by our seafaring vessels
about a marriage; we here are not bad matchmakers for you.'

This is startlingly reminiscent of the narrative's commentary on the unavailing efforts or attributes of those transient minor warriors who surface and disappear, but whose point of view, surprisingly, is made part of their brief history.[33]

[33] E.g., "He left these men, and went on after Polyidos and Abas, sons of the aged dream-interpreter, Eurydamas; yet for these two as they went forth the old man did not answer their dreams, but Diomedes the powerful slew them" (τοὺς μὲν ἔασ', ὁ δ' Ἄβαντα / μετῴχετο καὶ Πολύειδον / υἱέας Εὐρυδάμαντος ὀνειροπόλοιο γέροντος· / τοῖς οὐκ ἐρχομένοις ὁ γέρων ἐκρίνατ' ὀνείρους, / ἀλλά σφεας κρατερὸς Διομήδης ἐξενάριξε·, *Iliad* V 148–151); and "Diomedes of the great war cry cut down Axylos, Teuthras' son, who had been a dweller in strong-founded Arisbe, a man rich in substance and a friend to all humanity since in his house by the wayside he entertained all comers. Yet there was none of these now to stand before him and keep off the sad destruction, and Diomedes stripped life from both of them, Axylos and his henchman Kalesios" (Ἄξυλον δ' ἄρ' ἔπεφνε βοὴν ἀγαθὸς Διομήδης / Τευθρανίδην, ὃς ἔναιεν ἐϋκτιμένῃ ἐν Ἀρίσβῃ / ἀφνειὸς βιότοιο, φίλος δ' ἦν ἀνθρώποισι· / πάντας γὰρ φιλέεσκεν ὁδῷ ἔπι οἰκία ναίων. / ἀλλά οἱ οὔ τις τῶν γε τότ' ἤρκεσε λυγρὸν ὄλεθρον / πρόσθεν ὑπαντιάσας, ἀλλ' ἄμφω θυμὸν ἀπηύρα / αὐτὸν καὶ θεράποντα Καλήσιον *Iliad* VI 12–18); as well as *Iliad* II 871ff., V 9ff., 49–55, 54–64, etc.

It is here, perhaps, that the poem shows the discourse of the battlefield in all of its overwhelming power. The ironizing taunt of the warrior to the dead victim is in fact the final blow; it inflicts *achos* 'anguish' on the survivors as though the taunt had drawn blood, had caused the fatal wound.[34] Yet this is not because it is, like the rebukes and challenges, necessarily overtly hostile. One might easily imagine a taunt in which the warrior boasts of his superior ability and disparages his victim's inadequacy. But to the extent to which the victor and vanquished are compared in these speeches, the difference between them is, often, that the latter's expectations of the future were not justified.

Ultimately, it is that capacity of language to confuse categories, to render friends as enemies and the reverse, that puts an instrument of shattering effectiveness into the heroes' hands. What words can do on the battlefield, beyond any weapon, is indicated in the hortatory rebukes that, figuratively rendering the *philoi* as enemies, challenge them continually to reaffirm their status as *philoi*. But the fullest demonstration of their ability is in these parting taunts, which exploit the singular—indeed, unique—linguistic resource, the essential condition of language: the metaphor. Consider the words of Patroklos to Kebriones at *Iliad* XVI:[35]

τὸν δ' ἐπικερτομέων προσέφης, Πατρόκλεες ἱππεῦ·
ὢ πόποι ἦ μάλ' ἐλαφρὸς ἀνήρ, ὡς ῥεῖα κυβιστᾷ.
εἰ δή που καὶ πόντῳ ἐν ἰχθυόεντι γένοιτο,
πολλοὺς ἂν κορέσειεν ἀνὴρ ὅδε τήθεα διφῶν
νηὸς ἀποθρῴσκων, εἰ καὶ δυσπέμφελος εἴη,
ὡς νῦν ἐν πεδίῳ ἐξ ἵππων ῥεῖα κυβιστᾷ.
ἦ ῥα καὶ ἐν Τρώεσσι κυβιστητῆρες ἔασιν.

> *Iliad* XVI 744–750

'See now, what a light man this is, how agile an acrobat.
If only he were somewhere on the sea, where the fish swarm,
he could fill the hunger of many men, by diving for oysters;
he could go overboard from a boat even in rough weather
the way he somersaults so light to the ground from his chariot
now. So, to be sure, in Troy also they have their acrobats.'

---

[34] E.g., *Iliad* XIII 581, XIV 458, 486.
[35] Or of Poulydamas at *Iliad* XIV 454–457, or Akamas at *Iliad* XIV 479–485: "Promachos sleeps among you," or of Odysseus at *Iliad* XI 439–455 to Sokos, whom he has speared in the back as Sokos was running away: "Death ran faster than you," among other examples.

Through his words the warrior has the power not simply to destroy but to transfigure—to bring the image of domesticity, of private existence, onto the battlefield, to reproduce a world beyond the dusty plain of Troy. Above all, they allow the hero to keep on fighting after his enemy is dead—to address him as though he could hear, to bring him back to life.

Works Cited

Bourdieu, P. 1972. *Esquisse d'une théorie de la pratique.* Travaux de droit, d'économie, de sociologie et de sciences politiques 92. Paris.

Dunkel, G. 1979. "Fighting Words: Alcman *Partheneion* 63 μάχονται." *Journal of Indo-European Studies* 7:249–272.

Fenik, B. 1968. *Typical Battle Scenes in the Iliad: Studies in the Narrative Techniques of Homeric Battle Description.* Hermes, Einzelschriften 21. Wiesbaden.

Latacz, J. 1977. *Kampfparänese, Kampfdarstellung und Kampfwirklichkeit in der Ilias, bei Kallinos und Tyrtaios.* Zetemata 66. München.

Létoublon, F. 1983. "Défi et combat dans l'Iliade." *Revue des études grecques* 96:27–48.

Loraux, N. 1987. "Le lien de la division." *Cahier du Collège international de philosophie* 4:101–124.

———. 1989. "La politique des frères." In *Aux Sources de la puissance. Sociabilité et parenté. Actes du colloque de Rouen, 12'13 novembre 1987,* ed. F. Thélamon, 21–36. Mont-Saint-Aignan. Revised version reprinted as Chapter 8 of N. Loraux, *La Cité Divisée. L'oubli dans la mémoire d'Athènes* (Paris, 1997).

Monsacré, H. 1984. *Les larmes d'Achille.* Paris.

Muellner, L. 1976. *The Meaning of Homeric EYXΩMAI Through its Formulas.* Innsbrucker Beiträge zur Sprachwissenschaft 13. Innsbruck.

Nagy, G. 1979. *The Best of the Achaeans: Concepts of the Hero in Archaic Greek Poetry.* Baltimore.

Sacks, R. 1987. *The Traditional Phrase in Homer.* Columbia Studies in the Classical Tradition 14. Leiden.

Sinos, D. 1980. *Achilles, Patroklos and the Meaning of Philos.* Innsbrucker Beiträge zur Sprachwissenschaft 29. Innsbruck.

Vermeule, E. 1981. *Aspects of Death in Early Greek Art and Poetry.* Sather Classical Lectures 46. Berkeley.

Composition by Theme and the
Mêtis of the *Odyssey*

W HY IS THE NARRATIVE STRUCTURE of the *Odyssey* so complicated? Although the plot of the poem is perfectly straightforward—Aristotle observed that it was the imitation of a single action—nevertheless the ordering of its narrative is elaborately nonlinear. The *Iliad* gets under way with a question from which ensues a linear, chronological account of the events the poem presents: so much so that, for example, even material that one might have expected to be presented in a flashback—the identification and history of the Greek leaders and their relationship to Helen—is told by her in the *Teichoskopia*, in a present continuous with that of the ongoing narration of events. The *Iliad* demarcates its subject—the wrath of Achilles— at the outset and organizes its story from the onset of the wrath to Achilles' renunciation of it in Book 19 and the consequent episodes of the death and ransoming of Hector, according to the literal order in which those events take place.

The *Odyssey*, by contrast—to summarize what is familiar—begins in the proem with a proleptic reference to Odysseus' loss of his companions and to the specific episode of the eating of the cattle of Helios, then appeals to the Muse to begin *hamothen ge*—"from somewhere";[1] and the response is to locate Odysseus on Kalypso's island, where we will not actually meet him until Book 5. The action then proceeds with Poseidon going off to the Aethiopians, while the rest of the gods hold a council on Olympus in which Odysseus is not the first order of business: Agamemnon, Orestes, and Aegisthus are. Once Athena enjoins the Olympians to turn their attention to Odysseus, Zeus is immediately willing, asserting that he hasn't forgotten Odysseus. But the latter's way home, explains Zeus, has been barred by Poseidon, who maintains his grievance over the blinding of his son the Cyclops—another of a number of allusions to an

---

[1] See Clay 1976.

episode that the poem treats as past history although it is in the future from the narrative's standpoint. The narrative then takes up events in the human sphere on Ithaca, and the *Telemachia* takes the hero's son to Pylos and as far as Sparta in search of information about his father. In Book 5 the poem at last introduces us to its hero—with, in effect, another beginning, another discussion on Olympus—but *not* in fact at his last stop, as we might have assumed from the council of the gods in Book 1. Rather, Odysseus is only at the penultimate stage of his return home, so that the narrative will then move forward chronologically for a while—Books 5-8—before turning backward in Book 9. Thus we discover eventually, for example, that by the time Odysseus rejects the immortality Kalypso offers, he has already been to the underworld, has seen death, and has heard Achilles' evaluation of it.

Telemachus' journey, moreover, frames Books 5-15. The narrative, leaving Odysseus' son after his first day in Sparta in Book 4, proceeds from Kalypso on Ogygia to the Phaeacians on Scheria, where we hear the whole retrospective account of Odysseus' travels, covering the past ten years. The Phaeacians then return Odysseus to Ithaca, where he makes his way to Eumaios' hut and converses with him—at which point, at the opening of Book 15, we return to Telemachus, just waking up on Sparta: for him, only one night has passed. And the vacuum created by Odysseus' absence in Books 1-4 is filled by stories about him in which the past—a past extended for us by the memories of those in Ithaca, Pylos, and Sparta to include at least a second decade: that of the Trojan War with its antecedent events and immediate aftermath—is recalled against and vividly contrasted with a shadowy and enigmatic present.

As this brief summary illustrates, the *Odyssey*, as it moves back and forth, gives us the simultaneous perspective of many time-frames: the limitless framework of the gods, the lifetime of Odysseus (Penelope pointedly establishes this in Book 23, reflecting that "the gods begrudged that we should spend our youth together"[2]), the protracted return, the sudden maturation of Telemachus. The narrative sequence of the remainder of the poem, though more strictly chronological, displays a complementary virtuosity of concentration, counterpointing discretion and disclosure in the actions of Odysseus and Penelope until the *Odyssey*'s ultimate closure is achieved in the crucial convergence of events on a single day.[3]

---

[2] *Odyssey* 23.210-211.
[3] See Finley 1978, especially chapter 7.

How are we to understand the significance of the complex structure sketched here? Tz. Todorov, in a well-known essay, cites the *Odyssey* as the best means of dispelling illusions about the transparent simplicity of "primitive narrative": "Few contemporary works reveal such an accumulation of 'perversities,' so many methods and devices which make this work anything and everything but a simple narrative."[4] In recent years, indeed, the *Odyssey* has found a special place in influential writings on narrative theory aimed, as a rule, at modern fiction. In G. Genette's study of "narrative discourse," for example, the *Odyssey*, notably, is the paradigm that serves to introduce the defining terms by which the author establishes categories of a systematic theory of narrative at the same time as he develops an analysis of Proust's formidable masterpiece.

In order to proceed from basic distinctions among the possible meanings of the word *narrative*, Genette offers the *Odyssey* to illustrate how "narrative" can be used to refer to 1) "the narrative statement that undertakes to tell of an event or a series of events: thus we would term '*narrative of Ulysses*' the speech given to the Phaeacians in Books ix-xii of the *Odyssey*, and also these four books themselves"; 2) "the succession of events, real or fictitious, that are the subjects of this discourse...: an example would be the adventures experienced by Ulysses from the fall of Troy to his arrival on Calypso's island"; and 3) an event, "not, however, the event that is recounted, but the event that consists of someone recounting something: the act of narrating taken in itself. We thus say that Books IX-XII of the *Odyssey* are devoted to the narrative of Ulysses in the same way that we say that Book XXII is devoted to the slaughter of the suitors." These separate denotations among which the *Odyssey* allows such lucid discrimination enable an analysis "which constantly implies a study of relationships: on the one hand the relationship between a discourse and the events that it recounts (narrative in its second meaning), on the other hand the relationship between the same discourse and the act that produces it, actually (Homer) or fictively (Ulysses) (narrative in its third meaning)."[5]

It is a fundamental perception that any narrative is relational: that it both represents, and itself constitutes, a set of flexible, nonstatic interrelations, involving narrator (actual or fictive), audience (actual or fictive), process of communication, and substance of communication. To the configurations fruitfully identified by Genette, however, any discussion of the *Odyssey*

---

[4] Todorov 1977:53.
[5] Genette 1980:25–27.

must contribute an additional component, if its aim is not simply to view Homeric epic as illustrative background material but to bring the *Odyssey* itself into focus. This element is the relationship of an oral poem to the poetic tradition—the tradition of discourse, in Genette's terms—in which it participates: the tradition in which it was shaped and which it transmits.

Since the pioneering studies of Milman Parry, the traditional basis of oral poetry has received much meticulous scrutiny. Beyond the level of inherited meter, diction, and phraseology, however, a facet of the relationship between the epic and its tradition that bears particularly on the question of narrative complexity is that of "theme," elucidated by the work of Parry and especially by that of Albert Lord, where considerations of theory and practice intersect.

Lord uses the term *theme* to designate "a recurrent element of narration or description."[6] Based on his and Parry's fieldwork, Lord demonstrates that the theme serves as crucial a function as the formula in developing the oral poet's technique of composition in performance:

> Although the themes lead naturally from one to another to form a song which exists as a whole in the singer's mind with Aristotelian beginning, middle, and end, the units within this whole, the themes, have a semi-independent life of their own. The theme in oral poetry exists at one and the same time in and for itself and for the whole song. This can be said both for the theme in general and also for any individual singer's forms of it. His task is to adapt and adjust it to the particular song that he is re-creating.[7]

As the accomplished oral poet regenerates the tradition in which he sings, his use of recognizable themes allows him—indeed, requires him—to situate his song in the context of other narratives on the same subject, within the same genre:

> [The theme] does not have a single "pure" form either for the individual singer or for the tradition as a whole. Its form is ever changing in the singer's mind, because the theme is in reality *protean* [emphasis mine]; in the singer's mind it has many shapes, all the forms in which he has ever sung it.... It is not a static entity, but a living, changing, adaptable artistic creation. Yet it exists for the sake of the song. And the shapes that it has taken in the

---

[6] See, for example, Lord 1951:73 as well as Lord 1960:68. Lord's terminology follows Parry, who used *"theme"* to refer to *"repeated incidents or descriptive passages."*

[7] Lord 1960:94.

past have been suitable for the song of the moment. *In a traditional poem, therefore, there is a pull in two directions: one is toward the song being sung and the other is toward the previous uses of the same theme* [emphasis mine].[8]

The oral poem, therefore, continuously repositions itself with respect to a tradition made up of alternative narrative possibilities: "The substitution of one multiform of a theme for another, one kind of recognition scene for another kind, for example, one kind of disguise for another, is not uncommon...as songs pass from one singer to another."[9] This means that there will inevitably be diverse "versions" and "variants" of a single song that exist, as it were, in an implicit dialogue with each other.[10]

Each performance-composition of a song must necessarily reflect, and participate in, the evolution of possible alternatives to the version it actually presents. We know that there were other treatments of Odysseus' return to Ithaca, as the *Theogony*[11] suggests and the *Telegony* reminds us[12] and, moreover, that there were other *nostoi*, which the epic cycle also preserves, and which the *Odyssey* itself refers to. The *Odyssey*, therefore, needs to be approached in the context of a tradition of singing about the return of the hero, a tradition comprised of multiforms—equal thematic variants, which do not presuppose an Ur-form—that interact with each other on the level of theme, of story-pattern, and of narrative arrangement.

In the light of these observations, the *Odyssey* can be seen to have assimilated patterns of other return-stories to its own cast of characters and its own set of concerns. The evidence of traditional patterns, as demonstrated by the South Slavic material, indicates that in return stories the hero's son plays a limited role, although he is essential in revenge stories of the Agamemnon-Orestes type.[13] The *Odyssey* has combined two distinct (though overlapping) structural arrangements into one: the pattern of the son avenging

---

[8] Lord 1960:94.

[9] Lord 1960:119.

[10] "In some respects the larger themes and the song are alike. Their outward form and their specific content are ever changing. Yet there is a basic idea or combination of ideas that is fairly stable. We can say, then, that a song is the story about a given hero, but its expressed forms are multiple, and each of these expressed forms or tellings of the story is itself a separate song, in its own right, authentic and valid as a song unto itself." Lord 1960:100.

[11] *Theogony* 1011–1018.

[12] For a general argument on the archaic provenance of the epic cycle, see Kullmann 1960. Sacks 1982 has convincingly demonstrated the presence of traditional material in the *Telegony*. On the indications within the *Odyssey* of other return possibilities for Odysseus, see West 1981.

[13] Lord 1960:159ff.

the father, central to the Agamemnon-Orestes story, is modulated into the rescue and return of the imprisoned hero—the fundamental scheme of the *Odyssey*, whose hero returns not in the company of his son, but alone and in disguise.[14]

What I wish to draw attention to in this context is that the *Odyssey* acknowledges the Agamemnon story not just as a parallel set of events but precisely as an *alternative narrative model*. It does this from the very outset, when Book 1 opens the action with Zeus saying, in effect,[15] "I can't help thinking about the Agamemnon story, especially the part about the foolish suitor upon whom the hero's son took vengeance." To which Athena replies, in effect, "Yes, that certainly is a *model story*" and adds, "Let all foolish suitors perish *in the same way*"—*hôs*—that is, at the hands of the hero's son.[16] Athena, later in the same book, adduces Orestes as an example of established heroic renown, a model to Telemachus of what his story might be. Orestes is a son whose *kleos*—epic fame—already has wide circulation.[17] In Book 3 Telemachus confirms explicitly that he has taken the point. On hearing another injunction to him—this time from Nestor—to achieve fame like that of Orestes, Telemachus agrees that Orestes certainly did punish the murderous suitor and avenge his father, and that this will be an epic song for posterity. "But the gods," he asserts (to paraphrase 3.208–209), "haven't spun such fortune for me as to be able to punish the Suitors and have an Orestes-like story." The story the gods have spun for Telemachus, although it might have proceeded like that of Orestes—that is, they have themes in common—takes a different turn.

The juxtaposition of different narrative models is identified as such by the *Odyssey* itself, which even alludes to other representations, other versions and treatments, of its own subject matter. We can go a step further, to emphasize that the *Odyssey*'s overt acknowledgment of alternative story-patterns is part of a larger strategy by means of which the poem insists on the complexity of its own narrative structure and thereby draws attention to the very *process* of singing tales, of generating and regenerating epic song. The *Odyssey* may be said to treat narrative, or narrative discourse, as a subject in itself.

Albert Lord writes:

---

[14] Lord 1960:121.
[15] I am paraphrasing here to refer in summary to *Odyssey* 1.32–41.
[16] To paraphrase 1.45–47.
[17] 1.298ff.

While recognizing the fact that the singer knows the whole song before he starts to sing (not textually, of course, but thematically), nevertheless, at some time when he reaches key points in the performance of the song he finds that he is drawn in one direction or another by the similarities with related groups [of songs] at those points. The intensity of that pull may differ from performance to performance, but it is always there and the singer always relives that tense moment.[18]

My point is that the *Odyssey* incorporates an explicit awareness of the creative tension of composition, an awareness of the existence of possibilities that could become other songs; and this implies a claim that alternative treatments have been rejected and that the path taken to create *this* song, the one being sung—our *Odyssey*—is the ultimate and preemptive path.

The *Odyssey* underscores these issues as a poem of audiences in a post-Iliadic world, audiences for whom the preeminent narrative is the narrative of Troy. Telemachus attests to this when, lamenting his father's disappearance, he asserts that if Odysseus had been celebrated for his exploits like the heroes who perished fighting at Troy, the grief of his survivors would have been lessened. It is in part the *Odyssey*'s relationship to the epic about Troy, as the *Odyssey* represents it, that returns the poem continually to the issue of narrative. For in the Odyssean world of audiences, every new song must presuppose the existence of songs about Troy—of an *Iliad*—whose prestige is the narrative ideal.

In this context the *Odyssey* poses the question, "What kind of song can be sung about Odysseus?" by creating an internal audience for whom the answer is a matter of urgent suspense. In *Odyssey* 1, the bard Phemius entertains the Suitors with a return-song of the Achaean heroes. Penelope interrupts him, objecting that this song is always too painful for her to listen to. Telemachus, even as he argues with her, specifies Penelope's objection: that there is no place for Odysseus in a *nostos*-song. The unvoiced corollary remains: Might there be a *kleos*-epic about Odysseus? Athena complicates the answer: in the guise of Mentes, she first assures Telemachus that his father is still alive, casts doubt on this information shortly thereafter, and ends by sending Telemachus in search of either the *kleos* or the *nostos* of his father. Will the song about him be correspondingly complicated?

---

[18] Lord 1960:123. He continues, "Even though the pattern of the song he intends to sing is set early in the performance, forces moving in other directions will still be felt at critical junctures, simply because the theme involved can lead in more than one path."

The *Odyssey*'s own audience knows things that Telemachus does not—his father's whereabouts and Athena's plan, for example. Yet the multiple audiences within the *Odyssey* allow its listeners to reflect on what it means to be in the position of audience. There are many narrators; from the opening of the poem, in the absence of Odysseus, and before the poem has even introduced him directly, he is variously represented by narratives from a range of sources. Different Odysseus stories are delivered by Nestor, by Menelaos, by Helen, by Athena as Mentes and Mentor; the Suitors have their recollections, and Telemachus his secondhand version. Menelaos and Helen, who claim to be telling the same story but offer diametrically conflicting ones, make it clear that it is not easy for an audience to get a straight story, to discriminate among stories, or even to know what a straight story is.

By putting the story of Odysseus' return finally into the mouth of the hero, the *Odyssey* highlights the audience's role as active participants in the creation of the narrative, collaborators in the opening of alternative narrative paths and the pressures of tradition, which are the conditions of poetic composition. The demands that are subtly integrated in the production of narrative emerge as Odysseus recites his return-story to the Phaeacian connoisseurs of the epic of Troy, temporarily disrupting and displacing the epic perspective before rejoining and being reincorporated into it; so that the *Odyssey*'s assertion of superiority is expressed in part by allowing us to see the transitions it absorbs—that is, its use of the traditional operations of selection and combination of themes—but also by contrast to Odysseus' own recitation, or, to put it another way, in answer to Odysseus' challenge to the epic viewpoint.

Odysseus' recital is incomplete when he terminates it at 11.332. Alkinoos encourages him to continue by offering an approving assessment of the story that compares Odysseus explicitly to an *aoidos*, although he admits an audience's susceptibility to the seductiveness of false tales deceptively intended. It has been observed that one function of the proposed pause in the tales is to underscore the larger-than-life scale of the *Odyssey* itself, which far surpasses that of an evening's entertainment.[19] Alkinoos' expressed readiness to stay awake all night, listening to the end, confirms that the quality of the story matches its extraordinary length.

But the "intermezzo" provides a commentary on other aspects of the procedure of epic storytelling (performance-composition) as well. Alkinoos' remarks address the content (composition) in addition to the form (perfor-

---

[19] See Nagy 1979:18–20.

mance) of Odysseus' "song." We remember that in Book 8, Odysseus praised Demodokos in the context of asking him to change the *content* of his singing. He requested a song—of the Trojan horse—that would attest to the singer's access to the Muses. As the *Odyssey's* audience perceives, Odysseus himself could provide confirmation of this.[20] Now Alkinoos' praise of Odysseus as *aoidos* prefaces his request for a different kind of song. Alkinoos says, "You're like an *aoidos*"—and asks for a song about the heroes who died at Troy, that is, for a *kleos*-song. Odysseus' tales until this point have made only peripheral mention of Troy and have included no account of the *klea* of the heroes in the Trojan war. Instead, the encounters in uncharted territory that Odysseus has so far described are intriguing but alien; although like what an *aoidos* would sing, they are outside the conventional repertory of heroic experience, and equally that of epic song.

Alkinoos' reminder to Odysseus of the *topoi* of the Trojan heroes both acknowledges a conventional hierarchy of subjects within epic and reverts to it as a touchstone of poetic truth. Demodokos, responding to Odysseus' challenge to sing *kata moiran* about the episode of the Trojan horse, will prove whether he sings the *truth*; similarly, recounting stories of the heroes at Troy will authenticate, for Alkinoos and the Phaeacians, Odysseus' claims about himself—and, by extension, his unprecedented adventures outside the Trojan sphere (that is, outside the realm of common human history). But the premise that assigns value to verifiable authenticity based on conventional expectations of canonical, recognizable *topoi*, or familiar representations, is called into question by the implications of the interruption itself: by Odysseus' ending and resuming his recitation, taking up his tale again with precisely what Alkinoos has asked for, incorporating the transition into the narrative without a break, as though it were a feature of the story; by his elision and abridgment of the recitation, the *Odyssey* alerts *its* audience to question the idea of a "fixed or authentic version" of a story, reminds listeners of the multiformity of themes, and invites them to think about the role of ambiguity, multiplicity of tradition, revision, and point of view in telling (and hearing) stories. Alkinoos' invoking of the poetic process in the context of what turns out to be an interruption, an artificial ending and *re*-beginning, draws the audience's attention to the actual ending of Odysseus' tales and possibly to the actual beginning as well. When Odysseus brings his recitation to a close at the end of Book 12, is this the real ending or is it another pause? Could there be more to tell? These questions are brought to the fore by the

---

[20] Nagy 1979:100ff.

way Odysseus breaks off at that point, after a mere two and a half lines on his adventure with Kalypso. The half line is suggestive, because Odysseus seems to stop in midsentence, where more might have followed, in order to ask why he should *mûthologeuein* a story he has told the previous day?

His reference here is to the remarks addressed to Arete at 7.244–266 in which he summarized his stay on Ogygia—an abbreviated enough passage; but even more fleeting is the two-line, passing allusion to Kalypso at the outset of Book 9 that occurs in the course of Odysseus' reflection on the preciousness of one's own homeland. This initiates a kind of inverted ring-structure around Books 9–12, ending with the two and a half "broken" lines on Kalypso noted above. It is an inverted one in that both passages, rather than enclosing Odysseus' "bardic" recitation of the adventures, have their backs to it, as it were—opening outward to a frame of reference external to Odysseus' own account of this episode.

The version in Book 7, which the abruptly truncated mention of the Kalypso story at the end of Book 12 refers us to, offers in itself a kind of false start. Arete has asked Odysseus who he is and where he comes from, and his answer's opening phrase, *Ôgugiê tis nêsos*, is misleadingly like the conventional introduction to an account of one's origins. As has been observed, it is deceptively like Eumaios telling Odysseus where he comes from (*nêsos tis Suriê...*, 15.403), or Odysseus telling Penelope that he comes from Crete (*Krêtê tis gai' esti...*, 19.172).[21] In other words, it looks as though Odysseus is about to lie, thus confirming the suspicions of Arete, who thinks he has already lied. Just where the ironies reside in this exchange can be discerned, of course, solely by the Homeric audience. In a precisely parallel way, it is apparent only to the Homeric audience just how partial and limited Odysseus' version of the encounter with Kalypso is—because only they have heard Book 5. Odysseus' tales are displayed to the audience of the *Odyssey* as dazzling yet perhaps inadequate: incomplete by the standard that the *Odyssey* itself has set for us.

These versions of the Kalypso story constitute a unique instance of the inner narrative of Odysseus' first-person recitation referring to the outer narrative of the epic. When Odysseus reminds the Phaeacians that they have heard this episode before, he links together for the poem's audience its two disparate experiences of his adventure on Ogygia. With the version of the Kalypso episode as Odysseus tells it, we are aware of a story that is not only attenuated but actually fails in some of its information, although its literal

---

[21] Fenik 1974:16–17.

audience, the Phaeacians, cannot realize this. Odysseus, at 7.262–263, says that Kalypso let him go but that he doesn't know why. The outer epic narrative, however, has put *us*, as *its* listeners, in a position to know the entire sequence of events from Olympus on down.

The effect of presenting this disparity is to accord to the outer Homeric narrative the authority of absolute reality. The *Odyssey* becomes the intrinsic standard of validity by which we perceive the fictive potential of Odysseus' tales. To put it another way, Homeric poetics urges the paradoxical unreliability of the first-person eyewitness, the need for interpretation—and also the shifting perspectives that inhere in the relation between singer and audience and stand to be exploited by narrative virtuosity.

Alkinoos' request expresses an audience's assumption that what will authenticate a story is what the audience can recognize: that is, the piece of the puzzle they already possess. But the *Odyssey* compels us to acknowledge the limitations of this point of view, although we are led to understand it from the inside and to sympathize with it. The *Odyssey* encourages us to see that one's involvement inherently precludes one's seeing the whole picture—that, in a sense, you are the last person who can tell your own story. Far closer to Alkinoos than the heroes of Troy is the prophecy from Nausithoos, which he quotes at the end of Book 7: that Poseidon will someday be angry with the Phaeacians and end their seafaring. Odysseus then proceeds to describe, over the course of three books, how and why *he* is Poseidon's bitterest enemy; at the end of which Alkinoos, with considerable naïveté, wishes the Phaeacians conveying Odysseus back to Ithaca smooth sailing. Correspondingly, Odysseus fails to recognize and hence cannot communicate Athena's agency behind his return home; moreover, the same Odysseus who has told Alkinoos that one's homeland is the sweetest thing in life to see (and that he has spent years on Kalypso's island picturing Ithaca to himself) wakes up on Ithaca with no idea where he is or what he is looking at. The view that can reorient the audience and establish appropriate bearings for determining the poem's proper sphere is not one that reverts to the Trojan war—as Alkinoos does, or as Odysseus describes Aiolos doing at 10.14–15. It is rather the view that the poem assigns to Athena in Book 13 when she answers the mystified Odysseus' inquiry about his surroundings by saying:

> You are naïve, stranger, or you have come from far away,
> if you really are asking about this country. It is not
> so very nameless after all. A great many people know it,
> whether all who live eastward toward the dawn

or those who dwell toward the shadowy west.

. . . .

[S]o the name of Ithaca has reached even to Troy,
which they say is far from Achaean land.

(13.237–241, 248–249)

"You must be very ignorant if you ask about Ithaca. It is hardly obscure.... In fact, Ithaca is such a distinguished place that its fame has reached to Troy—which they say is very far away."[22] Decisively, the focus has shifted.

These questions posed by the *Odyssey* about authenticity, about point of view, about the integrity of the discourse, about which tradition is the relevant one, are raised in part formally—by the juxtaposition of the many endings and beginnings—and in part by the poem's recurrent themes of deception, disguise, and recognition.[23] They are questions to be answered by the totality of the epic itself, built up of many perspectives beyond what the various audiences can request or the multiple eyewitnesses can report. The *Odyssey* encompasses them all, both involved and uninvolved, including that of the Olympians. It can integrate a multiplicity of traditions and can lay claim to an encompassing authority.

I observed above that the interruption of Odysseus' recitation and the invitation by Alkinoos to resume draws the audience's attention to the actual ending of the tales and perhaps to their actual beginning as well. Odysseus begins his story in the first place in answer to Alkinoos' request that he identify himself. In the course of the *Odyssey*, we remember, many people ask Odysseus who he is and where he is from; but the question that initiates the telling of the tales is a special one, with special diction. Alkinoos inquires at the end of Book 8:

Come then, tell me this and recount accurately,
in what direction you were driven off course and what places you
came to belonging to
humans, both them and their well-inhabited cities—
as many as were savage and violent, and without justice,
and those who were hospitable to strangers with a god-fearing
mind.

(8.572–576)

---

[22] 13.237–239, 248–249.
[23] On these subjects see especially Murnaghan 1987, and also Slatkin 2005.

"Tell me, where were you driven off course, and which men and cities did you come to, and what were their minds?"

Here we are emphatically recalled not only to the beginning of the recitation but to the beginning of the *Odyssey*:

> Tell me, Muse, of the man of many turns, who was driven
> far and wide, after he sacked Troy's sacred citadel;
> many were those whose cities he saw, whose minds he learned of.
>
> (1.1–3)

For the synthesis of perspectives and traditions that these questions demand can be answered only by the Muse—which is to say, only by the epic as a whole.

With this passage we also double back to recognize the echoed diction of Telemachus' speech about Orestes—"the gods haven't spun such fortune for me as to have *kleos* and *aoidê* like that of Orestes"—in that Alkinoos' speech at the end of Book 8 not only returns us to the beginning of the poem overall but, a little further on, makes a statement about the imperative of epic song as the motivator of human events. The king here asks Odysseus why he weeps and laments to hear the fate of the Greeks and of Troy. "Don't you know," says Alkinoos, "that the gods have spun this so that it might be a subject of song for mortals to come?" If the *Odyssey* chooses epic narrative as a subject, it is for no lesser reason than the view voiced by Alkinoos: epic is itself the justification for human endeavor and suffering.

That the threads of human suffering spun by the gods become the fabric of epic song is reinforced by the distribution of diction that joins spinning or weaving[24] and poetic composition in an image of artisan production that complements the convention of the *aoidos* as divinely inspired.[25] This artisan aspect can, moreover, coexist with a vision of the singer as divinely affiliated and may have done so for a long time. Not only is there a divine craftsman among the Olympians,[26] but even in an archaic cosmogony like that of Alcman the primordial creative power is a demiurge (specifically a metal-worker).[27] Certainly the association of weaving and poetic composition is ancient.[28] Not

---

[24] Spinning and weaving are treated interchangeably by the two Homeric poems; in the *Odyssey* the *klôthes*, the spinsters themselves, are said to weave with thread.

[25] This image may represent the craft of learning performance-composition. Lord 1960:13–29 has described the conditions and the stages of developing singing techniques among modern-day singers that may not have been very different for those of an earlier era.

[26] See Frontisi-Ducroux 1975 on Olympian craftsmen.

[27] Alcman fr. 5 (Page).

[28] For a valuable discussion of the association of weaving and singing in archaic poetry, see Snyder 1981.

only do we see it elsewhere in early Greek—as in *Iliad* 3, where Helen weaves the *klea andrôn*; in the Hesiodic fragment 357 Merkelbach-West; in Sappho, Bacchylides, and Pindar—but it has been shown to have an Indo-European provenance.[29]

These interpenetrating associations are particularly resonant in the *Odyssey*, however, because the *Odyssey* gives weaving special prominence. Penelope's weaving and unweaving of the shroud for Laertes—the account of which is given, remarkably, three times in the poem—is the intricate device, or device of intricacy, by which Penelope manipulates the Suitors' attention and keeps them under control; it is the ruse by which time can be turned back and brought forward again. This ploy, proclaimed by the Suitors themselves (after the fact) as assuring Penelope's *kleos*, is the stratagem that Penelope refers to as her *mêtis* (19.158).

We remember here that in the *Odyssey* the word *mêtis* occurs formulaically in conjunction with *huphainô* in expressions that mean "to weave a scheme." When, for example, at 13.303, Athena, having asserted the bond of *mêtis* between herself and Odysseus, declares:

> Now again I am here, to weave a scheme with you,

to which Odysseus responds at 13.386:

> Come then, weave a scheme, the way I will pay [the Suitors] back,

these expressions confirm the appropriateness of Penelope's use of *mêtis* to denote the weaving scheme. As, in the literal act of weaving,[30] material and design emerge simultaneously from a single process, so with Penelope the action of weaving and unweaving does not fashion a device but constitutes the device itself.

The dual movement of Penelope's scheme—weaving and unweaving—leads us to look more closely at the properties of *mêtis*, an element crucial to the working out of events in the *Odyssey* and fundamental to its values. The meaning and role of *mêtis*, as it is represented from Hesiod and Homer through late antiquity, have been illuminated by M. Detienne and J.-P. Vernant in their 1974 study, *Les Ruses de l'intelligence: La Métis des grecs*.[31] Examining the structure and operations of *mêtis* as it is presented on a variety of levels and in a wide range of contexts from archaic poetry to the

---

[29] See Schmitt 1967:298–301.

[30] Frontisi-Ducroux 1975, chapter 3, p. 52ff.

[31] References below are to the English translation, Detienne and Vernant 1978.

second century A.D. treatises on fishing and hunting ascribed to Oppian, they point out that the terminology associated with *mêtis* has regularly to do with techniques of weaving, especially weaving nets, plaiting ropes or coils, fitting together traps—verbs like *huphainô, plekein, tektainesthai, strephein*—and they distinguish a number of its essential and consistent features, especially its mobility, flexibility, multiplicity, and diversity.[32]

Mêtis *is naturally attributed to such shape-shifters as Proteus, Nereus, and Thetis; according to Apollodorus, the divinity Mêtis herself has the power of metamorphosis. Zeus, therefore, observe Detienne and Vernant, "masters Mêtis by turning her own weapons against herself. These are premeditation, trickery, the surprise attack, the sudden assault."[33] Similarly, Menelaos has to outmaneuver Proteus by becoming a shape-shifter himself, temporarily, pretending to be a seal in order to get the better of the clever old fellow.*

In the world of natural history, *mêtis* is the property of such creatures as the octopus, with its polymorphy and its capacity for disguise through camouflage. The fox is called the most scheming of animals, considered a master of *mêtis* especially, it seems, in its ploy of reversing its own position.[34] It is said to *epistrephein*—to reverse itself suddenly, to turn back on itself to capture its unsuspecting prey or to escape from adversaries. This "secret of reversal" possessed by the fox is said to be "the last word in craftiness."[35] Another creature deserves to be singled out: a fish, aggrandized with the name of "foxfish" because of its behavior, which is described as follows by Plutarch: "It generally avoids bait (*dolos*), but if it is caught it gets rid of it. Thanks to its energy and flexibility (*hugrotêta*), it is able to change its body (*metaballein to sôma*) and turn it inside out (*strephein*) so that the *interior* becomes the *exterior* [emphasis mine]: the hook falls out (*hôste ton entos ektos genomenon apopiptein angkistron*)."[36] And more from Aelian: "It unfolds its internal organs and turns

---

[32] Detienne and Vernant 1978:20 write: "Why does *mêtis* appear as multiple (*pantoiê*), many-colored (*poikilê*), shifting (*aiolê*)? Because its field of application is the world of movement, of multiplicity, and of ambiguity. It bears on fluid situations which are constantly changing and which at every moment combine contrary features and forces that are opposed to each other. In order to seize upon the fleeting *kairos*, *mêtis* had to make itself even swifter than the latter. In order to dominate a changing situation, full of contrasts, it must become even more supple, even more shifting, more polymorphic than the flow of time: it must adapt itself constantly to events as they succeed each other and be pliable enough to accommodate the unexpected so as to implement the plan in mind more successfully."

[33] Detienne and Vernant 1978:21.

[34] Detienne and Vernant 1978:36 quote Aelian, *On the Nature of Animals* 6.24.

[35] Detienne and Vernant 1978:36.

[36] *On the Cleverness of Animals* 977b, as quoted at Detienne and Vernant 1978:37.

them inside out, divesting itself of its body as if it were a shirt"; or as Vernant and Detienne put it, "This fish turns itself inside out like a glove."[37]

The tricks of reversal exhibiting the *mêtis* of these creatures have clear affinities not only with Penelope's weaving and unweaving the web, but with the ingenious stroke of that supreme figure of *mêtis*, Hermes, who in the *Homeric Hymn to Hermes*, when he wants to effect the theft of the cattle of Apollo and elude discovery, drives the herd backward so that their tracks will look as though they had gone the other way; he turns them *prosthen opisthen*, as the Hymn says.[38] These few indications suggest some of the qualities of Odysseus, the ultimate man of *mêtis*. Eustathius actually calls him an octopus.[39]

Polumêtis is Odysseus' most frequently occurring distinctive epithet and *mêtis* his preeminent attribute, which Athena, the daughter of Mêtis, enthusiastically endorses and claims as the source both of their unity and of their *kleos*. She declares:

> For you are far the best of all mortals
> in planning and speaking, and I among all the gods
> am famous for cleverness and schemes.
>
> (13.297–299)

Odysseus the dissembler, the man who assumes many identities, is called superior in *mêtis* to all mortals—and is the only mortal bearer of the epithet *polumêtis* in the Homeric corpus, the others being the crafty Hermes (once) and the craftsman Hephaistos (once). Odysseus succeeds through *mêtis amumon*, as he himself calls it, in outwitting the Cyclops—and this of course is underscored by the pun through which that *mêtis* consists of *mê tis*.

The narrative of the *Odyssey*—which Albert Lord has called protean in its fundamental properties[40]—embodies, in its many weavings, its reversals, its twisting of time, a *mêtis* of its own. The epic song, and it alone, can see from all the angles, comprehend many points of view and many strands of tradition, even incorporating allusions to incompatible ones. It alone can disclose the identity of its hero, although it alone has not created him. More precisely, only the epic song can control that identity and that disclosure, whereas for all Odysseus' skill at disguising himself, he cannot have sufficient

---

[37] Detienne and Vernant 1978:37, quoting Aelian, *On the Nature of Animals* 9.12.
[38] *Homeric Hymn to Hermes* 77–78.
[39] Eustathius 1381.36ff., cited by Detienne and Vernant 1978:39, 52n91.
[40] See above, 26–28.

perspective on himself, on his own defining features, to anticipate or circumvent Eurykleia's recognition of him or to perceive that Penelope is testing *him* when she volunteers to have his bed moved. The narrative of the *Odyssey* asserts its own supremacy and justifies the assertion by inviting its audience to reflect on the process of storytelling. Like the fox-fish, it has turned its outside inside and made its framework its focus. As Detienne and Vernant observe, "The only way to get the better of a *polumêtis* one is to exhibit even more *mêtis*."[41] The singer of his own story, Odysseus, is indeed *polumêtis*; the traditional song that encompasses him and *all* his stories is *pan-mêtis*.[42]

Works Cited

Clay, J. S. 1976. "The Beginning of the *Odyssey*." *American Journal of Philology* 97:313–326.

Detienne, M., and J.-P. Vernant. 1978. *Cunning Intelligence in Greek Culture and Society*. Trans. J. Lloyd. Sussex and Atlantic Highlands, NJ. Originally published 1974, as *Les Ruses de l'intelligence: La Métis des grecs*. Paris.

Fenik, B. 1974. *Studies in the Odyssey*. Hermes Einzelschriften 30. Wiesbaden.

Finley, J. H., Jr. 1978. *Homer's Odyssey*. Cambridge, MA.

Frontisi-Ducroux, F. 1975. *Dédale: Mythologie de l'artisane en Grece ancienne*. Paris.

Genette, G. 1980. *Narrative Discourse: An Essay in Method*. Trans. J. Lewin. Ithaca, NY.

Kullman, W. 1960. *Die Quellen der Ilias (Troischer Sagenkreis)*. Hermes Einzelschriften 14. Wiesbaden.

---

[41] Detienne and Vernant 1978:30.

[42] A version of this paper was given at the Annual Meeting of the American Philological Association in December 1981, and the present version at a Homer symposium organized by Peter Bing at the University of Pennsylvania in March 1984. In the intervening years, numerous innovative directions in the study of Homeric narrative have been discovered. Although text and notes here have not been updated to include work published since this paper was originally delivered (with the exception of Sheila Murnaghan's study [above, n.23], which I had seen at an earlier stage), I hope that at least the questions offered here will be found compatible with those so illuminatingly posed by Homerist colleagues and others over the subsequent decade.

This paper was intended initially—and still is—as a tribute to the work of the late Albert B. Lord. As always, I benefited from the insights of Richard Sacks, Seth Schein, Amy Johnson, Gregory Nagy, and in particular Nelly Oliensis and the late Steele Commager.

Lord, A. B. 1951. "Composition by Theme in Homer and Southslavic Epos." *Transactions of the American Philological Association* 82:71–80.

———. 1960. *The Singer of Tales.* Repr. New York, 1965.

Murnaghan, S. 1987. *Disguise and Recognition in the Odyssey.* Princeton, NJ.

Nagy, G. 1979. *The Best of the Achaeans: Concepts of the Hero in Archaic Greek Poetry.* Baltimore.

Sacks, R. 1982. *Ending the Odyssey: Odysseus Traditions and the Homeric Odyssey.* Unpublished paper presented at the Columbia University Seminar in Classical Civilization.

Schmitt, R. 1967. *Dichtung und Dichtersprache in indogermanischer Zeit.* Wiesbaden.

Slatkin, L. 2005. "Homer's *Odyssey*." In *A Companion to Ancient Epic,* ed. J. M. Foley, 315-329. Oxford.

Snyder, J. M. 1981. "The Web of Song: Weaving Imagery in Homer and the Lyric Poets." *Classical Journal* 76:193–196.

Todorov, T. 1977. *The Poetics of Prose.* Ithaca, NY.

West, S. R. 1981. "An Alternative Nostos for Odysseus." *Liverpool Classical Monthly* 6-7:169-75.

Genre and Generation in the *Odyssey*

I N RECENT YEARS, much brilliant and invaluable work elucidating Greek
myths has been done by Jean-Pierre Vernant and Marcel Detienne,[1] who
have looked across texts and across historical periods in order to discern
and retrieve a given myth's dispersed but essential components, which, seen
in their relation to each other, yield meaning in every feature and become
comprehensible as a totality. Having acknowledged with admiration the
fruitfulness of looking for this material across the boundaries of literary
types, we might ask, from the standpoint of anthropology, "Can we learn
anything from where those boundaries are, in fact, established? Can the
boundaries themselves tell us anything? Do they form part of the regulation
of an economy of myth that they can help to identify?"

We may take as a starting point a statement by Louis Gernet: "What is
of particular interest in an anthropological study is the question about the
barrier between human and divine reality: what separates the human from the
divine and, conversely, what brings them together?"[2] I would like to suggest
that this barrier is reflected in different types of poetry, or more precisely
that the separation between types of poetry exists to express aspects of that
fundamental separation of which Gernet speaks. It may be appropriate for
classicists to follow suggestions implicit in the work of an ethnographer like
Pierre Smith in "Des genres et des hommes"[3] on the one hand, and a literary
theorist like Tzvetan Todorov in *Les genres du discours* on the other[4]—that is,
to treat genre itself as an institution, an aspect of society, and the distinct
relations among genres and sub-genres as charged with ideological content,
wherein the way that they are demarcated makes it possible to read the clas-

---

[1] Among their writings, see, for example (to cite only complete volumes): Vernant 1971, 1974;
Detienne 1967, 1972b, 1977; and Detienne and Vernant 1974.
[2] Gernet 1981:3.
[3] Smith 1974.
[4] Todorov 1978; especially p. 44–60.

sification of cultural phenomena, to see represented ways of organizing the world through distinct spheres of concern and distinct realms of reality. In this way literary studies and anthropological—especially structuralist-symbolic—studies can be mutually illuminating if we look at the meaning of genre distinctions or genre boundaries, when we recognize that genres can be viewed, like other cultural institutions, as existing in a relationship of interdependence, in which they have complementary functions in conveying different aspects of a coherent ideology or system of beliefs about the world. The crucial point about these distinctions or differentiations is their complementarity: they exist within, and serve to complete, a conception about the way the world is ordered.

Given the difficulties of applying anthropological methods of inquiry to mythology as rendered in ancient works of art, and of drawing anthropologically valid conclusions without fieldwork,[5] it may be useful to move back a step to see what we can learn from genre as a socially determined structure underlying a given work. To decode this properly would be a large project, but this paper will make a few suggestions of how such an effort might be relevant to seeing Homeric and Hesiodic poetry not just as "different except in the ways that they are similar (or vice versa)," but as fundamentally complementary institutions comprising a coherent world-picture.

Herodotus, at 2.53, speaks of Homer and Hesiod as being jointly responsible for having systematized the gods for the Greeks: he ascribes to them the authority for producing theogonies, naming the gods, identifying their attributes and functions, in sum for having explained in a certain sense how and why to worship the gods. What we know of Greek religious history and practice, of course, tells us that Homer and Hesiod are very far from constituting religious instruction in terms of practice. They do explain relations between men and gods, but from our modern critical standpoint it is curious that Herodotus should conjoin them as he does, in that the two traditions appear to do it in such different ways. What I would like to consider briefly is how we can see those differences as significant and also locate the differences themselves as part of a coherent cultural strategy within a larger integral system of viewing the social and cosmic order.

In order to bring this question into focus, we might consider one divergent feature that needs to be reconciled with Herodotus' statement, namely that the *Iliad* and the *Odyssey* do not present theogonic or cosmogonic material, except by way of allusion. It is clear that the *Iliad* and *Odyssey*, when they

---

[5] See the discussion in Burkert 1970.

speak of Zeus, son of Kronos, assume and refer to the same basis of cosmic order that is spelled out in Hesiod; that is, they presuppose material that is elaborated in Hesiodic poetry, but do not themselves make that material overt. For example, in the *Iliad* we find allusions to divine struggles on Olympus that, as Mabel Lang has shown, are linked together to form a kind of narrative beneath the surface level of the poem.[6] These would not be comprehensible without an understanding of the theogonic scheme as we are presented with it in Hesiod. Moreover, the *Iliad* takes as its central hero the son of Thetis, who, we know from any survey of her mythology, is a vehicle for divine succession. As is told elsewhere,[7] when Zeus was courting Thetis, intending to marry her, Themis, the guardian of order, intervened to prohibit the union because Thetis was destined to bear a son greater than his father. Themis urged the gods, therefore, to marry Thetis to a mortal, and to let her see her son die in battle. Hence Thetis' marriage to Peleus, and Achilles as the issue of an arrangement whereby he has to die, but Olympian stability is maintained. By looking at the diction and motifs associated with Thetis in the *Iliad*[8]—her connection with a divine conflict on Olympus in which Zeus is victorious and binds the losers;[9] her association there with Briareos the hundred-handed, to whom Hesiod assigns a prominent role in the Titanomachy;[10] the reference in *Iliad* I to ὁ γὰρ αὖτε βίῃ οὗ πατρὸς ἄμεινον;[11] her complaints about being forced to marry a mortal, and her lament about seeing her son die and being unable to help him[12]—from a constellation of allusions of this kind, we are able to perceive an underlying dimension to the Iliadic situation that, again, only makes sense in the light of the Hesiodic schema. From Hesiod we gain knowledge about divine intergenerational conflict and its massive consequences and implications; we learn what successive violent usurpation of the divine regime entails. Only through an account like that given by Hesiodic poetry are we enabled to understand that the *Iliad* is offering an explanation for human mortality in the paradigm of Achilles: in order to prevent perpetual violent overthrow, endless disorder, and for the sake of preserving Zeus' hegemony and cosmic stability, which as the *Theogony* shows us has been achieved—human beings must not

---

[6] Lang 1983.
[7] Pindar, *Isthmian* 8.28-50.
[8] See, for example, Slatkin 1986.
[9] *Iliad* 1.396-406.
[10] *Theogony* 617ff.
[11] *Iliad* 1.404.
[12] *Iliad* 18.429-443.

threaten to be stronger than their divine parents; that is, human beings must die. Embedded in the Homeric poems is the presumption of an evolved set of cosmic relations dependent on the myth of divine succession; yet if we look for such explicit material in the *Iliad* and *Odyssey*, we find that it is excluded, adverted to only in allusions. The question then becomes whether variant treatments of a given myth are developed in order to suit different genres, or whether, in the first place, alternative genres develop with exclusive parameters in order to suit the content of the myths?

We can examine another instance of differentiation and complementarity by looking at a problem in the *Odyssey*. It announces its subject as ἄνδρα with the first word, but defers the naming of its hero until line 21—an absence, a hiatus, that corresponds to the narrative strategy by which it does not introduce us to the missing hero until the fifth book. The epic thus invites its audience to ask the question, "who is this poem about?" and the response is twofold. The poem is about ἄνδρα, it is about a man and it is about man, or perhaps more pointedly, it is about a man who has "seen the cities of men and known their minds." The poem identifies its subject, then, in precise terms: man is both the viewer and the viewed; he is what he has seen. The poem proceeds to define its subject and object, man, along two axes: the vertical—who is man on the spectrum between gods at one end and beasts at the other?[13]—and the horizontal—who is a given man among men, how is he human among all the possible ways of living as a human being, as his place on the vertical axis has established the meaning of human?

Themes associated with the horizontal axis, framing the vertical, are presented in the opening and closing books of the poem, with Telemachus on Ithaca, at Pylos, in Sparta, and again on Ithaca. How does one society compare to another? Pylos, Sparta, and Ithaca are all alternative human communities juxtaposed for the sake of comparison. But the question of societal norms is put into a wider context by the central books of the *Odyssey*, V-XII, where the vertical range and man's place within it—that is, the terms for what is human—are established: the extremes being on the one hand the divine immortality offered by, and embodied in, Kalypso, and on the other hand, the pigs in the pen of Circe.[14] In between the extremes exists a range of alternatives, beings who are all in some ways recognizably human and in some

---

[13] For seminal discussions and applications of the gods-men-beasts model in the structural analysis of Greek myth and religion, see Vidal-Naquet 1970, Detienne 1972a, and Vernant 1974.

[14] See Vidal-Naquet 1970:1281.

ways monstrous. The fullest account is of the Cyclops, who is the most challenging to Odysseus of all the beings he encounters, and the most profoundly dismaying because he is "so human"; yet he lives without social organization, without laws, and most unspeakable, he is capable of practicing cannibalism without thinking that there is anything wrong with it.

This recalls a problem that the *Odyssey* has long presented for Homerists. They have puzzled over the fact that the *Odyssey* makes distinctions between right and wrong that the *Iliad* does not make, or as some scholars have put it, that the *Odyssey* is concerned with δίκη, in a way that the *Iliad* does not apparently help us to make sense of.[15] In the past this has been advanced as evidence against unity of authorship. Unlike the *Iliad*, in which Greeks and Trojans are not compared in terms of guilt and innocence—even Paris has his merits—in the *Odyssey* there are good and bad characters. There are the suitors, who are manifestly villains and whose behavior against the innocents in Ithaca amounts to criminality and clearly offends against everyone's sense of justice, except their own. From our standpoint it is useful to ask the question, where does that sense of justice, affronted by the suitors in the *Odyssey*, come from? Are there proto-legal notions to be uncovered here? How are we to understand what δίκη is, what norms of behavior it requires? Much as the idea of succession linked with cosmic order is not spelled out in the *Iliad* but fundamentally underlies it, similarly, I suggest, the answer to the question of Odyssean δίκη is to be found in reading the *Odyssey* in the light of the concept of δίκη as presented in the *Works and Days*.

Pierre Vidal-Naquet has pointed out that the places Odysseus visits in the course of his travels are distinguished by the absence of agriculture (and by the absence of sacrifice to the gods).[16] It is emphasized in Book IX that the Cyclops has nothing to do with agriculture: it is said that the Cyclopes "neither plow with their hands nor plant anything, / but all grows for them without seed planting, without cultivation, / wheat and barley and also the grapevines, which yield for them / wine of strength, and it is Zeus' rain that waters it for them."[17] Now, this description has special meaning when we consider that it is remarkably reminiscent of Hesiod's description of life in the Golden Age, under Kronos, before the separation of men and gods,[18] because men and gods (as Martin West puts it in his Commentary[19]) began

---

[15] See, for example, Reinhardt 1960:5ff.; Wilamowitz-Moellendorf 1884; Jaeger 1926.
[16] Vidal-Naquet 1970:1282–1283.
[17] *Odyssey* 9.108–111, trans. Lattimore 1967.
[18] This point is made by Vidal-Naquet 1970:1284.
[19] West 1978, repr. 1980, p. 49.

on the same terms. For those in the Golden Age, under Kronos, "all good things were theirs; ungrudgingly, the fertile land gave up her fruits unasked (αὐτομάτη)."[20] But as we know from Hesiod, the age of Kronos was the age of cannibalism as well, as Vidal-Naquet has pointed out[21]—after all, Kronos is the god who ate his own children! But thanks to the succession struggle by which Kronos was overthrown, Zeus is established in power on Olympus. Now gods and men are radically remote from each other; men have to labor and till the fields. But the *Works and Days* tells us that "Zeus the son of Kronos established this law for men, that it is for fishes and wild beasts and winged birds to eat each other, since δίκη is not in them; but to men he gave δίκη, which is much the best."[22] So we are again given a picture of an evolved set of relations between men and gods—costly for men, but beneficial as well. Man is no longer on a par with the gods, but neither is he to be identified with the beasts, and what determines this is δίκη.

So insofar as the *Odyssey* is concerned with exploring the nature of being human—its potentialities, limitations, and rough edges—it is concerned with δίκη as distinctive to that condition. It is on this basis, therefore, that the poem indicts the suitors, who, over and over again, are said to be eating up the substance of another man:[23] it is not so much that they are bad people as that, being without δίκη, they are, so to speak, not people at all—and from the travel books V-XII, we are prepared to appreciate what that means, as we remember the Cyclopes or the Laestrygones. It is striking, then, and worth noting, that the passage in the *Works and Days* about δίκη precluding ἀλληλοφαγία occurs specifically in the context of an exhortation to Perses to restrain his voracity in claiming someone else's patrimony.

Hesiod opposes δίκη and ὕβρις in the *Works and Days* so as to show, as J.-P. Vernant has pointed out, that they are in a perpetual deadlock over pride of place among men.[24] We may remember that three times in the course of his travels, upon arriving in unknown territory, Odysseus asks himself whether he has landed among men who are ὑβρισταί or δίκαιοι. Significantly these occur when he arrives on Scheria, that most humanly refined place where the inhabitants are ἀγχίθεοι; on the island of the Cyclops, that extreme of bestiality; and finally, when he reaches Ithaca, and does not know where he is.[25] It

---

[20] *Works and Days* 116–118.
[21] Vidal-Naquet 1970:1280, citing *Theogony* 459–467.
[22] *Works and Days* 276–279.
[23] *Odyssey* 1.160, 2.123, 11.116, 13.396 = 13.428, 15.32, etc.
[24] Vernant 1960.
[25] *Odyssey* 6.120 = 9.175 = 13.201.

is the ambiguity of the status of δίκη on Ithaca that is to be underscored here, in its Hesiodic sense.

If the suitors, like Polyphemos, behave as the absence of δίκη implies, they threaten to invert all the procedures by which men recognize each other as *beings of the same species*, and treat each other with respect as men. This means that on Ithaca no identity is secure. In shorthand, it means that Telemachus does not know who he is; so that when Athena says, "You certainly look like Odysseus! Are you his son?" he replies, "I don't know; no one ever knows his own father."[26] As for Laertes, he is less like a valued elder of the family than a superannuated retainer or discarded beast of burden. In Book II, the first assembly since Odysseus' departure is called. Mentor regrets the current state of affairs, which, he says, has come about because no one remembers the just king—the σκηπτοῦχος βασιλεύς—who was like a father.[27] When the disguised Odysseus later compares Penelope to a king who rules with δίκη,[28] the passage is, as Gregory Nagy has pointed out, particularly close in diction and purport to the Hesiodic description in the *Works and Days* of orderly right relations in the community where δίκη is upheld.[29] But at Odysseus' praise evoking such a community Penelope demurs—rightly, because in a Hesiodic sense δίκη cannot be said to exist on Ithaca. As Penelope replies, only Odysseus can make this happen, because only his return will restore δίκη; only his return will put all the pieces in place and restore the categories that δίκη exists to govern. In the *Works and Days*, Hesiod says that under δίκη women bear children who resemble their fathers,[30] so that it is the return of Odysseus that will allow Telemachus to know what he looks like, and will allow Laertes to be a father again—a father who recognizes his son.

Here I want to emphasize the importance of understanding *recognition* on Ithaca as a function of δίκη, which, as Hesiod shows us, allows us to identify members of our own species in general, and to know how we are related to them in particular—and to treat them appropriately. "It is for fishes and wild beasts and winged birds to eat each other, since δίκη is not in them; but to men [Zeus] gave δίκη, which is much the best."[31] If δίκη enables human beings to observe the distinction between their kind and other kinds, it makes those fundamental defining features explicit in the first place through

---

[26] *Odyssey* 1.206–209, 214–216.
[27] *Odyssey* 2.230–234.
[28] *Odyssey* 19.107–114.
[29] Nagy 1982.
[30] *Works and Days* 235.
[31] *Works and Days* 276–279.

the family. This is the entity that allows you to identify others as members of your own species, because in order to do that you must first know what you look like yourself. (We remember here that Penelope rejects the beggar Odysseus' characterization of her as a king upholding δίκη in telling terms: she responds by saying that in the present conditions on Ithaca she no longer looks the way she used to—she has become unrecognizable—but that were Odysseus to return, she would look like herself again.) Thus δίκη allows human beings, by recognizing species and family, to determine a distinction—with which the *Odyssey* is concerned throughout—between licit and illicit appetites, both for what one consumes and for sexual relations. Fishes, wild beasts, and birds do not make those distinctions, either within species or within family; they avoid neither ἀλληλοφαγία nor incest.

Given conditions on Ithaca, in the absence of Hesiodic δίκη resemblance between the generations of a family may indeed cease to be reliable, as in the case of the faithful Dolios and his treacherous offspring Melanthios and Melantho—so that we see a son who partakes of the wrong food (with the suitors), and a daughter who sleeps in the wrong bed (also with the suitors). To put it another way, in such conditions, how to avoid the threat realized in the *Telegony*, where Telegonos, Odysseus' son by Circe, kills his father without knowing who he is, and then proceeds to marry Penelope?

In this sense, the extended meeting scene between Odysseus and Laertes in Book XXIV is anything but gratuitous, despite objections to it by a number of scholars, famously, for example, Denys Page. For this scene asserts the coherence and continuity of generations guaranteed by and reinforcing δίκη; the token of their relationship, the orchard of Odysseus and Laertes, bears fruit unfailingly, as in the Hesiodic community where δίκη prevails, and women bear children who look like their fathers.

These illustrations of some ways in which Homeric and Hesiodic poetry exhibit a complementary distribution of subject matter within a relationship of interdependence could of course be reciprocally matched by illustrations from Hesiod vis-à-vis Homer: the Hesiodic poems assume heroic events and situations—at Troy and at Thebes—but do not elaborate or recreate them. The level at which we need to see Homeric and Hesiodic poetry as participating jointly in the systematization of the gods for the Greeks, as Herodotus claims, must precisely identify the differentiation between the two traditions—their very distinctions—as a crucial part of the system. The separation between them reinforces and institutionalizes the proposition inherent in the mythological totality: namely that the order of things is organized, based on a prior evolution, according to a separation between human and divine, a breach that is complete, and must continually be recapitulated, as with the institution of sacrifice. But if we can see both a symbolic and an effective function for genre boundaries in this way, we can understand as well why Homeric poetry and Hesiodic poetry occasionally, if only tangentially, extend into each other's territories: to incorporate another genre, as the *Odyssey* has been shown to do with "instruction poetry,"[32] is not just to be more sophisticated as poetry, but to be more encompassing as a representation of social and cosmic order; in this sense Homeric epic seeks to preempt other genres, to be the "genre of genres." But this must be done with great tact and subtlety: otherwise, as with the strategy of the succession myth, the attempt to devour the alternatives may be indigestible and self-defeating, not only for the poem but for the audience. The anthropologist Mary Douglas in her essay on "Deciphering a Meal" quotes Allan Tate saying, "Formal versification is the primary structure of poetic order, the assurance to the reader and to the poet himself that the poet is in control of the disorder both outside him and within his own mind."[33] Perhaps the same can be said of the function of genre, if for poet we substitute society.[34]

Works Cited

Burkert, W. 1970. "Jason, Hypsipyle, and New Fire at Lemnos: A Study in Myth and Ritual." *Classical Quarterly* 20:1–16.

Detienne, M. 1967. *Les maîtres de vérité dans la Grèce ancienne.* Paris.

———. 1972a. "Entre bêtes et dieux." *Nouvelle revue de psychanalyse* 6:231–246. Reprinted as Chapter 3 in Detienne 1977.

———. 1972b. *Les jardins d'Adonis: la mythologie des aromates en Grèce.* Paris.

———. 1977. *Dionysos mis à mort.* Les essais (Gallimard) 195. Paris.

Detienne, M. and J.-P. Vernant. 1974. *Les ruses de l'intelligence: la métis des grecs.* Paris.

Douglas, M. 1975. *Implicit Meanings: Essays in Anthropology.* London.

---

[32] See the convincing argument of Martin 1984.

[33] Douglas 1975:273.

[34] An early version of this paper was delivered at a symposium in honor of George E. Dimock, Jr. at Smith College in November 1985. My ongoing thinking about the subject owes much to stimulating discussions with M.D. Carroll, A.E. Johnson, N. Loraux, and L. Muellner, and to valuable suggestions from P.E. Easterling, P.-Y. Jacopin, and S.L. Schein.

Gernet, L. 1981. *The Anthropology of Ancient Greece.* Trans. J. Hamilton and B. Nagy. Baltimore.

Jaeger, W. 1926. "Solons Eunomie." *Sitzungsberichte der Preussischen Akademie der Wissenschaften. Philosophisch-historische Klasse* 11:69–85.

Lang, M. L. 1983. "Reverberation and Mythology in the *Iliad.*" In *Approaches to Homer,* ed. C. A. Rubino and C. W. Shelmerdine, 140–164. Austin.

Lattimore, R., trans. 1967. *The Odyssey of Homer.* New York.

Martin, R. 1984. "Hesiod, Odysseus, and the Instruction of Princes." *Transactions and Proceedings of the American Philological Association* 114:29–48.

Nagy, G. 1982. "Hesiod." In *Ancient Writers: Greece and Rome,* ed. T. J. Luce, 1:43-73. New York.

Reinhardt, K. 1960. *Tradition und Geist: Gesammelte Essays zur Dichtung.* Ed. C. Becker. Göttingen.

Slatkin, L. M. 1986. "The Wrath of Thetis." *Transactions and Proceedings of the American Philological Association* 116:1–24.

Smith, P. 1974. "Des genres et des hommes." *Poétique* 19:294–312.

Todorov, T. 1978. *Les genres du discours.* Paris.

Vernant, J.-P. 1960. "Le mythe hésiodique des races: Essai d'analyse structurale." *Revue de l'histoire des religions* 157:21–54. Reprinted as Chapter 1 in Vernant 1971.

———. 1971. *Mythe et pensée chez les Grecs.* 3rd ed. Paris.

———. 1974. *Mythe et société en Grèce ancienne.* Paris. See especially "Le mythe prométhéen chez Hésiode," 177–194.

Vidal-Naquet, P. 1970. "Valeurs religieuses et mythiques de la terre et du sacrifice dans l'Odyssée." *Annales. Économies, Sociétés, Civilisations* 25:1278–1297. Reprinted 1981 in *Le chasseur noir.* Paris.

West, M. L., ed. 1978. *Hesiod: Works and Days.* Oxford.

Wilamowitz-Moellendorf, U. von. 1884. *Homerische Untersuchungen.* Philologische Untersuchungen 7. Berlin.

The Poetics of Exchange in the *Iliad* [1]

ξένια γὰρ Ἄρεος τραύματα, φόνοι

—scholia Sophocles *Electra* 96

T HE FAR-REACHING IMPLICATIONS of Marcel Mauss's *Essai sur le Don*,[2] much admired by ethnographers and anthropological theorists, have contributed greatly to our grasp of how thoroughly a code of reciprocity, expressed especially in the institution of gift-exchange, organizes social and economic relations in archaic societies in which, as Mauss made clear, social relations are economic relations. Mauss did not use archaic Greece as an example, and his conclusions initially served to inform scholarship on gift-giving in the contexts of marriage and hospitality, primarily as attested in the *Odyssey*. But there have been stimulating studies of reciprocity, early on by Louis Gernet and subsequently by M. I. Finley, Walter Donlan, and others,[3] that encourage us to go beyond those Odyssean contexts; to see gift-exchange as containing and regenerating competition, both constituting and challenging social contract; and to understand that reciprocity is a fundamental organizing principle of the Iliadic world, underlying both heroic behavior and heroic discourse.

A full-scale discussion of this topic would need to examine the interrelated notions of value, price and honor, portion and "destiny," and to investigate distribution by booty, proposals of ransom, awards of prizes. What I would like to do in this essay is something more modest, having acknowledged the larger scheme in which it belongs: that is, simply to suggest one aspect of how the *Iliad* thematizes reciprocity, by indicating the ways in which an encompassing system—or economy—of reciprocal exchange structures the representation of social interactions and, more particularly, how a paradigm

---

[1] This paper was delivered at the first UCLA "Homeric Dialogues" conference, organized by Ann Bergren, in May 1989.
[2] First published in *l'Année Sociologique*, seconde série, 1923–1924.
[3] See now the work of King (forthcoming), van Wees 1992, von Reden 1995, and Wilson 2002.

of exchange is embedded in the language of social relations through a dense network of metaphor, one that makes significant interactions into transactions. Emile Benveniste, in his analysis of "Don et échange" in early Greek,[4] determined that diction having to do with gifts embraces a wide range of exchanges, or, to put it the other way, that a range of procedures, motivations, and goals is subsumed within the language of giving. In the *Iliad* we see the sphere of operation extending itself not so much lexically as metaphorically, as the poem proposes models of exchange and equilibrium that it unsettles, subjects to ironic transformations, restores, and again disturbs. Thus the poem constructs out of the war itself an overall social order as a process of exacting and meeting economic obligations within an ever-renewed accounting.

The dynamics of the *Iliad*'s paradigm of exchange may be introduced against the background of those figures in which equilibrium and disequilibrium, parity and disparity, are represented in similes of measurement and balance, vivid for their depiction of a strained, taut symmetry, as at *Iliad* XV 410–413:

> ἀλλ' ὥς τε στάθμη δόρυ νήϊον ἐξιθύνει
> τέκτονος ἐν παλάμῃσι δαήμονος, ὅς ῥά τε πάσης
> εὖ εἰδῇ σοφίης ὑποθημοσύνῃσιν Ἀθήνης,
> ὣς μὲν τῶν ἐπὶ ἶσα μάχη τέτατο πτόλεμός τε·

> But as a chalkline straightens the cutting of a ship's timber
> in the hands of an expert carpenter, who by Athene's
> inspiration is well versed in all his craft's subtlety,
> so the battles fought by both sides were pulled fast and even.

Here the battle is compared to a carpenter's chalkline (στάθμη), a line drawn even, to allow a true measurement for hewing δόρυ νήϊον—timber that will be used to build the "balanced ships."

As at *Iliad* XII 436 and XV 413 (ὣς μὲν τῶν ἐπὶ ἶσα μάχη τέτατο πτόλεμός τε), the battle is stretched out equally from both sides once again at XVII 543–544:

> Ἀψ δ' ἐπὶ Πατρόκλῳ τέτατο κρατερὴ ὑσμίνη
> ἀργαλέη πολύδακρυς...

> Once again over Patroklos was close drawn a strong battle
> weary and sorrowful...

---

[4] Benveniste 1969:65–80.

Here an introductory simile of the kind that introduces the image in the earlier passages is elided or else has been displaced into the subsequent verses in which Zeus stretches out a rainbow as a portent of war.

These images of the war in balance recapitulate the metaphor of Zeus pulling the battle evenly from both sides, at *Iliad* XI 336:

> Ἔνθά σφιν κατὰ ἶσα μάχην ἐτάνυσσε Κρονίων

> There the son of Kronos strained the battle even between them

and at *Iliad* XVI 661–662:

> ...πολέες γὰρ ἐπ’ αὐτῷ
> κάππεσον, εὖτ’ ἔριδα κρατερὴν ἐτάνυσσε Κρονίων.

> ...since many others had fallen
> above him, once Zeus had strained fast the powerful conflict.

as well as at *Iliad* XVII 400–401:

> τοῖον Ζεὺς ἐπὶ Πατρόκλῳ ἀνδρῶν τε καὶ ἵππων
> ἤματι τῷ ἐτάνυσσε κακὸν πόνον·

> such was the wicked work of battle for men and for horses
> Zeus strained tight above Patroklos that day

The war is drawn out into equilibrium, yet not attenuated; on the contrary, it is intensified in its evenness. Hector and Poseidon, from opposite sides, are said at *Iliad* XIV 388–391 to stretch to its deadliest (αἰνοτάτην) the conflict of battle:

> Τρῶας δ’ αὖθ’ ἑτέρωθεν ἐκόσμει φαίδιμος Ἕκτωρ.
> δή ῥα τότ’ αἰνοτάτην ἔριδα πτολέμοιο τάνυσσαν
> κυανοχαῖτα Ποσειδάων καὶ φαίδιμος Ἕκτωρ,
> ἤτοι ὁ μὲν Τρώεσσιν, ὁ δ’ Ἀργείοισιν ἀρήγων.

> On the other side glorious Hektor ordered the Trojans,
> And now Poseidon of the dark hair and glorious Hektor
> strained to its deadliest the division of battle, the one
> bringing power to the Trojans, and the god to the Argives.

The figure of the stretched rope may recall a powerful metaphor earlier in the poem, in which Zeus and Poseidon pull and tie a cable around both armies. Paradoxically, it loosens or "unstrings" the limbs of many warriors:

τοὶ δ᾽ ἔριδος κρατερῆς καὶ ὁμοιΐου πτολέμοιο
πεῖραρ ἐπαλλάξαντες ἐπ᾽ ἀμφοτέροισι τάνυσσαν,
ἄρρηκτόν τ᾽ ἄλυτόν τε, τὸ πολλῶν γούνατ᾽ ἔλυσεν.

Iliad XIII 358–360

So these two had looped over both sides a crossing
cable of strong discord and the closing of battle, not to be
slipped, not to be broken, which unstrung the knees of many.

But the general image of strained evenness is made hideously specific in the simile, at *Iliad* XVII 389–395, of men stretching an oxhide, pulling equally from both sides—where it is not the battle itself that is stretched, but the body of the dead Patroclus:[5]

ὡς δ᾽ ὅτ᾽ ἀνὴρ ταύροιο βοὸς μεγάλοιο βοείην
λαοῖσιν δώῃ τανύειν, μεθύουσαν ἀλοιφῇ·
δεξάμενοι δ᾽ ἄρα τοί γε διαστάντες τανύουσι
κυκλόσ᾽, ἄφαρ δέ τε ἰκμὰς ἔβη, δύνει δέ τ᾽ ἀλοιφὴ
πολλῶν ἑλκόντων, τάνυται δέ τε πᾶσα διαπρό·
ὡς οἵ γ᾽ ἔνθα καὶ ἔνθα νέκυν ὀλίγῃ ἐνὶ χώρῃ
εἵλκεον ἀμφότεροι·

As when a man gives the hide of a great ox, a bullock,
drenched first in deep fat, to all his people to stretch out;
the people take it from him and stand in a circle about it
and pull, and presently the moisture goes and the fat sinks
in, with so many pulling, and the bull's hide is stretched out
        level;
so the men of both sides in a cramped space tugged at the body
in both directions...

In figures depicting the battle as pulled taut to its extreme limit by equal force from either end, then, warriors are both subject and object of the stretching (the dead warrior lies τανύθεις, e.g., *Iliad* XIII 392 = XVI 485; XX 483; τανύσσας, XXIII 25), just as the poem shows enemies as both divided (οἵ τε πανημέριοι στυγερῷ κρίνονται Ἄρηϊ, *Iliad* XVIII 209) and dividing (ἐν μέσῳ ἀμφότεροι μένος Ἄρηος δατέονται, *Iliad* XVIII 264)—dividing "between

---

[5] Cf. Zeus' dispensation for his son: Sarpedon is spared not death, but the battle over his body. Compare the gentle, coordinated effort of Sleep and Death, which specifically exempts Sarpedon's body from having the battle enacted on it, as it is on so many others, including Patroclus.

them the strength of Ares." In these terms (as on the level of the narrative itself) the poem shows all its warriors to be at once agents and victims of destruction. War is ὁμοίϊος 'equalizing' as, elsewhere, only old age or death are ὁμοίϊος (*Iliad* IV 315 and *Odyssey* iii 236 respectively). The war god, as Hector says (*Iliad* XVIII 309), is even-handed, and slays the slayer.

Images of equilibrium freeze the volatility, the turmoil and clamor of fighting, into tableau-like immobility, portraying the battle as a dire tug-of-war in which, as Nicole Loraux has elucidated,[6] enemies are inextricably linked together at the same time as they are profoundly divided from each other—a paradox that corresponds to the Iliadic representation of warriors opposed in conflict as mirror-images of each other, never resembling each other more closely than when locked together in passionate strife.[7] An indelible image that belongs in this category is that of two men running—Hector and Achilles: the one fleeing, the other pursuing, as in a dream; the one unable to escape, the other unable to overtake him:

ὡς δ' ἐν ὀνείρῳ οὐ δύναται φεύγοντα διώκειν·
οὔτ' ἄρ' ὁ τὸν δύναται ὑποφεύγειν, οὔθ' ὁ διώκειν·

Iliad XXII 199–200

As in a dream a man is not able to follow one who runs
from him, nor can the runner escape, nor the other pursue him...

Yet, for all that the war renders its participants equal at one level of description, when it reveals a disparity between them, that disparity is definitive, and fatal. Thus, for example, Diomedes rightly says, "Unhappy are they whose sons match themselves against me in strength" (δυστήνων δέ τε παῖδες ἐμῷ μένει ἀντιόωσιν, *Iliad* VI 127);[8] and of Achilles' pursuit of Hector, the narrative says, "It was a great man who fled, but far better he who pursued him rapidly" (πρόσθε μὲν ἐσθλὸς ἔφευγε, δίωκε δέ μιν μέγ' ἀμείνων / καρπαλίμως, *Iliad* XXII 158–159).

The language of gauging—as when Helenus says of Diomedes, "It is not possible for anyone to equal him in strength" (οὐδέ τίς οἱ δύναται μένος ἰσοφαρίζειν, *Iliad* VI 101)—resumes the *Iliad*'s preoccupation with determining value as a function of relative measurement: warriors are compared not to an absolute standard, but to each other. Such language expresses the

---

[6] Loraux 1987 = Loraux 1997:109–114.
[7] Loraux 1997:111ff.
[8] Similarly, Achilles at *Iliad* XXI 151: δυστήνων δέ τε παῖδες ἐμῷ μένει ἀντιόωσι. Everything must be measured, but to measure is dangerous.

fundamental character of social relations in the context of war, where the only meaningful categories are "greater than" or "less than" and where to be "greater than" is to kill and to be "less than" is to be killed.[9] Between them there appear no gradations; there is no such status as—and no hypothetical meaning offered to the notion of being—"almost as great as" or "slightly less good than" your antagonist.

More disturbing is that the poem seems to call into question the meaning of "equal". How does the action of the *Iliad* allow us to understand what constitutes the term "equal to" or even whether it can have a meaning? An unsettling illustration of the problem is offered by the poem's use of the phrase δαίμονι ἶσος 'equal to a divinity'. When a hero entering the fray is described as δαίμονι ἶσος, the phrase introduces an encounter in which the term ἶσος can be tested, because the antagonist who confronts him is in fact a god. In each of the episodes in which this occurs, it becomes devastatingly clear with the destruction (or near-destruction) of the mortal fighter how utterly unequal to a god, in reality, the hero is. Apollo himself makes this explicit in his encounter with Diomedes. Diomedes may come close to fighting on the gods' terms, but Apollo warns him:

'φράζεο, Τυδεΐδη, καὶ χάζεο, μηδὲ θεοῖσιν
ἶσ' ἔθελε φρονέειν, ἐπεὶ οὔ ποτε φῦλον ὁμοῖον
ἀθανάτων τε θεῶν χαμαὶ ἐρχομένων τ' ἀνθρώπων.'

Iliad V 440–442

'Take care, give back, son of Tydeus, and strive no longer
to make yourself like the gods in mind, since never the same is
the breed of gods, who are immortal, and the men who walk
      groundling.'

Apollo admonishes as if to correct a misapprehension or to dispel a familiar illusion—such as the one embodied in the very appellation δαίμονι ἶσος.

The problem extends beyond exposing the irreconcilable differences between the human and the divine. On the human level, the duel in Book VII between Hector and Ajax suggests the profound complexity that inheres in the

---

[9] Achilles may be the best warrior but is "less kingly" than Agamemnon; Diomedes and Ajax are called the best of the Achaean warriors after Achilles; the Trojans describe their terror of Diomedes by saying they fear him even more than they did Achilles. Agamemnon, moreover, wishes to keep Chryseis because she is "not inferior to Clytaemnestra"; and of course the worth of women can be measured, as at *Iliad* XXIII 704–705. See Felson and Slatkin 2004.

theoretically unambiguous status of "equal." In this episode, in which Hector challenges "the best of the Achaeans" to meet him in single combat, the warriors themselves articulate the process of taking the measure of individual fighters, specifically assessing each compared to the others, to determine which one will be equal to—which, in the event, means greater than—Hector's threat. Although the duel is designed to distinguish which of two antagonists is the greater, its actual outcome is prefigured in the prayer to Zeus uttered by the Achaeans on the sidelines as Ajax arms himself for combat:

'δὸς νίκην Αἴαντι καὶ ἀγλαὸν εὖχος ἀρέσθαι·
εἰ δὲ καὶ Ἕκτορά περ φιλέεις καὶ κήδεαι αὐτοῦ,
ἴσην ἀμφοτέροισι βίην καὶ κῦδος ὄπασσον.'

Iliad VII 203–205

'Grant that Aias win the vaunt of renown and the victory;
but if truly you love Hektor and are careful for him,
give to both of them equal strength, make equal their honour.'

Yet the narrative describes the duel inevitably doing what it must, progressively revealing the superior might of Ajax over Hector. Hector's spear fails to penetrate Ajax' shield, while Ajax successfully pierces Hector's shield completely, so that blood gushes from his wound. Hector retaliates by striking Ajax' shield with a stone, but Ajax hurls a far larger one, which crushes Hector's shield and Hector with it. The narrative leaves no doubt that, while they may have met on equal ground initially, Ajax would overpower Hector and kill him were their contest to take its natural course. The wished-for ἴση βίη, an ideal resisted by the intrinsic capacities of the antagonists, grows more and more remote. It is a notion that can be made to correspond to reality only by the intervention of a truce, diplomatically arranged and superimposed. The enforced stalemate that concludes their encounter suggests not only that equilibrium is fragile and fleeting, but that, if it is to be maintained even temporarily, it must be socially constructed. Or it may, in rare instances, be divinely manipulated. Thus Aeneas in his confrontation with Achilles uses the narrative's metaphor to voice the hope that he might stand a chance against Achilles if only Poseidon were to stretch out an 'equal outcome' (ἴσον τέλος) to the war:

'εἰ δὲ θεός περ
ἴσον τείνειεν πολέμου τέλος, οὔ κε μάλα ῥέα
νικήσει', οὐδ' εἰ παγχάλκεος εὔχεται εἶναι.'

Iliad XX 100–102

> 'But if the god only
> would pull out even the issue of war, he would not so easily
> win, not even though he claims to be made all of bronze.'

And indeed it is only the intervention of Poseidon that allows Aeneas to emerge intact from a meeting remarkable for its elaborate, competitive rehearsal of claims to superior genealogical status and worth but, in the event, predictably familiar in its demonstration of the superiority of Achilles' native ability. As a function of the intrinsic abilities of individuals, equilibrium between those at war appears fugitive, at best.

But within the narrative's broad perspective, individual gains and losses are subsumed in a view of the aggregate, so as to produce the similes of the evenness of battle cited above. The balanced symmetry of war they describe is a stasis built out of the unrelenting, ongoing fluctuation of triumphs and defeats—a rhythm wherein there emerges at every moment a victor and a vanquished, yet through which, by turns, each side overbalances, and then is overbalanced by, the other.

This continuous process is given expression in the poem's most memorable, recurring motif of measurement: that of the scales of Zeus, poised to determine survival or destruction for those who are, by a scarcely fathomable process, placed in the balance and weighed against each other. It is an image at once mysterious and transparent, enigmatic in blurring the lines between the literal and the figurative, between description and prediction—yet instantly comprehensible in what it signifies. The battle narrative of Book VIII introduces the image:

> Ὄφρα μὲν ἠὼς ἦν καὶ ἀέξετο ἱερὸν ἦμαρ,
> τόφρα μάλ' ἀμφοτέρων βέλε' ἥπτετο, πῖπτε δὲ λαός.
> ἦμος δ' Ἠέλιος μέσον οὐρανὸν ἀμφιβεβήκει,
> καὶ τότε δὴ χρύσεια πατὴρ ἐτίταινε τάλαντα·
> ἐν δὲ τίθε δύο κῆρε τανηλεγέος θανάτοιο,
> Τρώων θ' ἱπποδάμων καὶ Ἀχαιῶν χαλκοχιτώνων,
> ἕλκε δὲ μέσσα λαβών· ῥέπε δ' αἴσιμον ἦμαρ Ἀχαιῶν.
>
> *Iliad* VIII 66–72

> So long as it was early morning and the sacred daylight
> increasing,
> so long the thrown weapons of both took hold and men dropped
> under them.
> But when the sun god stood bestriding the middle heaven,

then the father balanced his golden scales, and in them
he set two fateful portions of death, which lays men prostrate,
for Trojans, breakers of horses, and bronze-armoured Achaians,
and balanced it by the middle. The Achaians' death-day was
heaviest.

The image recurs in the climactic account of the confrontation between Hector and Achilles in Book XXII, as though the weighing were itself the decisive event:

ἀλλ' ὅτε δὴ τὸ τέταρτον ἐπὶ κρουνοὺς ἀφίκοντο,
καὶ τότε δὴ χρύσεια πατὴρ ἐτίταινε τάλαντα,
ἐν δ' ἐτίθει δύο κῆρε τανηλεγέος θανάτοιο,
τὴν μὲν Ἀχιλλῆος, τὴν δ' Ἕκτορος ἱπποδάμοιο,
ἕλκε δὲ μέσσα λαβών·

Iliad XXII 208–212

But when for the fourth time they had come around to the well
        springs,
then the father balanced his golden scales, and in them
he set two fateful portions of death, which lays men prostrate,
one for Achilleus, and one for Hektor, breaker of horses,
and balanced it by the middle...

Zeus holds the scales, as the balance shifts between Achaeans and Trojans, but does not intervene; destinies are calibrated independent of divine favor, according to an impartial principle of discrimination that allows them, as it were, to find their own level. The scales tip, ineluctably; never do they remain in equipoise.

In a passage in Book XVI, the scales of Zeus reappear when, intriguingly, the narrative describes with a brief comment Hector's decision to retreat:

ἐς δίφρον δ' ἀναβὰς φύγαδ' ἔτραπε, κέκλετο δ' ἄλλους
Τρῶας φευγέμεναι· γνῶ γὰρ Διὸς ἱρὰ τάλαντα.

Iliad XVI 657–658

He climbed to his chariot and turned to flight, and called to
        the other
Trojans to run, for he saw the way of Zeus' sacred balance.

This cannot refer to the only prior appearance of the scales in Book VIII because there they inclined otherwise, with the Trojans' fortunes in the ascendant. What is it that Hector perceives? Does he actually see something,

something that the narrative assumes but omits to describe except through his reaction? Or does the narrative ascribe to him its own figurative mode of cognition and representation? Does the poem show him in the process of creating (and itself recreating) a metaphor?[10]

What is implicit in Hector's reaction is not simply a reference to the previous instance of the motif's occurrence (when in fact the Trojans, by contrast, were successful), but an interpretation of the dynamics of battle, one that recapitulates the narrative's vision of the ceaseless movement in heroic relations between balance and imbalance, equal and unequal measure. That vision can be invoked by allusion, as here, because the recurring figures of equilibrium have prepared us for it, providing a framework in which to locate the motif of the scales.

The full implication of the motif's place in a larger system becomes clearer from a passage in Book XIX, in which Odysseus makes reference to the scales of Zeus as part of an admonition to Achilles, urging him not to send men into battle hungry.

> τῶ τοι ἐπιτλήτω κραδίη μύθοισιν ἐμοῖσιν.
> αἶψά τε φυλόπιδος πέλεται κόρος ἀνθρώποισιν,
> ἧς τε πλείστην μὲν καλάμην χθονὶ χαλκὸς ἔχευεν,
> ἄμητος δ' ὀλίγιστος, ἐπὴν κλίνῃσι τάλαντα
> Ζεύς, ὅς τ' ἀνθρώπων ταμίης πολέμοιο τέτυκται.
>
> *Iliad* XIX 220–224

> Therefore let your heart endure and listen to my words.
> When there is battle men have suddenly their fill of it
> when the bronze scatters on the ground the straw in most
>   numbers
> and the harvest is most thin, when Zeus has poised his balance,
> Zeus, who is administrator to men in their fighting.

Here what it means to "know" or "recognize" the scales of Zeus is clear. Although his image is not easy to decipher precisely, for Odysseus the scales of Zeus are part of a metaphor, one that coincides with the narrative's representation, in which Achaeans and Trojans are poised as seemingly indistinguishable counterweights. Here they are sheaves of wheat—resources in a process of winnowing and weighing that, when complete, will finally, irre-

---

[10] It is worth noting here, although the point has received little attention, that Hector's language is the most figurative of any Iliadic character; he even glosses his own figures of speech.

vocably, discriminate between them. We are made to see the act of weighing set within broader procedures of harvesting, husbanding, and dispensing, in which Zeus performs as steward (ταμίης) of war.

For the primary context, the function of scales is, crucially, that of economic activity.[11] Therefore, the presence of the motif must evoke, however generally, a process of transaction. It is explicit in a memorable simile at *Iliad* XII 433–438, where an honest widow employs a pair of scales to balance her wool so that she may eke out a pittance in wages for her children. As equal as her measures are, so evenly balanced was the fighting between Trojans and Achaeans:

> ἀλλ' ἔχον ὥς τε τάλαντα γυνὴ χερνῆτις ἀληθής,
> ἥ τε σταθμὸν ἔχουσα καὶ εἴριον ἀμφὶς ἀνέλκει
> ἰσάζουσ', ἵνα παισὶν ἀεικέα μισθὸν ἄρηται·
> ὣς μὲν τῶν ἐπὶ ἶσα μάχη τέτατο πτόλεμός τε,
> πρίν γ' ὅτε δὴ Ζεὺς κῦδος ὑπέρτερον Ἕκτορι δῶκε
> Πριαμίδῃ...

> but held evenly as the scales which a careful widow
> holds, taking it by the balance beam, and weighs her wool evenly
> at either end, working to win a pitiful wage for her children:
> so the battles fought by both sides were pulled fast and even
> until that time when Zeus gave the greater glory to Hektor,
> Priam's son...

The fighting remained evenly balanced, that is, until Zeus gave κῦδος to Hector.

Other mechanisms and instruments supplement and reinforce the image of the scales in a pervasive model of transaction and distribution, as in the urgent struggle—with measuring ropes—in our earlier simile of the dispute over the division of a field:

> ἀλλ' ὥς τ' ἀμφ' οὔροισι δύ' ἀνέρε δηριάασθον
> μέτρ' ἐν χερσὶν ἔχοντες, ἐπιξύνῳ ἐν ἀρούρῃ,
> ὥ τ' ὀλίγῳ ἐνὶ χώρῳ ἐρίζητον περὶ ἴσης,
> ὣς ἄρα τοὺς διέεργον ἐπάλξιες·

> *Iliad* XII 421–424

---

[11] N.B. the indispensability of scales as an implement determining currency in a pre-monetary economy and the evolution of the meaning of τάλαντα—from 'scales' to 'money'.

> but as two men with measuring ropes in their hands fight
> bitterly
> about a boundary line at the meeting place of two
> cornfields,
> and the two of them fight in the strait place over the
> rights of division,
> so the battlements held these armies apart...

Armed conflict becomes the striking of a bargain in which the terms are continually subject to reevaluation as elements are added and subtracted, though the goal is a constant one. The poem's figurations of parity and disparity participate in a representation of the war, not as random and chaotic disintegration, but as an economy of reciprocal exchanges—coherent, encompassing, self-perpetuating.

Warriors on the battlefield refer their life-and-death confrontations to a model of reciprocal economic claims, which means that they represent their actions in dialogue that takes place almost exclusively in a figurative mode. In Book XIII, Idomeneus kills the Trojan ally Asios together with his charioteer. Priam's son Deiphobos, grieving for Asios, casts his spear at Idomeneus; he misses his target, but strikes Hypsenor nearby and cries out that the death of Asios has not gone unpaid (ἄτιτος). Idomeneus responds by killing a third Trojan fighter, Alkathoos, and calls out to Deiphobos to ask, "Do we agree this is a suitable return, three men killed in exchange for one?" as though they were negotiating together the terms for a bargain:

> 'Δηΐφοβ', ἦ ἄρα δή τι ἐΐσκομεν ἄξιον εἶναι
> τρεῖς ἑνὸς ἀντὶ πεφάσθαι; ἐπεὶ σύ περ εὔχεαι οὕτω.'
>
> *Iliad* XIII 446–447

> 'Deiphobos, are we then to call this a worthy bargain,
> three men killed for one? It was you yourself were so boastful.'

The diction of exchange is similarly explicit at *Iliad* XIV 470ff, where the Trojan Poulydamas boasts of killing Prothoënor, an Argive warrior. Ajax, in turn, kills a Trojan fighter and replies, "Consider, Poulydamas, whether this man isn't equivalent in exchange for Prothoënor?":

> 'φράζεο, Πουλυδάμα, καί μοι νημερτὲς ἐνίσπες·
> ἦ ῥ' οὐχ οὗτος ἀνὴρ Προθοήνορος ἀντὶ πεφάσθαι
> ἄξιος;'
>
> *Iliad* XIV 470–472

'Think over this, Poulydamas, and answer me truly.
Is not this man's death against Prothoënor's a worthwhile
exchange?'

In the poem's descriptions of ransom arrangements—all enacted in
the past or imagined for the future—materials valued as treasure are trans-
ferred between individuals as recompense based on equivalent worth:[12] one
of Priam's sons, Lykaon, for example, describes having been sold in the past
by his captor Achilles for one hundred oxen and subsequently ransomed for
treasure worth three hundred oxen. But in such battlefield dialogue as I have
been referring to, warriors' *deaths* are figuratively measured against each
other to meet a standard of parity, as though with an eye to making an appropriate exchange.

Thus—as in the examples of Agamemnon and Nestor cited above—
characters in the *Iliad* do not speak of inflicting punishment on each other,
or even of hurting each other or making each other suffer, but rather of
making each other *pay*. They exact payment for sorrow endured, for
outrage borne. The priest Chryses, at the opening of the poem, appeals to
Apollo to "make the Danaans pay for his tears" by visiting a plague on them
(τίσειαν Δαναοὶ ἐμὰ δάκρυα σοῖσι βέλεσσιν, *Iliad* I 42). Ares threatens to
exact payment for the death of his son Askalaphos (*Iliad* XV 116), Achilles
for Patroclus' death (*Iliad* XIX 208; XXI 134); Menelaos will make Paris pay
(*Iliad* III 28, 351, 366). Most stunning is the dialogue in Book XI between the
two sons of the Trojan ally Antimachos and Agamemnon, who captures
them together. Antimachos, the narrative tells us, had been bought off by
Paris, and so opposed the return of Helen to the Argives. His sons plead for
their lives, offering 'appropriate' ransom (ἄξια... ἄποινα) and 'boundless'
ransom (ἀπερείσι' ἄποινα). This, they say, their father will be glad to pay.
Agamemnon replies that their father will not pay for their lives; *their lives*
will be payment for his outrage (λώβη):

'εἰ μὲν δὴ Ἀντιμάχοιο δαΐφρονος υἱέες ἐστόν,
ὅς ποτ' ἐνὶ Τρώων ἀγορῇ Μενέλαον ἄνωγεν,

---

[12] Gernet 1968:93–137 points out the parallel between objects used in gift-exchange and those
used for ransom: "Les objets donnés en prix appartiennent à une catégorie assez large, mais
assez définie. On les retrouve, eux ou leurs analogues, dans plusieurs séries parallèles—
cadeaux coutumiers, présents d'hospitalité, rançons, offrandes aux dieux, part du mort et
objets déposés dans des tombes des chefs. Dans l'ensemble, ce sont ceux qui font la matière
d'un commerce noble" (96).

ἀγγελίην ἐλθόντα σὺν ἀντιθέῳ 'Οδυσῆϊ
αὖθι κατακτεῖναι μηδ' ἐξέμεν ἂψ ἐς Ἀχαιούς,
νῦν μὲν δὴ τοῦ πατρὸς ἀεικέα τείσετε λώβην.'

Iliad XI 138–142

'If in truth you are the sons of wise Antimachos,
that man who once among the Trojans assembled advised them
that Menelaos, who came as envoy with godlike Odysseus,
should be murdered on the spot nor let go back to the Achaians,
so now your mutilation shall punish the shame of your father.'

A specific kind of payment is that designated by the term ποινή. Ποινή in actual practice denotes a specific recompense, often in gold, paid by an individual as a blood-price to the next-of-kin of a man who has been slain. The practice is referred to, for example, by Ajax, who reproaches Achilles for his rejection of Agamemnon's grandiose offer in Book IX. Achilles, Ajax says, is intransigent, impossible; for, after all, a man will accept a blood-price (ποινή) from the killer of his brother or his child:

νηλής· καὶ μέν τίς τε κασιγνήτοιο φονῆος
ποινὴν ἢ οὗ παιδὸς ἐδέξατο τεθνηῶτος·

Iliad IX 632–636

Pitiless. And yet a man takes from his brother's slayer
the blood price, or the price for a child who was killed.

Or again, a ποινή is at issue in the famous scene on the shield made by Hephaestus for Achilles:

λαοὶ δ' εἰν ἀγορῇ ἔσαν ἀθρόοι· ἔνθα δὲ νεῖκος
ὠρώρει, δύο δ' ἄνδρες ἐνείκεον εἵνεκα ποινῆς
ἀνδρὸς ἀποφθιμένου· ὁ μὲν εὔχετο πάντ' ἀποδοῦναι
δήμῳ πιφαύσκων, ὁ δ' ἀναίνετο μηδὲν ἑλέσθαι.

Iliad XVIII 497–500

The people were assembled in the market place, where a quarrel
had arisen, and two men were disputing over the blood price
for a man who had been killed. One man promised full restitution
in a public statement, but the other refused and would accept
nothing.

But ποινή generates a metaphor that encapsulates the economy of the battle-field, recalling the kind of negotiation Idomeneus questions Deiphobus about, in which one death is weighed against another with the question "is this a suitable exchange?" When Patroclus enters the battle in Achilles' place, he is said to kill many Trojans to exact ποινή for many Achaean deaths:

Πάτροκλος δ' ἐπεὶ οὖν πρώτας ἐπέκερσε φάλαγγας,
ἂψ ἐπὶ νῆας ἔεργε παλιμπετές, οὐδὲ πόληος
εἴα ἱεμένους ἐπιβαινέμεν, ἀλλὰ μεσηγὺ
νηῶν καὶ ποταμοῦ καὶ τείχεος ὑψηλοῖο
κτεῖνε μεταΐσσων, πολέων δ' ἀπετίνυτο ποινήν.

Iliad XVI 394–398

But Patroklos, when he had cut away their first battalions,
turned back to pin them against the ships, and would not allow
    them
to climb back into their city though they strained for it, but
    sweeping
through the space between the ships, the high wall, and the river,
made havoc and exacted from them the blood price for many.

When the Trojan Akamas kills the Argive Promachos as the latter attempts to drag off the corpse of Akamas' brother, Akamas asserts that his opponent's death means that the ποινή for his fallen brother does not remain unpaid (ἄτιτος) for long:

'φράζεσθ' ὡς ὑμῖν Πρόμαχος δεδμημένος εὕδει
ἔγχει ἐμῷ, ἵνα μή τι κασιγνήτοιό γε ποινὴ
δηρὸν ἄτιτος ἔῃ·'

Iliad XIV 482–484

'Think how Promachos sleeps among you, beaten down under
my spear, so that punishment for my brother may not go
long unpaid.'

Because the language in which these exchanges are figured belongs to the narrative as well as to the divine and human characters, the *Iliad* enlarges its perspective to view such transactions not as isolated, but as integrated in an ongoing cycle sustained by its own momentum. Thus the poem says that the ποινή for Patroclus' death at Hector's hands will be the deaths of many Trojan fighters. Yet Hector's success itself constituted recompense in the first place. At *Iliad* XVII 201–208 Zeus meditates on Hector's dressing for battle in Achilles' armor and foresees Hector's death. He reflects:

181

'ἆ δείλ', οὐδέ τί τοι θάνατος καταθύμιός ἐστιν,
ὃς δή τοι σχεδὸν εἶσι· σὺ δ' ἄμβροτα τεύχεα δύνεις
ἀνδρὸς ἀριστῆος, τόν τε τρομέουσι καὶ ἄλλοι·
τοῦ δὴ ἑταῖρον ἔπεφνες ἐνηέα τε κρατερόν τε,
τεύχεα δ' οὐ κατὰ κόσμον ἀπὸ κρατός τε καὶ ὤμων
εἵλευ· ἀτάρ τοι νῦν γε μέγα κράτος ἐγγυαλίξω,
τῶν ποινὴν ὅ τοι οὔ τι μάχης ἐκ νοστήσαντι
δέξεται Ἀνδρομάχη κλυτὰ τεύχεα Πηλεΐωνος.'

'Ah, poor wretch! There is no thought of death in your mind now,
     and yet death stands
close beside you as you put on the immortal armour
of a surpassing man. There are others who tremble before him.
Now you have killed this man's dear friend, who was strong and
     gentle,
and taken the armour, as you should not have done, from his
     shoulders
and head. Still for the present I will invest you with great
     strength
to make up for it that you will not come home out of the fighting,
nor Andromache take from your hands the glorious arms of
     Achilleus.'

When Akamas refers to the ποινή for his brother, therefore, or when Euphorbos takes aim at Menelaos and calls out, "Then, lordly Menelaos, you must now pay the penalty for my brother, whom you killed" (νῦν μὲν δή, Μενέλαε διοτρεφές, ἦ μάλα τείσεις / γνωτὸν ἐμόν, τὸν ἔπεφνες, *Iliad* XVII 34–35), they reaffirm their participation in a system where debit and credit are constantly renegotiated, toward a settlement that is perpetually readjusted, a system that can function only because it is reciprocal—and collaborative.

The collaborative basis of these transactions is fundamental to their role within a larger framework of exchange. It represents enmity as partnership, in which each "pays the other back"—a searing irony that the warriors exploit in their dialogue. We see it in recurrent formulations: (to paraphrase) "you'll give me εὖχος but your ψυχή will go to Hades" or "you'll give me εὖχος and I'll give you φόνος"; these describe an economy of circulation where everything is redistributed and nothing, so to speak, is lost.[13]

---

[13] These formulations of recycling recall the warnings repeatedly issued to one's allies that consist of reminding them that what is pain for them will be the enemy's χάρμα 'joy'.

The implications of such a relationship of collaboration in exchange between enemies are extended in the ironizing, metaphorical treatment of the notion of κόρος as 'satisfaction'. For the response to the enemy's demands for payment is the offer to give him satisfaction, however insatiable he may be. Agamemnon, in Book VII, says that the Achaean chiefs who volunteer to meet Hector in a μονομαχία will make Hector happy, *happy to run*, for all that he cannot get *enough* of battle. Idomeneus, at *Iliad* XIII 315ff, says that the two Ajaxes will give Hector a sufficiency of war—*enough* war. And Achilles in Book XIX promises that he will not cease fighting until he has driven a sufficiency of war on the Trojans, whom Menelaos in his harangue in Book XIII calls ἀκόρητοι μαχῆς 'insatiable of battle' and ἀκόρητοι ἀυτῆς 'insatiable of the war cry'. Achilles will give them "enough."

But to give your enemy "enough," we understand, means to give him too much. To satiate his insatiability means to overwhelm him, to destroy him. And this, we learn, is how the Iliadic economy functions—equilibrium is destabilized, preventing the scales from settling evenly into those freeze-frames described above; thus more payments can be called for, more exchanges generated. Your struggle with the enemy for equal shares will always remain a struggle in which neither antagonist is finally satisfied.

And it is through the figure of Achilles that we learn it—Achilles whom the narrative calls, to his face, insatiable, in one of the few instances when it addresses him in the second person. For it is Achilles who says to the Trojans at *Iliad* XXI 128ff, "Die, perish, until you all pay for the death of Patroclus": only the deaths of *all* the Trojans will pay for the death of Patroclus. But to say this is as much as to say that Achilles does not buy in, so to speak, to the figurative trades, the rhetoric of reciprocity, and the constructed system of even exchange that the warriors presuppose and reinforce.

Achilles, who begins the poem by being preoccupied with the problem of appropriate distribution and, in particular, adequate compensation, is brought to see—and to expose—the incommensurability of what any hero does and what he receives. In his speech to the embassy from Agamemnon in Book IX, he rejects the "deal" Agamemnon proposes:[14]

---

[14] Through Achilles' hyperboles—like those at *Iliad* IX 379ff, or at XXI 128ff—and through his refusal, we are reminded of Mauss' emphatic observation that in archaic societies exchange procedures must above all appear to be "voluntary, disinterested, and spontaneous," while in fact giving, receiving, and return-giving are precisely calculated and entirely "obligatory and interested," compelled by the most stringent sanctions (1954:1); that reciprocal giving, moreover, must be treated as though it were perfectly symmetrical, as though gift and

οὐδ' εἴ μοι δεκάκις τε καὶ εἰκοσάκις τόσα δοίη
ὅσσα τέ οἱ νῦν ἔστι, καὶ εἴ ποθεν ἄλλα γένοιτο,
οὐδ' ὅσ' ἐς Ὀρχομενὸν ποτινίσεται, οὐδ' ὅσα Θήβας
Αἰγυπτίας, ὅθι πλεῖστα δόμοις ἐν κτήματα κεῖται,
αἵ θ' ἑκατόμπυλοί εἰσι, διηκόσιοι δ' ἀν' ἑκάστας
ἀνέρες ἐξοιχνεῦσι σὺν ἵπποισιν καὶ ὄχεσφιν·
οὐδ' εἴ μοι τόσα δοίη ὅσα ψάμαθός τε κόνις τε,
οὐδέ κεν ὣς ἔτι θυμὸν ἐμὸν πείσει' Ἀγαμέμνων

Iliad IX 379–386

Not if he gave me ten times as much, and twenty times over
as he possesses now, not if more should come to him
    from elsewhere,
or gave all that is brought in to Orchomenos, all that is brought in
to Thebes of Egypt, where the greatest possessions lie up
    in the houses,
Thebes of the hundred gates, where through each of the
    gates two hundred
fighting men come forth to war with horses and chariots;
not if he gave me gifts as many as the sand or the dust is,
not even so would Agamemnon have his way with my spirit...

For Achilles only μοῖρα is ἴση—that is, only the destiny that comes to us all in the end is "equal"—and distributes payments evenhandedly:

ἴση μοῖρα μένοντι, καὶ εἰ μάλα τις πολεμίζοι·
ἐν δὲ ἰῇ τιμῇ ἠμὲν κακὸς ἠδὲ καὶ ἐσθλός·
κάτθαν' ὁμῶς ὅ τ' ἀεργὸς ἀνὴρ ὅ τε πολλὰ ἐοργώς.

Iliad IX 318–320

---

counter-gift were on a par; whereas in fact they will always be unequal; and all-important shifts in prestige and authority will depend upon, and reflect, that differential. One giver (or one community of givers) will inevitably outgive, and dominate, the other. Pierre Bourdieu, based on his field work in Algeria, speaks of this disjunction between the "social representation" of exchange or the formal behavior governing it, and its exigent, compulsory reality, as necessary "misrecognition"—"*méconnaissance*": "If the system is to work, the agents must not be entirely unaware of the truth of their exchanges...while at the same time they must refuse to know and above all to recognize it." Achilles forces acknowledgement of the fiction of exchange or, as Bourdieu puts it, the "authorized oversight," the "collectively maintained and approved self-deception without which symbolic exchange, a fake circulation of fake coin, could not operate" (1977:3–6).

Fate is the same for the man who holds back, the same if he
    fights hard.
We are all held in a single honour, the brave with the
    weaklings.
A man dies still if he has done nothing, as one who has
    done much.

But the other "misrecognition" that the poem identifies, also through the figure of Achilles, is the one supported by the metaphors of economic activity, whereby one death can be viewed as traded for, or as "paying for," another—as though there could be parity, recuperation of damages, a stable, balanced reciprocity in the world of the battlefield, in the realm of suffering. The imagery of economic exchange makes that notion possible, concealing the harrowing, irremediable losses. For Achilles the only equation is that between himself and Patroclus, for whom he laments:

Πάτροκλος, τὸν ἐγὼ περὶ πάντων τῖον ἑταίρων,
ἶσον ἐμῇ κεφαλῇ·

Iliad XVIII 81–82

Patroklos, whom I loved beyond all other companions,
    as well as my own life...

Achilles, by the end of the poem, exposes the deficiencies of a conventional calculus expressed in the language of exchange—in metaphors of trading with weights and measures. As he explains to Priam in the description of the two πίθοι, suffering mortals share what is distributed unequally—and they suffer alike.

We might say that Achilles, by repudiating the economy of social relations and its metaphors, finally removes himself from the life of the poem. For the others, however, the metaphors of exchange have their own regenerative momentum. We see this in the paradox of the theme of enemies as partners who give each other what each needs. Your friends pity you, grieve for you, avenge you; but it is your enemy—your killer—who speaks your disappointed hopes. Idomeneus, for example, addresses the corpse of Othryoneus, whom he has just slain. He tells Othryoneus' story: the promises, now never to be fulfilled, by which Othryoneus was to have received Priam's daughter in marriage in return for beating the Greeks back from the city. He suggests to the corpse that the Achaeans will act as matchmakers for him in return for his services:

"Ὀθρυονεῦ, περὶ δή σε βροτῶν αἰνίζομ' ἀπάντων,
εἰ ἐτεὸν δὴ πάντα τελευτήσεις ὅσ' ὑπέστης
Δαρδανίδῃ Πριάμῳ· ὁ δ' ὑπέσχετο θυγατέρα ἥν.
καί κέ τοι ἡμεῖς ταῦτά γ' ὑποσχόμενοι τελέσαιμεν,
δοῖμεν δ' Ἀτρεΐδαο θυγατρῶν εἶδος ἀρίστην
Ἄργεος ἐξαγαγόντες ὀπυιέμεν, εἴ κε σὺν ἄμμιν
Ἰλίου ἐκπέρσῃς εὖ ναιόμενον πτολίεθρον.
ἀλλ' ἔπε', ὄφρ' ἐπὶ νηυσὶ συνώμεθα ποντοπόροισιν
ἀμφὶ γάμῳ, ἐπεὶ οὔ τοι ἐεδνωταὶ κακοί εἰμεν.'

Iliad XIII 374–382

'Othryoneus, I congratulate you beyond all others
if it is here that you will bring to pass what you promised
to Dardanian Priam, who in turn promised you his daughter.
See now, we also would make you a promise, and we would fulfill it;
we would give you the loveliest of Atreides' daughters,
and bring her here from Argos to be your wife, if you joined us
and helped us storm the strong-founded city of Ilium.
Come then with me, so we can meet by our seafaring vessels
about a marriage; we here are not bad matchmakers for you.'

Such parting taunts as that of Idomeneus (or we might think of Patroclus' taunt to the corpse of Cebriones at *Iliad* XVI 745ff.) assume, in the metaphors they draw out, the intimacy of a shared code with a common currency, both economic and linguistic. But, as I have argued elsewhere,[15] the language that renders enemies as friends, and the reverse, puts an instrument of shattering effectiveness into the heroes' hands. Such densely figurative language evokes a complex lifeworld precisely to annihilate it. And such exchanges dramatize the terrible power of a reciprocity exercised unto and beyond death: the triumphant hero will address his dead enemy precisely to recall him back into life to be perpetually destroyed—because perpetually imaginable, sharable, and thus annihilable in mutually recognized terms.

---

[15] *Les Amis mortels* (this volume).

Works Cited

Benveniste, E. 1969. *Le Vocabulaire des Institutions Indo-Européennes.* Paris.

Bourdieu, P. 1977. "The Objective Limits of Objectivism." Chapter 1 of P. Bourdieu, *Outline of a Theory of Practice*, trans. R. Nice, 1-58. Cambridge Studies in Social Anthropology 16. Cambridge.

Felson, N. and L. Slatkin. 2004. "Gender and Homeric Epic." In *The Cambridge Companion to Homer*, ed. R. Fowler, 91-114. Cambridge.

Gernet, L. 1968. *Anthropologie de la Grèce antique.* Paris.

King, B. Forthcoming. *The End of Adventure.*

Loraux, N. 1987. "Le lien de la division." *Le cahier du Collège international de Philosophie* 4:101-124. Reprinted as Chapter 4 of N. Loraux, *La Cité Divisée: l'oubli dans la mémoire d'Athènes* (Paris, 1997), 90–130. Also reprinted as "The Bond of Division," in N. Loraux, *The Divided City. On Memory and Forgetting in Ancient Athens* (New York, 2002), trans. C. Pache and J. Fort, 93–123.

Mauss, M. 1954. *The Gift: Forms and Functions in Archaic Societies.* Trans. I. Cunnison. Reprint 1970. London. Originally published as "Essai sur le Don. Forme et raison de l'échange dans les sociétés archaïques." *L'Année sociologique* seconde série 1:30–186.

Reden, S. von. 1995. *Exchange in Ancient Greece.* London.

Wees, H. van. 1992. *Status Warriors: War, Violence, and Society in Homer and History.* Dutch Monographs on Ancient History and Archaeology 9. Leiden.

———. 2004. *Greek Warfare: Myths and Realities.* London.

Wilson, D. F. 2002. *Ransom, Revenge, and Heroic Identity in the Iliad.* Cambridge.

Measuring Authority, Authoritative Measures
Hesiod's *Works and Days*[1]

Observe due measure: and best in all things is the right time and right amount.[2]

Hesiod, *Works and Days* 694

Ἥλιος οὐχ ὑπερβήσεται μέτρα· εἰ δὲ μή,
Ἐρινύες μιν Δίκης ἐπίκουροι ἐξευρήσουσιν...

Heraclitus fr. 94D-K

The sun will not transgress his measures. If he does, the Furies, ministers of Justice, will find him out.[3]

I F IN GREEK TRAGEDY, the Furies pursue human beings who violate the laws of kinship—of family exchanges properly conducted, taboos properly observed—they pursue, in Heraclitus, the potentially transgressive sun. Fragment 94 of this pre-Socratic philosopher (c. 500 BCE) offers an apparent paradox, not so much in its use of mythological personae to formulate a theory of cosmic structure (a practice common to all surviving 6th century natural philosophy) as in its account of the relations among these figures. Throughout early Greek literature, the all-seeing and all-revealing sun bears witness to every action in both the human and the divine domains, functioning as the ultimate monitor of events that even the gods wish to conceal. Here, however, the sun's own celestial operations are themselves subject to the scrutiny of the shadowy, chthonic Furies, irascible informants whose realm lies deep within the earth.

---

[1] This is a slightly revised version of Chapter 1, *The Moral Authority of Nature* eds. L. Daston and F. Vidal (Chicago: 2002).
[2] μέτρα φυλάσσεσθαι· καιρὸς δ' ἐπὶ πᾶσιν ἄριστος. Translations of the *Works and Days* are based on Evelyn-White 1929.
[3] As translated by Kahn 1993:49.

Why then, in Heraclitus' book on the structure of the cosmos, are these dark and vengeful spirits imagined to oversee the movement of the sun? And equally puzzling, why is Justice concerned with the passage of the day? At the center of this conjunction of radiance and obscurity, of sky and land, of the ephemeral journey of the sun (who, as Heraclitus tells us in another passage, is new every day) and the eternal, inflexible reckoning of the Furies, allies of Justice, is the element on which everything is staked: measure (*metra*).

Heraclitus's formulation posits terms, concepts, and problematic relations that I propose to consider in the following pages, in exploring the relationship of nature to morality within the context of the philosopher's antecedents among the poets of early (pre-classical) Greece. I hope to show that in early Greek thought and poetics, both values and norms—whether proposed as "cultural" or "natural" or "divine"—are derived through and embedded in a rich discourse and figurative complex of what Hesiod invokes as "due measure," which Heraclitus revisits here. For Greek thinkers of the archaic period, right order—in the cosmos, between gods and men, among humans, between men and the earth—is not, as it were, *given* or transparently natural, but is rather in need of extensive poetic elaboration and explanation. For these writers, the processes and patterns of nature are read as a system ideally in equilibrium. Human beings are enjoined to model their behavior on, and to accord their actions with, the equilibrating logic of nature. That nature is seen to manifest such equilibrium, however violently its upheavals may appear at any time, is of course a feat of human cognition.[4] The values encoded in the notion of measure thus involve a transference from the nature that is their imagined source, to the social and ethical order that is the explicit concern of such poets as Hesiod. To examine the reciprocity of nature and human values, I follow Heraclitus back to the tradition of didactic literature represented by the earliest extant Greek example of what is classified as a "wisdom" text: Hesiod's *Works and Days*, a poem from the Greek mainland in the 8th century BCE, which stands as the first Greek text we possess that is overtly and explicitly moralizing.

In contrast to the reticence of Homeric epic, which is free of narrative judgment about, for example, the origins and conduct of the Trojan War, the *Works and Days* offers instruction on how to live an orderly and productive life. Hesiod's poem imagines a personal dispute as the occasion for a meditation on ethical behavior and on the role of justice in the construction of social

---

[4] For archaic thinkers' turn to nature as a cognitive model as well as a field for perception, see Finley 1965.

order. The *Works and Days*, in some eight hundred verses, takes the form of a set of instructions delivered by the poet to his brother Perses, who, in the division of their joint inheritance (so the poet tells us), has unfairly seized an unequal share. In making his illegitimate grab, the poem complains, Perses has been supported by corrupt leaders (kings) who also function, as was customary, as arbiters and judges; both Perses and the judges constitute the poem's purported addressees:

> ...let us settle our dispute here with true judgment which is of Zeus
> and is perfect. For we had already divided our inheritance, but you
> seized the greater share and carried it off, greatly swelling the glory
> of our bribe-swallowing lords who love to judge such a cause as this. [5]
> *Works and Days* 35–39

In enjoining its audience(s), both within the poem and outside it,[6] to eschew the fecklessness of a Perses and the greed of those in power, the poem invokes cosmic patterns of the natural world within the context of defining human nature and the human condition.

Notably, there is no abstract term "Nature" to designate the natural world in the literature of this period in Greece; the word *phûsis* never appears in Hesiod, nor ever in this sense in Homer.[7] What "nature" is and how it operates emerges from accounts of its specific, concrete individual elements, and from their presence in a range of tropes, including metaphor, personification, riddle, fable, and proverb. Nature is most often represented by the characteristics and seasonal processes of "the earth," through which the poem figures questions of morality and social order. Thus the poem tells us that

> Neither famine nor disaster ever haunt men who do true justice,
> but light-heartedly they tend the fields which are all their care.
> The earth bears them victual in plenty, and on the mountains the
> oak bears acorns upon the top and bees in the midst. Their woolly

---

[5] ...ἀλλ' αὖθι διακρινώμεθα νεῖκος
ἰθείῃσι δίκῃς, αἵ τ' ἐκ Διός εἰσιν ἄρισται.
ἤδη μὲν γὰρ κλῆρον ἐδασσάμεθ', ἀλλὰ τὰ πολλὰ
ἁρπάζων ἐφόρεις μέγα κυδαίνων βασιλῆας
δωροφάγους, οἳ τήνδε δίκην ἐθέλουσι δίκασσαι.

[6] On the issue of the audiences (external and internal) of the *Works and Days*, as well as questions of persona and identity, see Griffiths 1983.

[7] Similarly, neither Hesiod nor Homer uses the term *kosmos* (κόσμος) as an abstraction meaning "unified world order," as do sixth-century natural philosophers.

sheep are laden with fleeces; their women bear children who resemble their parents...[8]

Works and Days 230–235

Significantly, the man who is identified as practicing "true justice" is not a judge but a farmer. Because humankind must toil to earn a livelihood from the earth, farming serves, in the *Works and Days*, as the governing trope for the human condition. The "Works" of the poem's title translates the (plural) noun *erga*, which in early Greek poetry specifically denotes agricultural work and also occurs with the meaning of "tilled fields." The *Works and Days*, however, does not aim to teach lessons about farming.[9] In its concern with justice and ethical behavior, the poem uses the farmer to think with because it is through farming that humans are most immersed in natural processes, and the farmer is the human type who most obviously must accord his behavior with the exigencies and contingencies of nature's patterns.

Although Hesiod refers to "true justice," justice itself is never defined in the literature of this period; rather, justice emerges in the passage above as homologous with the order of nature, which it both generates and imitates. Nature cooperates with, as well as rewards, the man who does "true justice." Here we see a crucial conceptual link: the order of justice and the order of nature reciprocally substantiate each other.

Hesiod's account of the just farmer rewarded by plenty resembles the poem's vision of life in the earliest phase of mortal existence, the Golden Age:

First of all the immortal gods who dwell on Olympus made a golden race of mortal men who lived in the time of Kronos when he was reigning in heaven. And they lived like gods without sorrow of heart, remote and free from toil and grief: wretched age rested not on them; but with legs and arms never failing they took pleasure in feasting beyond the reach of all evils...and they had all good things; for the fruitful earth of its own accord bore them fruit in abundance and unstinting. They lived at ease and peace upon

---

[8] οὐδέ ποτ' ἰθυδίκῃσι μετ' ἀνδράσι λιμὸς ὀπηδεῖ
οὐδ' ἄτη, θαλίης δὲ μεμηλότα ἔργα νέμονται.
τοῖσι φέρει μὲν γαῖα πολὺν βίον, οὔρεσι δὲ δρῦς
ἄκρη μέν τε φέρει βαλάνους, μέσση δὲ μελίσσας·
εἰροπόκοι δ' ὄιες μαλλοῖς καταβεβρίθασιν·
τίκτουσιν δὲ γυναῖκες ἐοικότα τέκνα γονεῦσιν·
[9] See Nelson 1998.

their lands with many good things, rich in flocks and loved by the blessed gods.[10]

Works and Days 109–120

In what way can our collaboration with nature in that long-vanished past be reproduced through the efforts of the farmer, laboring in the here-and-now? What is the relationship between the world measured by days and structured by work, in which Hesiod's poem plants us, and that golden era of spontaneously flourishing nature and proximity to the divine, in which aging—the passage of time—was not a burden?

From the very outset, the *Works and Days* establishes our relationship to nature by framing it temporally, locating it within a mythic history of the evolved human condition—or to put it another way, the poem represents the evolution of the human condition precisely as a function of our changed relationship to "the earth" and its productions. And indeed it is this change that creates the very notion and experience of temporality and the dependence of human circumstances upon it. The *Works and Days* presents both work and the day as governing conditions for our lives; yet both work and the day—our laboring condition and the temporality in and through which we live, work, sacrifice, reproduce, and die—require explanation. What is presented as given, then, must also be explained.

The Hesiodic tradition—encompassing both the *Works and Days* and the *Theogony*—is both cosmological and didactic: it accounts for the way things are (what is), how they came to be so, and what this cosmic arrangement requires of us. In the *Works and Days*, description and explanation shift almost imperceptibly into prescription; the "is" modulates into the "ought," the given into the enjoined. Although Hesiod presents his narratives—the mythic content of the *Works and Days*—and his injunctions as equally authoritative, this modulation between mythic explanation and normative exhortation is

---

[10] χρύσεον μὲν πρώτιστα γένος μερόπων ἀνθρώπων
ἀθάνατοι ποίησαν Ὀλύμπια δώματ' ἔχοντες.
οἳ μὲν ἐπὶ Κρόνου ἦσαν, ὅτ' οὐρανῷ ἐμβασίλευεν·
ὥστε θεοὶ δ' ἔζωον ἀκηδέα θυμὸν ἔχοντες
νόσφιν ἄτερ τε πόνων καὶ ὀιζύος· οὐδέ τι δειλὸν
γῆρας ἐπῆν, αἰεὶ δὲ πόδας καὶ χεῖρας ὁμοῖοι
τέρποντ' ἐν θαλίῃσι κακῶν ἔκτοσθεν ἁπάντων·
...ἐσθλὰ δὲ πάντα
τοῖσιν ἔην· καρπὸν δ' ἔφερε ζείδωρος ἄρουρα
αὐτομάτη πολλόν τε καὶ ἄφθονον· οἳ δ' ἐθελημοὶ
ἥσυχοι ἔργ' ἐνέμοντο σὺν ἐσθλοῖσιν πολέεσσιν.
ἀφνειοὶ μήλοισι, φίλοι μακάρεσσι θεοῖσιν.

not seamless: the coordination of explanation and prescription constitutes, in fact, the work of the poem's measures.

For Hesiod, the discourse of measure mediates between the "is" and the "ought," coordinating notions of timeliness and seasonality, as well as prescriptions for good conduct. The supreme ought of the *Works and Days* is expressed in the poet's exhortation to his brother Perses: "Work, foolish Perses! Work the work which the gods ordained for men..."[11] This imperative marks not only the route Perses should take but also the condition human beings have had thrust upon them—for as Hesiod makes plain, human beings did not always have to work. The authority of the poem's injunction to work thus requires an explanation, an accounting, not only of why Perses should work but indeed why we all must do so. It is not only that men should work; they must work, as human beings who are now subject to need. Hesiod's *Works and Days* thus conjoins a mode of explanation (why we must work) to a rhetoric of exhortation (work!).

For, as Hesiod tells us, it was not always so. From the description of life in the Golden Age, we learn that originally humankind feasted with the gods and lived as the gods do, without toil or sorrow or old age, sharing all good things that the earth shared with them. In the Golden Age, men lived in effortless harmony with the earth, in which the "ground" of their lives was spontaneous bounty. In that epoch, there was no need for work; scarcity was unknown, as were contention, "toil and grief," and aging.

This glorious myth of origins is to be read as the negative image of the *now*:

For the gods keep [the means of] life (*bios*) hidden from men. Otherwise in a day you would easily accomplish enough to have a living for a full year even without working; immediately you could put away your rudder over the smoke, and the work of the ox and patient mule would be over.[12]

Works and Days 42–46

The circumstance that necessitates work also necessitates the explanation of both work and life: namely, that the gods have hidden from mortals

---

[11]   ...ἐργάζευ, νήπιε Πέρση,
ἔργα, τά τ' ἀνθρώποισι θεοὶ διετεκμήραντο... (397–398)

[12]   κρύψαντες γὰρ ἔχουσι θεοὶ βίον ἀνθρώποισιν·
ῥηιδίως γάρ κεν καὶ ἐπ' ἤματι ἐργάσσαιο,
ὥστε σε κεἰς ἐνιαυτὸν ἔχειν καὶ ἀεργὸν ἐόντα·
αἶψά κε πηδάλιον μὲν ὑπὲρ καπνοῦ καταθεῖο,
ἔργα βοῶν δ' ἀπόλοιτο καὶ ἡμιόνων ταλαεργῶν.

their means of life—*bios* is the term that designates both livelihood and life itself. The *bios* of human beings—life, and the means of life—is concealed from them, such that they must discover both the means of life and the *meaning* of it; they must learn where *bios* is located in the cosmic scheme—or, to put it more precisely, where it has been relocated. For at one time, the *Works and Days* recounts, men and gods began on the same terms:[13]

> ...I will sum you up another story well and skillfully—and you lay it up in your heart—how the gods and mortal men sprang from one source. [14]
>
> *Works and Days* 106–107

Now, however, the defining condition of human existence is not only that men must age, suffer, and die, but that first they must struggle to achieve their *bios*. Men, moreover, must strive to understand the arrangement by which they and the gods now coexist; no longer is this arrangement self-evident.

Why have the gods hidden the *bios* from men? The answer begins with a story of bad measuring, of distorted equilibrium, which provokes a quarrel between Zeus and Prometheus. Hesiodic tradition narrates the story twice. It has been demonstrated that the account of Zeus and Prometheus in *Works and Days* presupposes and alludes to the version of the story as given in Hesiod's *Theogony*; it is from the combined accounts that we may assemble the entire narrative.[15] From the two poems we learn that the unity of men and gods was disrupted by an unequal division of a feast that was held at a place called Mekone:

> For when the gods and mortal men were making a division at Mekone, even then Prometheus eagerly cut up a great ox and set portions before them, trying to deceive the mind of Zeus. Before the rest he set flesh and innards rich with fat upon the hide, covering them with an ox paunch; but for Zeus he put the white bones dressed up with treacherous skill and covered with shining fat. Then the father of men and of gods said to him:

[13] At fr. 1, Merkelbach and West 1967, men and gods are said originally to have taken their places together at shared feasts.
[14] ...ἕτερόν τοι ἐγὼ λόγον ἐκκορυφώσω
εὖ καὶ ἐπισταμένως· σὺ δ' ἐνὶ φρεσὶ βάλλεο σῇσιν.
ὡς ὁμόθεν γεγάασι θεοὶ θνητοί τ' ἄνθρωποι.
[15] See the valuable study in Vernant 1988.

"Son of Iapetus, most glorious of all lords, my dear, how unevenly you have divided the portions!"[16]

Theogony 535–544

Prometheus' intervention on men's behalf, whereby he misrepresents the shares to their benefit, prompts Zeus to retaliate by withholding the power of fire from men, reserving it for the gods' use; whereupon Prometheus in turn steals it for men. As the *Works and Days* tells us:

But Zeus angered in his heart hid it, because scheming Prometheus deceived him; so Zeus devised calamitous sorrows against men. He hid fire; but the clever son of Iapetus stole it again for men from Zeus the contriver in a hollow narthex, so that Zeus who delights in thunder did not notice it. But afterwards cloud-gathering Zeus said to him in anger:

"Son of Iapetus, beyond all others in cunning, you rejoice that you have outsmarted me and stolen fire—a great bane for you yourself and for men who shall come after. But I will give men in exchange for fire [*anti puros*] an evil thing in which they may all take pleasure in their hearts while they embrace their own destruction."

So said the father of men and gods, and laughed out loud. And he bade renowned Hephaestus as speedily as possible to mix earth with water and to put in it the voice and strength of a human being, likening her face to the immortal goddesses, a beautiful, desirable maiden...And he called this woman Pandora, because all those who live on Olympus gave her as a gift, a bane to men who eat bread....

---

[16] καὶ γὰρ ὅτ' ἐκρίνοντο θεοὶ θνητοί τ' ἄνθρωποι
Μηκώνῃ, τότ' ἔπειτα μέγαν βοῦν πρόφρονι θυμῷ
δασσάμενος προέθηκε, Διὸς νόον ἐξαπαφίσκων.
τοῖς μὲν γὰρ σάρκας τε καὶ ἔγκατα πίονα δημῷ
ἐν ῥινῷ κατέθηκε καλύψας γαστρὶ βοείῃ,
τῷ δ' αὖτ' ὀστέα λευκὰ βοὸς δολίῃ ἐπὶ τέχνῃ
εὐθετίσας κατέθηκε καλύψας ἀργέτι δημῷ.
δὴ τότε μιν προσέειπε πατὴρ ἀνδρῶν τε θεῶν τε·
Ἰαπετιονίδη, πάντων ἀριδείκετ' ἀνάκτων,
ὦ πέπον, ὡς ἑτεροζήλως διεδάσσαο μοίρας.

...For before this the tribes of men lived on earth remote and free
from troubles and hard toil and painful sicknesses which bring
upon men their deaths...[17]

Works and Days 47–63, 80–82, 90–92

The autonomy of mortals as a group, their separateness, thus begins over
an asymmetrical apportionment. Because of an unequal division, men must
live divided from the gods; men must also begin their vexed relationship
with Pandora and her kind. We may understand the Prometheus/Pandora
story, in the Hesiodic version, as prompting Zeus to establish not only justice
but a new mechanism for relations between gods and men, profoundly far-
reaching both in itself and as an example for human relations.

This cosmic reorganization simultaneously moves men farther
from the gods but, as it were, closer to each other; they become each
others' neighbors. Separated from the gods, they become (relative to life
in the Golden Age) more dependent on the gods, but also on each other.
All-encompassing consequences, needless to say, result from this situation, prominent among which is the development that, separated from the
gods, men will now not only labor by themselves among themselves, but

---

[17] ἀλλὰ Ζεὺς ἔκρυψε χολωσάμενος φρεσὶν ᾗσιν,
ὅττι μιν ἐξαπάτησε Προμηθεὺς ἀγκυλομήτης·
τοὔνεκ' ἄρ' ἀνθρώποισιν ἐμήσατο κήδεα λυγρά.
κρύψε δὲ πῦρ· τὸ μὲν αὖτις ἐὺς πάις Ἰαπετοῖο
ἔκλεψ' ἀνθρώποισι Διὸς πάρα μητιόεντος
ἐν κοΐλῳ νάρθηκι λαθὼν Δία τερπικέραυνον.
τὸν δὲ χολωσάμενος προσέφη νεφεληγερέτα Ζεύς·
Ἰαπετιονίδη, πάντων πέρι μήδεα εἰδώς,
χαίρεις πῦρ κλέψας καὶ ἐμὰς φρένας ἠπεροπεύσας,
σοί τ' αὐτῷ μέγα πῆμα καὶ ἀνδράσιν ἐσσομένοισιν.
τοῖς δ' ἐγὼ ἀντὶ πυρὸς δώσω κακόν, ᾧ κεν ἅπαντες
τέρπωνται κατὰ θυμὸν ἑὸν κακὸν ἀμφαγαπῶντες.
ὣς ἔφατ'· ἐκ δ' ἐγέλασσε πατὴρ ἀνδρῶν τε θεῶν τε.
Ἥφαιστον δ' ἐκέλευσε περικλυτὸν ὅττι τάχιστα
γαῖαν ὕδει φύρειν, ἐν δ' ἀνθρώπου θέμεν αὐδὴν
καὶ σθένος, ἀθανάτῃς δὲ θεῇς εἰς ὦπα ἐΐσκειν
παρθενικῆς καλὸν εἶδος ἐπήρατον·
          ...ὀνόμηνε δὲ τήνδε γυναῖκα
Πανδώρην, ὅτι πάντες Ὀλύμπια δώματ' ἔχοντες
δῶρον ἐδώρησαν, πῆμ' ἀνδράσιν ἀλφηστῇσιν.
. . . .
Πρὶν μὲν γὰρ ζώεσκον ἐπὶ χθονὶ φῦλ' ἀνθρώπων
νόσφιν ἄτερ τε κακῶν καὶ ἄτερ χαλεποῖο πόνοιο
νούσων τ' ἀργαλέων, αἵ τ' ἀνδράσι Κῆρας ἔδωκαν.

will, among themselves, attempt to rectify or overcome unequal apportionment, all the while perpetually recapitulating that original imbalance. Only
through and over time—rather than within any given exchange—is equilibrium achieved.

Hesiod thus represents our mortal, laboring human condition not
simply as a fall—an ontological change—but rather as a qualitative change in
relations between gods, men, and the bounty of the earth. In the new mortal
condition of separation from the gods, the previous model of commen-
sality and sharing equally is replaced by a mode of transaction that will be
the distinctive paradigm for relations at every level and in every arena of
our existence: not collectivity and common property and sharing, Golden
Age-style, nor theft, as practiced by Prometheus, but exchange. Zeus' gift
of Pandora "in exchange for fire" (*anti puros*) or, as the *Theogony* says, "in
exchange for good,"[18] is nothing less than the first, originary gift-exchange.

Because Zeus will now withhold natural fire—the thunderbolt—Pandora
is given in exchange for fire. The emphasis on Pandora as a gift is reiterated a
number of times throughout this passage; the *Works and Days* names her and
etymologizes her name in a line that means not that the gods gave her a gift,
but that they gave her as a gift.[19] In this exchange the gods get their unique and
undivided status as immortals who receive sacrifices and live at ease without
suffering or cares, and men get Pandora—and all the contents of her jar:

> For ere this the tribes of men lived on earth remote and free from
> ills and hard toil and heavy sicknesses which bring the Fates upon
> men; for in misery men grow old quickly. But the woman took
> off the great lid of the jar with her hands and scattered all these
> and her thought caused sorrow and mischief to men. Only Hope
> remained there in an unbreakable home within under the rim of
> the great jar, and did not fly out at the door; for ere that, the lid of
> the jar stopped her, by the will of Aegis-holding Zeus who gathers
> the clouds. But the rest, countless plagues, wander amongst men;
> for earth is full of evils, and the sea is full. Of themselves diseases
> come upon men continually by day and by night, bringing mischief
> to mortals silently...[20]
>
> *Works and Days* 90–104

---

[18] *Theogony* 585. See the important article Arthur 1982, discussing reciprocity in the *Theogony*
with implications for the *Works and Days*.
[19] West 1978:166.
[20] Πρὶν μὲν γὰρ ζώεσκον ἐπὶ χθονὶ φῦλ᾽ ἀνθρώπων

Pandora is given to men "in exchange for fire"; now she and her kind will sear and scorch and consume men. As Zeus puts it, men will embrace their own ruin. In the *Theogony*, Pandora is called a "sheer deception":[21] woman is an insidious subterfuge; a Trojan horse. But Pandora is also given "in exchange for fire" in another sense: in exchange for the pyre. Although men must die and be given to the funeral flames, through Pandora they will generate offspring and be provided with a means of overcoming that burning finality, that ultimate oblivion.[22] In this way the *Works and Days* explains that the quarrel between Zeus and Prometheus alters the terms on which the prerogatives of immortality will be accessible to men. Immortality for mortals will henceforth consist of fame through celebration in epic—of poetic immortalization—and of the capacity to reproduce their own kind, a capacity the immortal gods no longer possess.

Interestingly, how men were produced in the Golden Age in the first place is not clear, but that does not mean that it was a mystery; in Hesiod's account their existence simply doesn't require explanation. On the contrary, it is through the introduction of woman that one's progeny (or the relation

---

νόσφιν ἄτερ τε κακῶν καὶ ἄτερ χαλεποῖο πόνοιο
νούσων τ᾽ ἀργαλέων, αἵ τ᾽ ἀνδράσι Κῆρας ἔδωκαν.
[αἶψα γὰρ ἐν κακότητι βροτοὶ καταγηράσκουσιν.]
ἀλλὰ γυνὴ χείρεσσι πίθου μέγα πῶμ᾽ ἀφελοῦσα
ἐσκέδασ᾽· ἀνθρώποισι δ᾽ ἐμήσατο κήδεα λυγρά.
μούνη δ᾽ αὐτόθι Ἐλπὶς ἐν ἀρρήκτοισι δόμοισιν
ἔνδον ἔμιμνε πίθου ὑπὸ χείλεσιν, οὐδὲ θύραζε
ἐξέπτη· πρόσθεν γὰρ ἐπέλλαβε πῶμα πίθοιο
[αἰγιόχου βουλῇσι Διὸς νεφεληγερέταο.]
ἄλλα δὲ μυρία λυγρὰ κατ᾽ ἀνθρώπους ἀλάληται·
πλείη μὲν γὰρ γαῖα κακῶν, πλείη δὲ θάλασσα·
νοῦσοι δ᾽ ἀνθρώποισιν ἐφ᾽ ἡμέρῃ, αἳ δ᾽ ἐπὶ νυκτὶ
αὐτόματοι φοιτῶσι κακὰ θνητοῖσι φέρουσαι
σιγῇ...

[21] See *Odyssey* 4.92 where δόλον αἰπὺν, the *Theogony*'s term for Pandora, is applied to the Trojan horse.

[22] See Arthur 1982:74 on Pandora as the principle of reproduction. As Froma Zeitlin points out to me, the *Works and Days* does not explicitly associate Pandora with immortality through reproduction; it is suggestive, though, that the *Catalogue of Women* links Pandora—as parent—with the ultimate progenitors of mankind, Deucalion and Pyrrha, and so with the prospect of future generations and the inextinguishability of humankind. According to a scholion at Apollonius Rhodius 3.1086, "Hesiod says in the *Catalogue*" that Deucalion is the son of Prometheus and Pandora. In the text the name of Pandora is badly corrupt (Fr.2 in Merkelbach and West 1967), but Fr.4 maintains the connection, calling her the mother of Pyrrha.

of progeny to paternity) can become a mystery, once the *bios* is hidden from men. What has also required explanation, the poem attests, is the appearance of the race of women and of human progeny—that is, our contemporary situation as sexually dimorphic, reproductive, mortal beings.[23]

As inaugurated by the gods' gift of Pandora, the dynamic of reciprocal exchange becomes fundamental to the condition of a redefined human existence, and is tied to the struggle for survival. Human existence, now for the first time, involves *need*—as well as the need for explanation. Precariously dependent on cosmic forces and natural phenomena, men are obliged both to extrapolate patterns from nature and to impose them in turn, in the task of cultivation. No longer does the earth spontaneously bear for mortals what they need in order to keep themselves alive. As a sign of their difference from the gods rather than as a punishment,[24] human beings are compelled to work—they must cultivate their food. In their changed relationship with nature, they now must contend with cooking and culture. The anthropologist Lévi-Strauss says of myths that sometimes "[they]...do not seek to depict what is real, but to justify the shortcomings of reality, since the extreme positions are only *imagined* in order to show that they are *untenable*."[25] From an anthropological perspective, the Mekone story is perhaps a prototypical example of such a mythic thought-experiment: why must we sacrifice? Must we sacrifice? "The mythic narrative founds sacrifice, whereby we transform our relation with nature (meat-eaters, but cooked meat) into our relation with the gods, which turns out to be founded on our failure to take advantage of Zeus (our because Prometheus is our agent, and ancestor as well). We commemorate this failure every time we eat meat, and suffer for it every time we labor, die, and have children."[26]

The Hesiodic tradition thus authorizes agricultural work as the right relation of men to the earth, sacrifice as the proper exchange relation between men and the gods, sexual reproduction as the constitutive relation between

---

[23] On women imagined as a race apart, see the definitive discussion in Loraux 1993.

[24] It is important to observe that in the Greek tradition work is not meted out simply as a punishment, as it is in ancient Near Eastern (including Mesopotamian and Hebrew) traditions. It is true that the need to work emerges in Hesiodic explanation as part of a series of contentious exchanges between Zeus and Prometheus, and that, as part of this serial "payback" for theft and bad-apportioning, it can resemble punishment—yet the archaic Greek tradition is more ambiguous about how and whether to valorize aspects of the human condition (e.g., work, sex, death) than a reading of work-as-punishment will allow.

[25] Lévi-Strauss 1967:30.

[26] In J.M. Redfield's formulation (private communication). See Redfield 1993.

male and female, and economic transactions as the relations required among men. All these relations require men to take the measure of their actions.

The definition of the human condition as a laboring condition is installed, as we have seen, after a crisis of bad apportioning, mis-taking, and mismeasure. The primordial conflict between Zeus, the greatest of the gods, and men's agent Prometheus—the quarrel to begin all quarrels, which is responsible for the irrevocable change from the Golden Age—is the prototype of which the quarrel between Hesiod and Perses is a distant, but direct, descendant. The *Works and Days* begins with strife (*eris*), in a passage that serves as a programmatic introduction to the poem as a whole. The poet's grievance with his brother purports to be the occasion for the poem, but the address to his brother, enjoining him to *work*, is also, more broadly, an order that he desist from destructive conflict. What the poem introduces at the outset is not a particular strife; it provides instead a reflection on the nature of strife:

> So there was not only one kind of Strife [*eris*], after all—but in fact on earth there are two. The one Strife, a man would praise once he knew her; but the other is blameworthy: and they are different at heart. For one fosters evil war and conflict, cruel as she is: no mortal cares for her; but of necessity, through the will of the immortals, mortals give honor to harsh Strife. But the other Strife dark Night bore first, and the son of Kronos who sits on high, dwelling in the aether, placed her in the roots of the earth: and she is much better for men; she rouses even the feckless man. For a person grows eager to work when he looks at his neighbor...[27]
>
> *Works and Days* 11–21

Hesiod tells us that there is not one strife, one *eris*, but two—namely, the one that produces wars and violence and the one that produces work. He makes it clear

---

[27] οὐκ ἄρα μοῦνον ἔην Ἐρίδων γένος, ἀλλ' ἐπὶ γαῖαν
εἰσὶ δύω· τὴν μέν κεν ἐπαινέσσειε νοήσας,
ἣ δ' ἐπιμωμητή· διὰ δ' ἄνδιχα θυμὸν ἔχουσιν.
ἣ μὲν γὰρ πόλεμόν τε κακὸν καὶ δῆριν ὀφέλλει,
σχετλίη· οὔτις τήν γε φιλεῖ βροτός, ἀλλ' ὑπ' ἀνάγκης
ἀθανάτων βουλῇσιν Ἔριν τιμῶσι βαρεῖαν.
τὴν δ' ἑτέρην προτέρην μὲν ἐγείνατο Νὺξ ἐρεβεννή,
θῆκε δέ μιν Κρονίδης ὑψίζυγος, αἰθέρι ναίων,
γαίης ἐν ῥίζῃσι, καὶ ἀνδράσι πολλὸν ἀμείνω·
ἥτε καὶ ἀπάλαμόν περ ὁμῶς ἐπὶ ἔργον ἔγειρεν.
εἰς ἕτερον γάρ τίς τε ἰδὼν ἔργοιο χατίζει...

that in a kind of *mise en abîme*, the two strifes (or *erides*) are in contention with each other, bespeaking their primal character: strife was always already there.

Each *eris* herself needs to outdo the other; so, for example, Hesiod insists that it is the bad *eris* that is keeping Perses from activating her good counterpart. The personification of destructive Strife with a capital S (or *Eris* with a capital epsilon) appears in the *Iliad*, stirring up the contending armies on either side to a greater pitch of violence. But the realm of the beneficent strife (*eris*) is adversarial as well: she does not exist to promote (so to speak) self-motivation or auto-competition; there is no notion of bettering one's own record. There is, in fact, no "one" in this realm (any more than in that of her counterpart)—only two. Thus each participant in an *eris*, reciprocally, keeps the other one productive:

> For a man is eager to work when he looks at his neighbor, a rich man who hurries to plough and plant and put his house in good order; and neighbor vies with his neighbor as he hastens after wealth. This Strife is good for men.[28]
>
> *Works and Days* 21–24

In a sense, *strife* defines both the problem and the solution for the human condition.

Through its story of the two strifes, the *Works and Days* divides strife and theorizes its various actions; the division of strife also provides the opportunity for the poem to valorize one kind of conflict and to authorize some human activities (e.g., work) and not others.[29] The *Iliad* juxtaposes them and renders the parallelism between them in a passage that describes a particularly grueling phase of the fighting between Greek and Trojan warriors, where an impasse in the battle is compared to a scene of agricultural activity, a dispute between neighbors over the common boundary of a field:[30]

---

[28] εἰς ἕτερον γάρ τίς τε ἰδὼν ἔργοιο χατίζει
πλούσιον, ὃς σπεύδει μὲν ἀρώμεναι ἠδὲ φυτεύειν
οἶκόν τ' εὖ θέσθαι· ζηλοῖ δέ τε γείτονα γείτων
εἰς ἄφενος σπεύδοντ'· ἀγαθὴ δ' Ἔρις ἥδε βροτοῖσιν.

[29] Greek culture develops, we might say, a poetics of strife, out of which competing and conceptually interdependent genres emerge: one (Hesiodic) oriented toward proper conduct given the limits of the human condition and the regular measures of the cosmos, the other genre (Homeric epic) oriented toward exceptional conduct, which aims at transcending the very limits that the other genre has theorized.

[30] This is one of a number of similes throughout the *Iliad* which liken the warriors' efforts on the battlefield to scenes in the wheatfield, or the vicinity thereof. See also e.g., *Iliad* 11.67–72, as well as the striking passage at *Odyssey* 18.365–380, in which Odysseus equates the *eris* of work (using the phrase *eris ergoio*) with that of warfare, in proposing the terms of a contest between himself and Eurymachus.

For neither were the powerful Lycians able to break through the wall of the Danaans and make a path to the ships, nor could the Danaan spearmen push the Lycians back from the wall, once they had reached it. But as two men holding measuring ropes in their hands quarrel over boundaries in a shared field, and in a narrow space contend [*erizeto* = have an *eris*] each for his equal share...[31]

Iliad 12.417–423

Although a consideration of the competition between poetic genres, to which Hesiodic poetry alludes,[32] leads beyond the scope of this discussion, we may note that both the *Works and Days* and the *Iliad* generate their measures out of what they take to be a given, primordial crux: strife. And if strife is a generative matrix for early Greek poetry—its competing valorizations of warfare and work, its reflections on exchanges between gods, men, and the earth, its theory of the origin of two sexes and reproduction—it is not surprising that we see, accompanying the endless work of strife, the endless work of measure, since what is struggled over, what is labored for, what is contended, is always, literally or metaphorically, a "share" or "portion."[33]

Because the earth no longer of its own accord unstintingly provides human beings their *bios* in all seasons, the ultimately pressing question for them becomes, how much will it provide, and when? Thus their existence also comes to be bound up with calculation and measurement, and with the exigencies of the calendar. If human existence were still as it had been in the Golden

---

[31] οὔτε γὰρ ἴφθιμοι Λύκιοι Δαναῶν ἐδύναντο
τεῖχος ῥηξάμενοι θέσθαι παρὰ νηυσὶ κέλευθον,
οὔτε ποτ' αἰχμηταὶ Δαναοὶ Λυκίους ἐδύναντο
τείχεος ἂψ ὤσασθαι, ἐπεὶ τὰ πρῶτα πέλασθεν.
ἀλλ' ὥς τ' ἀμφ' οὔροισι δύ' ἀνέρε δηριάασθον
μέτρ' ἐν χερσὶν ἔχοντες ἐπιξύνῳ ἐν ἀρούρῃ,
ὥ τ' ὀλίγῳ ἐνὶ χώρῳ ἐρίζητον περὶ ἴσης...

[32] *Works and Days* 24–26.

[33] In a world where destiny expresses a notion of allotment—where the word "fate" (*moira*) is used to denote a serving of meat, a share of land, a portion of the spoils of war, as well as to refer to the final shape of a man's life—we understand that the largest framework in which human lives are viewed is that of division and apportionment. Throughout the Homeric poems, for instance, we observe that a basis in appropriate distribution and reciprocal exchange is explicitly invoked by formal procedures such as honorific feasting, distribution of booty, awards of prizes, return for specific services, ransom arrangements and other transactions, where equitable division is the inflexible requirement. But this exigent imperative bespeaks a comprehensive view of social relations, in the *Iliad* as well as in the *Works and Days*, among human beings and between humans and gods. See 167–187 in this volume.

Age (pre-mortal, as it were) there would be no calendar and no measuring. There would be, in a sense, no difference between a day and a year.[34]

> For the gods keep [the means of] life (*bios*) hidden from men. Otherwise in a day you would easily accomplish enough to have a living for a full year even without working...[35]
>
> *Works and Days* 45–47

As it is, time and timing must be measured—and the seasons and days take on a distinctive character and significance. The farmer performs a precarious balancing act, adjusting to the forces of nature and the rhythm of the year. These adjustments are mirrored by the ceaseless imperative of reciprocal exchanges with his neighbors on the land.

If resources are no longer unlimited, they must be carefully weighed and protected; thus relations with others who have a claim on them become fraught. Skill in conducting social and economic transactions thus becomes as crucial to survival as work itself:

> Invite your friend to a meal; but leave your enemy alone; and especially invite the one who lives near you: for if any trouble happens in the place, your neighbors come ungirt, but your kin stay to gird themselves. A bad neighbor is as great a disaster as a good one is a great blessing; whoever enjoys a good neighbor has a precious possession. Not even an ox would die if your neighbor weren't a bad one.[36]
>
> *Works and Days* 342–348

Hesiod's advice is to make sure that your neighbor needs you more than you need him:

---

[34] Hamilton 1989:84.

[35] κρύψαντες γὰρ ἔχουσι θεοὶ βίον ἀνθρώποισιν·
ῥηιδίως γάρ κεν καὶ ἐπ' ἤματι ἐργάσσαιο,
ὥστε σε κεἰς ἐνιαυτὸν ἔχειν καὶ ἀεργὸν ἐόντα·

[36] τὸν φιλέοντ' ἐπὶ δαῖτα καλεῖν, τὸν δ' ἐχθρὸν ἐᾶσαι·
τὸν δὲ μάλιστα καλεῖν, ὅς τις σέθεν ἐγγύθι ναίει·
εἰ γάρ τοι καὶ χρῆμ' ἐγχώριον ἄλλο γένηται,
γείτονες ἄζωστοι ἔκιον, ζώσαντο δὲ πηοί.
πῆμα κακὸς γείτων, ὅσσον τ' ἀγαθὸς μέγ' ὄνειαρ.
ἔμμορέ τοι τιμῆς, ὅς τ' ἔμμορε γείτονος ἐσθλοῦ.
οὐδ' ἂν βοῦς ἀπόλοιτ', εἰ μὴ γείτων κακὸς εἴη.

> And so you will have plenty till you come to silvery springtime,
> and will not look wistfully to others, but another man will need
> your help.[37]

Works and Days 477–478

Need becomes its own measurable resource, a measurable share: debt. This logic of measurable shares, the ground of Hesiodic economics, presumes finite resources, as Paul Millett has observed:

> Certainly Hesiod sees it as being in every man's interest to get for
> himself as much wealth as possible; but he also assumes that the
> stock of wealth—effectively the quantity of land—is finite and fixed.
> So what one man gains, another must necessarily lose, and there is
> no scope for an overall growth in prosperity...And that is presum-
> ably why it is so important to work harder than your neighbor; it is
> a guarantee that his and not your *oikos*[38] will be the one to decline...
> This negative view of wealth and prosperity as being feasible only
> at the expense of other people is apparently typical of peasant
> societies.[39]

The line between cooperation and competition is thus constantly blurred and redrawn throughout the account of agricultural work:

> Give to one who gives, but do not give to one who does not give. A
> man gives to the giver, but no one gives to the non-giver.[40]

Works and Days 354–355

If the destructive strife—the war-producing kind—generates negative reciprocity, whereby social relations are frustrated and inhibited, the good strife promotes those sequences of exchanges through which in balanced reciprocity social relations are extended and made continuous; gift and counter-gift returns each party to the other's position: each is by turns giver and receiver. As described in detail by Marcel Mauss and other students of primitive exchange,[41] in a system of reciprocity, maintaining the system involves the paradox of equilibrium built on imbalance in that each strives to give more than he has

---

[37] εὐοχθέων δ' ἵξεαι πολιὸν ἔαρ, οὐδὲ πρὸς ἄλλους
αὐγάσεαι· σέο δ' ἄλλος ἀνὴρ κεχρημένος ἔσται.

[38] *oikos* = "household," "holdings."

[39] Millett 1983.

[40] καὶ δόμεν, ὅς κεν δῷ, καὶ μὴ δόμεν, ὅς κεν μὴ δῷ.
δώτῃ μέν τις ἔδωκεν, ἀδώτῃ δ' οὔτις ἔδωκεν.

[41] Mauss 1967.

received. It is not simply that giving is better than receiving—it is a better *way to receive*, that is, a guarantee of future receiving. This dialectic of giving and receiving, the transmutation of giving into good receiving, presents a problem for Perses, who does not understand the relation between *giving* and *receiving* in an exchange system. Thus his options have become, according to Hesiod, either to seize illegitimately or to beg; neither furthers the desired economy.

> But I will give you no more nor give you further measure. Work, foolish Perses! Work the work that the gods ordained for men, so that in the grief of your heart, you with your children and wife do not seek your livelihood among your neighbors, who do not care.[42]
>
> *Works and Days* 396–400

The daily, and perennial, effort undertaken by the farmer—an effort that informs all his activities—to achieve a balance between too early and too late, too hot and too cold, too dry and too wet, between too little and too much, is replicated in the necessary effort to equalize exchanges between himself and his neighboring farmers over time. The task of proper calculation and the perception of temporality are what together enable a productive economy of strife:

> to the best of your ability, sacrifice to the immortal gods purely and cleanly, and in addition burn glorious thigh-pieces...that they may be propitious to you in heart and spirit, and so you may buy another's holding and not another yours.[43]
>
> *Works and Days* 336–337, 340–341

In his prescriptions, Hesiod repeatedly articulates the essential character of reciprocal exchange, of gift and counter-gift, namely that it is inherently and perpetually in disequilibrium and must be continually rebalanced over time, so that every exchange begets a further exchange:

---

[42] ...ἐγὼ δέ τοι οὐκ ἐπιδώσω
οὐδ' ἐπιμετρήσω· ἐργάζευ, νήπιε Πέρση,
ἔργα, τά τ' ἀνθρώποισι θεοὶ διετεκμήραντο,
μή ποτε σὺν παίδεσσι γυναικί τε θυμὸν ἀχεύων
ζητεύῃς βίοτον κατὰ γείτονας, οἳ δ' ἀμελῶσιν.

[43] κὰδ δύναμιν δ' ἔρδειν ἱέρ' ἀθανάτοισι θεοῖσιν
ἀγνῶς καὶ καθαρῶς, ἐπὶ δ' ἀγλαὰ μηρία καίειν·
. . . .
ὥς κέ τοι ἵλαον κραδίην καὶ θυμὸν ἔχωσιν,
ὄφρ' ἄλλων ὠνῇ κλῆρον, μὴ τὸν τεὸν ἄλλος.

Take fair measure from your neighbor and pay him back fairly with
the same measure, or better, if you can; so that if you are in need
afterwards, you may find him reliable.[44]

Works and Days 349–351

We have seen that, after the crisis of bad apportioning—the scandal
at Mekone and the theft of Prometheus—exchange has become an imperative: the system of reciprocity, of paybacks conducted through time, is now,
we might say, what *is*. How one *ought* to behave, given these conditions,
returns Hesiod to the problem of measure. The *Works and Days* prescribes
adherence to due season and fair measure, both as literal mandates in daily
activity and—beyond practicality—as tropes of mortal temporality, mutual (if
agonistic) dependence, and the ethical ordering of society:

Observe due measure (*metra*): and best in all things is the right time
and right amount.[45]

Works and Days 694

When Hesiod insists that he will no longer help Perses if the latter is in
need—

But I will give you no more nor give you further measure.[46]

Works and Days 396–397

—Hesiod's "measure" may denote the actual material, the begrudged hand-
outs, that he announces he will no longer give Perses. But elsewhere, as in
the passage cited above, we see that "measure" functions as a more abstract,
mobile counter in Hesiod's normative economy of good relations:

Take fair measure from your neighbor and pay him back fairly with
the same measure, or better, if you can; so that if you are in need
afterwards, you may find him reliable.[47]

Works and Days 349–351

---

[44] εὖ μὲν μετρεῖσθαι παρὰ γείτονος, εὖ δ' ἀποδοῦναι,
αὐτῷ τῷ μέτρῳ, καὶ λώιον, αἴ κε δύνηαι,
ὡς ἂν χρηίζων καὶ ἐς ὕστερον ἄρκιον εὕρῃς

[45] μέτρα φυλάσσεσθαι· καιρὸς δ' ἐπὶ πᾶσιν ἄριστος.

[46] ...ἐγὼ δέ τοι οὐκ ἐπιδώσω
οὐδ' ἐπιμετρήσω...

[47] εὖ μὲν μετρεῖσθαι παρὰ γείτονος, εὖ δ' ἀποδοῦναι,
αὐτῷ τῷ μέτρῳ, καὶ λώιον, αἴ κε δύνηαι,
ὡς ἂν χρηίζων καὶ ἐς ὕστερον ἄρκιον εὕρῃς.

Or, more pessimistically,

> Do not make a friend equal to a brother; but if you do, do not injure him first, and do not lie to please the tongue. But if he injures you first, either by saying or doing something offensive, remember to repay him double...[48]

> *Works and Days* 708–711

The notions of due measure and right season are thus linked in ways that at first seem to be quite literal—

> ...but let it be your care to arrange your work in due measure, that in the right season your barns may be full of grain.[49]

> *Works and Days* 306–307

—but that also function as ramifying tropes that figure a system in equilibrium. "Fair measure" then represents not a precise equivalent, but a just amount—an amount that will continue the sequence of exchanges. And the "right season" takes account of those exchanges as part of a cycle, operating with and through the patterns of nature.

We see, then, that the Hesiodic etiology of work and exchange (the mythic narrative) and his prescriptions regarding proper conduct (the didactic discourse) both partake of the figurative system of the seasonable, the timely, the natural—that which is "in season" (*hôraios; hôra* = season). Life can be regulated according to calculable elements, says the Hesiodic tradition, and if you measure your actions and exchanges appropriately (*erga... metria kosmein*) you can recapitulate that order. Because of the predictability of at least some vital natural phenomena on which the life—the *bios*—of mortals depends, that which is "timely" (*hôraios*, e.g., the appearance and disappearance of constellations throughout the year, their rising and setting, the sequence of the seasons) becomes a figure both for the ordered life and for a standard of appropriateness within it. Thus Hesiod's recourse to the imperative of due season:

[48] μηδὲ κασιγνήτῳ ἶσον ποιεῖσθαι ἑταῖρον·
εἰ δέ κε ποιήσῃς, μή μιν πρότερος κακὸν ἔρξῃς.
μηδὲ ψεύδεσθαι γλώσσης χάριν· εἰ δὲ σέ γ᾿ ἄρχῃ
ἤ τι ἔπος εἰπὼν ἀποθύμιον ἠὲ καὶ ἔρξας,
δὶς τόσα τίνυσθαι μεμνημένος...

[49] ...σοὶ δ᾿ ἔργα φίλ᾿ ἔστω μέτρια κοσμεῖν,
ὥς κέ τοι ὡραίου βιότου πλήθωσι καλιαί.

But you, Perses, remember all works in their season...[50]

Works and Days 641–642

"Due measure"—a figure for fair treatment and appropriate interactions—and "seasonability," a figure for order, first reinforce each other and then function as metonyms of one another; so that in a passage on right conduct and relations, inappropriate, improper behavior (like harming a suppliant or sleeping with your brother's wife) is called "unseasonable," "untimely" (*parakairia*):

Alike with whoever wrongs a suppliant or a guest, or does acts contrary to nature [*unseasonable/untimely* acts], climbing into his brother's wife's bed in covert lust, or who thoughtlessly injures orphaned children, or who abuses his old father at the grim threshold of old age and attacks him with harsh words, with this one truly Zeus himself is angry, and in the end imposes on him a harsh requital for his unjust acts.[51]

Works and Days 327–334

Hence the poem's insistence on acting "in season," on the importance of the calendar and of observing the proper timing for accomplishing work—this is the *Days* part of the *Works and Days*.

But when Orion and Sirius are come into midheaven, and rosy-fingered Dawn sees Arcturus, then cut off all the grape-clusters, Perses, and bring them home. Show them to the sun ten days and ten nights: then cover them over for five, and on the sixth day draw off into vessels the gifts of joyful Dionysus. But when the Pleiades and Hyades and strong Orion begin to set, then remember to plough in season: and so the completed year will fitly pass beneath the earth.[52]

Works and Days 609–617

---

[50] τύνη δ', ὦ Πέρση, ἔργων μεμνημένος εἶναι
ὡραίων πάντων...

[51] ἶσον δ' ὅς θ' ἱκέτην ὅς τε ξεῖνον κακὸν ἔρξη,
ὅς τε κασιγνήτοιο ἑοῦ ἀνὰ δέμνια βαίνη
κρυπταδίης εὐνῆς ἀλόχου, παρακαίρια ῥέζων,
ὅς τέ τευ ἀφραδίης ἀλιταίνεται ὀρφανὰ τέκνα,
ὅς τε γονῆα γέροντα κακῷ ἐπὶ γήραος οὐδῷ
νεικείη χαλεποῖσι καθαπτόμενος ἐπέεσσιν·
τῷ δ' ἦ τοι Ζεὺς αὐτὸς ἀγαίεται, ἐς δὲ τελευτὴν
ἔργων ἀντ' ἀδίκων χαλεπὴν ἐπέθηκεν ἀμοιβήν.

[52] Εὖτ' ἂν δ' Ὠαρίων καὶ Σείριος ἐς μέσον ἔλθη

Another perspective on the problematic of seasonality is offered by the account of the history of humankind through time, as delineated in the myth of the Five Ages, of which the Golden Age is the first:

> Thereafter, I wish that I were not among the men of the fifth generation, but either had died before or been born afterwards. For now truly is a race of iron, and men never rest from labor and sorrow by day, and from perishing by night; and the gods will give them sore cares. But, notwithstanding, even they shall have some good mixed with their evils. And Zeus will destroy this race of mortal men also when they come to have grey hair on their temples at birth.[53]
>
> *Works and Days* 174–181

For the sign of the last stage of corruption among mortals, when they have become so degenerate that Zeus will destroy them, is a stunning one: the mark of their corruption is that their *timing* is *out of sync*. Hesiod says that Zeus will destroy this age when babies are born with grey hair, that is, when the seasons and generations of man have collapsed all together and become confused. When newborns have the features of old men, the seasons of our lives are truly out of joint. So to observe the due sequence of things—to pay attention to the calendar—is not only to bring temporality, that inescapable fact of our lives, in some small way under control, but it is also to resist such moral chaos as is envisaged for the end of the fifth age, the age of iron—our own.

If that which is "in season" (*hôraios*) emerges in Hesiod as a normative ground, the trope of due measure par excellence, we also know that it has required narrative explanation. Hesiod has, as we have seen, spent many

---

οὐρανόν, Ἀρκτοῦρον δ' ἐσίδῃ ῥοδοδάκτυλος Ἠώς,
ὦ Πέρσῃ, τότε πάντας ἀποδρέπεν οἴκαδε βότρυς·
δεῖξαι δ' ἠελίῳ δέκα τ' ἤματα καὶ δέκα νύκτας,
πέντε δὲ συσκιάσαι, ἕκτῳ δ' εἰς ἄγγε' ἀφύσσαι
δῶρα Διωνύσου πολυγηθέος. αὐτὰρ ἐπὴν δὴ
Πληιάδες θ' Ὑάδες. τε τό τε σθένος Ὠαρίωνος
δύνωσιν, τότ' ἔπειτ' ἀρότου μεμνημένος εἶναι
ὡραίου· πλειὼν δὲ κατὰ χθονὸς ἄρμενος εἶσιν.

[53] μηκέτ' ἔπειτ' ὤφελλον ἐγὼ πέμπτοισι μετεῖναι
ἀνδράσιν, ἀλλ' ἢ πρόσθε θανεῖν ἢ ἔπειτα γενέσθαι.
νῦν γὰρ δὴ γένος ἐστὶ σιδήρεον· οὐδέ ποτ' ἦμαρ
παύονται καμάτου καὶ ὀιζύος, οὐδέ τι νύκτωρ
φθειρόμενοι. χαλεπὰς δὲ θεοὶ δώσουσι μερίμνας·
ἀλλ' ἔμπης καὶ τοῖσι μεμείξεται ἐσθλὰ κακοῖσιν.
Ζεὺς δ' ὀλέσει καὶ τοῦτο γένος μερόπων ἀνθρώπων,
εὖτ' ἂν γεινόμενοι πολιοκρόταφοι τελέθωσιν.

measures explaining that time is, philosophically, a problem, not a given, for man; that the existence of the calendar measures, in fact, the distance men have come from their previous timeless ease; that the current measures of man, the conditions governing him—from temporality to mortality to work—are all developments requiring explanation.

Due measure and right season are invested with an ethical dimension, most fully realized as the basis for the operations of Justice.[54] In the poetic tradition transmitted by the *Works and Days*, Justice herself brings to the imagery of balance and fair measure—dealing "straightly" as opposed to askew—the dimension of appropriate temporality. For we discover that, in the cosmic genealogy narrated in Hesiod's *Theogony*, Justice herself is none other than one of the Seasons (*Hôrai*).[55] Thus Hesiodic etiology allows us to see what kind of norm justice is for archaic Greek thought: not just any norm, but an order; not just any order, but the cyclic order of the seasons, which defines time itself.[56]

The problem of measure thus informs justice as arbitration and calibration; it is brought equally to natural processes and to human affairs. Because days are more self-regulating than human works, it is not surprising that Hesiod orients us to the problem of measuring human transactions:

> But you, Perses, lay up these things within your heart and listen now to Justice, ceasing altogether to think of violence. For the son of Kronos has ordained this law for men, that fishes and beasts and winged fowls should devour one another, for Justice is not in them; but to mankind he gave Justice which proves far the best.[57]
>
> *Works and Days* 274–279

---

[54] "And there is virgin Justice, the daughter of Zeus, who is honored and reverenced among the gods who dwell on Olympus, and whenever anyone hurts her with lying slander, she sits beside her father, Zeus the son of Kronos, and tells him of men's wicked heart, until the people pay for the mad folly of their princes who, evilly minded, pervert judgment and give sentence crookedly. Keep watch against this, you princes, and make straight your judgments, you who devour bribes; put crooked judgments altogether from your thoughts." *Works and Days* 256–262.

[55] *Theogony* 901–902.

[56] I owe this formulation to the incisive editorial response of Raine Daston and Fernando Vidal.

[57] ὦ Πέρση, σὺ δὲ ταῦτα μετὰ φρεσὶ βάλλεο σῇσι,
καί νυ δίκης ἐπάκουε, βίης δ' ἐπιλήθεο πάμπαν.
τόνδε γὰρ ἀνθρώποισι νόμον διέταξε Κρονίων
χθύσι μὲν καὶ θηρσὶ καὶ οἰωνοῖς πετεηνοῖς
ἐσθέμεν ἀλλήλους, ἐπεὶ οὐ δίκη ἐστὶ μετ' αὐτοῖς·
ἀνθρώποισι δ' ἔδωκε δίκην, ἣ πολλὸν ἀρίστη
γίγνεται·

Hesiod's identification of Justice and seasonality, and his coordination of the right time and the right amount, in a metaphorical discourse of ethical behavior, help us to read Heraclitus' conjunction of the sun's measures, the avenging Furies and the Justice that administers their function. Heraclitus invokes the sun's measures—usually the very trope of regularity, of the predictable, of the obvious—*as a problem*; he does so, moreover, through a strikingly peculiar, counterfactual rhetoric, as though beginning the trope of the *adynaton*—the figure of impossibility (of the sort, "when rivers run back to their source, ..." "when fish fly, ..." etc.). Why is justice concerned with the passage of the day? Are (not) the sun's measures inviolable? The extended coordination of Justice with the sun's measures or with—more broadly—that which is seasonable (*hôraios*), must be seen as a complex, provocative wager: betting on the sun's regularity, troping norms out of nature, one gains in figurative power what one loses, perhaps, in ethical force. Heraclitus' imagined transgression, even if offered through a conditional rhetoric of the improbable—invites us to continue our explorations of the thought-experiments conducted through poetry as well as philosophy.

As I hope to have shown for the *Works and Days*, the measures of early Greek poetry accomplish their cognitive and ethical work through complex tropes and figurations: even if "nature" as such does not quite yet exist as a category in archaic epic, nevertheless the processes and ordination of the natural world—its measures from the seasons to cosmic rhythms—everywhere inform Hesiodic explanations of and prescriptions for the social and ethical orders of man and, indeed, of supra-human Justice. Any analysis of early Greek thought—whether construed as "pre-scientific," "mythological," "poetic," or in later periods, "philosophical"—requires an extensive investigation of such figurative textures. The present reading, restricted as it is, aims to offer an invitation for future comparative readings across periods and cultures: through sustained collaborative analyses of the figurative bases of representations of cultural order (whether figured as "natural" or not), we can refine our understanding of human value-making and the role of figurally-based ideologics in the constitution of communities.[58] We can also better approach the ways ancients, and indeed moderns, have chosen to represent themselves to themselves.

In the authoritative explanations and pronouncements of Hesiod, we have an example of archaic Greek culture thinking about itself, authorizing itself, taking its own measure. In archaic Greek poetry, man may not yet be

---

[58] For a powerful example of such a cultural reading, see Ferrari 2002 and 1990.

what he later becomes for the 5th century philosopher Protagoras, who called him the *measure of all things*, but as a worker, he is already what he must be first: the *measurer* of them.

Works Cited

Arthur, M. 1982. "Cultural Strategies in Hesiod's Theogony." *Arethusa* 15:63–82.

Evelyn-White, H. G., trans. 1929. *Hesiod, the Homeric Hymns, and Homerica.* Loeb Classical Library. London.

Ferrari, G. 1990. "Figures of Speech: The Picture of Aidos." *Metis* 5:185–200.

———. 2002. *Figures of Speech: Men and Maidens in Ancient Greece.* Chicago.

Finley, J. H., Jr. 1965. *Four Stages of Greek Thought.* Stanford, CA.

Griffiths, M. 1983. "Personality in Hesiod." *Classical Antiquity* 2 (1):47–62.

Hamilton, R. 1989. *The Architecture of Hesiodic Poetry.* Baltimore.

Kahn, C. H. 1993. *The Art and Thought of Heraclitus.* Cambridge.

Lévi-Strauss, C. 1967. "The Story of Asdiwal." In *The Structural Study of Myth and Totemism,* ed. E. Leach, 1-47. A.S.A. Monographs 5. London.

Loraux, N. 1993. "On the Race of Women and Some of Its Tribes: Hesiod and Semonides." In *The Children of Athena: Athenian Ideas about Citizenship and the Division between the Sexes,* trans. C. Levine, 72–110. Princeton. Originally published as "Sur la race des femmes et quelques-unes de ses tribus." *Arethusa* 11 (1978):43–88.

Mauss, M. 1967. *The Gift: Forms and Functions of Exchange in Archaic Societies.* Trans. I. Cunnison. New York. Originally published as *Essai sur le don,* 1925.

Merkelbach, R. and M. L. West, eds. 1967. *Fragmenta Hesiodea.* Oxford.

Millett, P. 1983. "Hesiod and his World." *Proceedings of the Cambridge Philological Society* 209:84–115.

Nelson, S. 1998. *God and the Land: The Metaphysics of Farming in Hesiod and Vergil.* Oxford.

Redfield, J. M. 1994. "The Sexes in Hesiod." In "Reinterpreting the Classics," ed. C. Stray and R. Kaster. Special issue, *Annals of Scholarship* 10(1):31–61.

Vernant, J.-P. 1988. "The Myth of Prometheus in Hesiod." In *Myth and Society in Ancient Greece*, trans. J. Lloyd, 183-201. New York.

West, M. L., ed. 1978. *Hesiod: Works and Days.* Cambridge.

Remembering Nicole Loraux Remembering Athens[1]

I WISH THIS MORNING TO OFFER A FEW REMARKS on method and memory, topics that this anthology asks us to recall and rethink. In the course of these remarks I wish as well to recall explicitly the work of our co-editor Nicole Loraux, whose astonishing series of books and essays—along with those of her colleagues J.-P. Vernant, P. Vidal-Naquet, and M. Detienne—enjoin us to reflect on the inescapable politics of memory as well as on the rigors and nuances of method.

An early favorable, if somewhat arch, review of Loraux described her as "one of the best, most prolific, and most solidly 'historical' of the Paris 'structuralists.'"[2] With scare quotes around both "historical" and "structuralist," the reviewer alluded to a methodological opposition that one might hope is now old news. It is by now a familiar criticism of structuralism, and the so-called structuralist "method," that it elides history, suppresses conflict, and hypostatizes process. This criticism is relevant, it seems, only to those works—largely Anglo-American, it must be admitted—that have seized upon structuralism as a kind of reification, a readymade toolkit built for breaking down a cultural system or classical text into its smallest constituent units. It is certainly true that structuralism—as manifested, for example, in the magisterial and highly influential work of Lévi-Strauss—has come in for its share of salutary criticism: one may think of contemporary critiques like Sartre's, or of Derrida's famous analysis of the illusory mechanics of structuralism in his "Structure, Sign, and Play in the Discourse of the Human Sciences" (1966). Yet the Anglo-American resistance to structuralism was

---

[1] This essay is a version of a talk presented at a conference in New York City in April 2001, on the occasion of the publication of *Antiquities: Post-War French Thought* (New York: The New Press, 2001), co-edited with Nicole Loraux and Gregory Nagy. I include it here as a tribute, however inadequate, to Nicole, who died in 2003. My thanks to Ramona Naddaff, general editor of the *Post-War French Thought* series, for her characteristic thoughtfulness and generosity, which greatly facilitated our collaboration.

[2] Fisher 1984.

more importantly, as we know, a resistance to things French, or—and perhaps this is the same—to things Parisian, and theoretical. What we see in the work of these French classicists in *Antiquities* is an imaginative dialogue with, never a vulgar appropriation or a reification of, structuralism. Leaving aside the question of defining "structuralism"—for this I refer you both to the anthology's introduction and to the vast literature surrounding the structuralist problematic—let us concede that those French classicists associated with newer "schools of thought" (anthropological, psychoanalytic, hermeneutic) have often been tarred with the structuralist label. What we see, however, when we turn to the work of these classicists, is their unflagging commitment to history, to politics, and, in the broadest sense, to committed reading.

It has been especially productive for those of us trained in the Anglo-American tradition to encounter the work of what was called, as early as 1982, "the Paris School" of classicists.[3] If we have felt simultaneously thrilled and puzzled by their work, this indicates the success of their collective venture, which seems nothing less than a wholesale defamiliarization of both antiquity and the study of antiquity. Not defamiliarization for its own sake, but for the sake rather of rigor and revelation, always undertaken under the sign of engaged reading. Consider David Schaps on this productive bewilderment: imagining the reception of Loraux's work by succeeding generations of scholars, he writes, "None of them [the next generation] will get from this book what it offers to mature scholars of our generation, the exhilarating experience of having the views they had learned from their teachers or from their own reading so penetratingly challenged."[4] We might say that, in her commitment to discovering and reconstructing (not, it must be emphasized, merely retrieving) antiquity, Nicole Loraux offered classicists a productive response to Sartre's famous and always urgent question: why write? For as she explained in her introduction to *The Invention of Athens*, "when confronted with democracy, with the word as well as the thing, and when confronted with antiquity, too, I feel that I am in a strange world, and thus entitled to attempt a new reading."[5]

The hostility that this work has sometimes encountered, particularly from British and German classicists, must be attributed, not only to national styles of scholarship or even to national chauvinism, but also to the profound challenge such brilliantly eclectic yet remorselessly argued books and essays

---

[3] Fisher 1982.
[4] Schaps 1996.
[5] Loraux 1986:7.

present to our received notions of democracy, rationality, the political: I think here of Vernant's "The Spiritual Universe of the Polis" and Loraux's *Invention of Athens*.

The crude rift between, say, classical philology and modern "schools of thought" is revealed to be precisely that, crude, in such works as *The Invention of Athens*, *Children of Athena*, *The Experiences of Tiresias*, and *Mothers in Mourning*, which ingeniously, imaginatively, and thrillingly illuminate the politics, myths, state genres, gendered discourses, and institutions of antiquity. As her work on gender and the body shows, Loraux pointedly rejected any reduction of "difference" into binaries—for example male/female—which could then be "subsumed under a 'law of symmetrical inversion.'" As she remarked, following Froma Zeitlin's work on transvestism in Greek drama,[6] this "overly mechanical process" must be resisted; it is our task rather to identify the complex layers, sometimes overlapping, sometimes not, of representations and institutions of difference. For indeed to invoke, as Loraux does, the vocabulary of the Prague school, if "male" emerges as unmarked and "female" as marked in the classical city, this marking bears always an ideological weight and a political meaning; however "structural" this opposition, it works in historical, political ways. So we see that, even as she found in structuralism, or in later work in exchange-theory, workable tools for approaching and describing systems, her sense of history and her alertness to the mobility of ideological formations always informed, we might even say governed, her use of these tools.

Confounding those who defensively police the boundaries of their disciplines, Loraux unapologetically ranged among history, philology, philosophy, psychoanalysis, literary studies, and studies of myth and ritual. She acknowledged the "risk that anyone working on the edges of a discipline must incur"[7]—namely, the risk of antagonizing other scholars who feel their discipline is not getting its due (she mentions historians and psychoanalysts who might take umbrage at *Tiresias*). Perhaps we might take Loraux's situating of herself as a model: "working of the edges of a discipline," as she put it, she forced us to reflect on the polyvalence of boundaries, on the ambiguous work that boundaries are meant to do, whether for the classical city or in our scholarly disciplines.

That mainstream classicists considered what we might call the structuralist turn in classics to be strange and alienating was not only surprising,

---

[6] See especially Zeitlin 1982 = 1996:375–416.
[7] Loraux 1995:17–18.

it was diagnostic. For the self-announced task of thinkers like Loraux was to defamiliarize what classicists had long conceived—dare we say, unconsciously?—to be their task: to curate the past, to display it honorifically, worshipfully, albeit philologically. Whether culturally triumphalist or culturally defensive, the curatorial function of classical scholarship is one Loraux and her colleagues have always regarded with skepticism, as she wrote in her Introduction to *The Invention of Athens*: "we no longer believe naively that we are the posterity whom the orators exhorted to remember Athens."[8]

And yet remembering Athens, and remembering antiquity more broadly, is, as Loraux suggested, the task undertaken not only by orators but also, of course, by ourselves. Focusing from the outset on the vicissitudes of scholarly remembering, Loraux launched her magisterial volume, *The Invention of Athens*, with a pointed "examination of three readings [of *epitaphios*] in which three Athenses emerge." "French Athens," as represented by G. Glotz, unsurprisingly emerges as a polis in which "fraternity" is a central democratic value alongside democracy and liberty; "[i]t is a short step from this," Loraux observes, the funeral oration in mind, "to seeing the *epitaphios* as the ancestor of the Declaration of the Rights of Man."[9] Hegel offers us a German Athens, "a democracy reduced to its spirit and excessively concerned with a love of the beautiful: a strange example [Loraux wryly remarks] of political life in which the political life is absent." And then there is the English Athens, in which the *epitaphios* is far more scrupulously read (her example is the work of Grote) but nevertheless becomes, in Loraux's words, "a hymn to the individual, positive, action-oriented liberty, and to classical Athens—a hardworking, expanding, imperialist Athens, like the British Commonwealth."

If the text of Athens inevitably becomes something of a culturally narcissistic reflecting pool, nevertheless Loraux does not invoke these readings simply to dismiss them. She recalls them, instead (we might say, anticipating her discussion of amnesty), in order to recall *against* them. These readings thus emerge as diagnostic of the predicament of reading, and more broadly of the historical project: "there is no such thing as an innocent reading," Loraux says in her first book, and all her work attests to her commitment to rigorously knowing readings.

From her first book, *The Invention of Athens*, to her final work, Nicole Loraux ceaselessly, remorselessly, and imaginatively explored Greek—and more particularly Athenian—self-representations. Positing a dynamic relationship

---

[8] Loraux 1986:14.
[9] Loraux 1986:6.

between what she persuasively reconstructed as a model institution and genre, the funeral oration, and its various exemplary instances in *epitaphioi*, Loraux observed that "a certain idea that the city wishes to have of itself emerges, beyond the needs of the present: within the orthodoxy of an official speech, there is a certain gap between Athens and Athens."[10]

There is a certain gap between Athens and Athens, between representations and the array of practices, institutions, and beliefs we call "the real"; the task of the classicist is to identify—to reconstruct, in fact—that critical, political gap. Loraux makes explicit the vocabulary of her method: "I have preferred to use the notion of the imaginary to designate the process by which, in the oration, an ideal of the polis, both opaque and dominant, is constituted."[11] Insisting that "the imaginary/*imaginaire*" is a constitutive element of the real, Loraux taught us to see not only the complexity and contradictions encoded within, for example, the funeral oration, or in the representation of the mourning mother, or in Greek discourse on gender: she shows us again and again how the field of representation, particularly as it emerges in a democratic terrain, is the field of contest. If the funeral oration worked to secure for the state the glorious deaths of its warriors, the oration, a double form—both a genre and an institution, as Loraux taught us—also accomplishes other cultural work. Announcing the dead warrior's embodiment of *arête* and securing this virtue for the city, the funeral oration also enacts a conspicuous silencing: the silencing of alternate genres (lament), emotions (anger), genders (women), roles (mothers), and histories. She pointedly remarks on "the silence observed by the funeral oration on the subject of slaves."[12] Such silences are paradigmatic, ultimately marking out the system of the city itself: "silence brings us back to a much more general omission: the oration ignores whatever does not belong to the sphere of war or politics, that is, everything related to the physical subsistence of the city."[13]

How the city represents itself, how it constitutes itself, how it remembers and members itself: these are among Loraux's central preoccupations. At the end of *The Experiences of Tiresias*, she turns from her anatomization of male appropriation of the feminine in Greek culture to the space of the city itself:

[10] Loraux 1986:14 = 2006:42.
[11] Loraux 1986:335–336 = 2006:417.
[12] Loraux 1986:334 = 2006:414.
[13] Loraux 1986:334 = 2006:415.

Let us leave the soul and return one last time to the city, to observe that the strict separation between feminine and masculine truly has no other place, no other boundaries than politics—or more exactly, the *ideology* of politics. For, in ancient Greece, politics is probably more extensive than is suggested in the singularly edifying official parlance that speaks of the peaceful functioning of the city of the *andres*. If the pertinence of this language is challenged at all, it becomes clear that this inner conflict represents, if not an adverse definition, at least an essential side to politics, even though politics in the form of *stasis* (sedition) is endlessly refused and rejected from the city just as it takes place in its midst. In a word, it is *denied*.[14]

Under the sign of the tellingly ambiguous seer Tiresias, Loraux excavates what official parlance buries; she ceaselessly uncovers its constitutive denials and procedures of denial, not to restore or to replace or to solace, but rather to *remember* and *recall*, to speak—insofar as it is possible—the whole text of Athens, as it were, even those lines "official parlance" refused to sanction.

And indeed it is no accident that Loraux zeroes in on that *topos* in which the boundaries and affiliations (all affiliations involving a recognition of difference) within the city are most violently contended: namely, the condition of *stasis*, of seditious dissent, culminating in civil war. "Stasis" emerges as a keyword in Loraux's corpus: stasis, this strife, this chaos, this *rejectamenta* within the political, the refusal of which guarantees the city's apparently seamless self-representations and foundational oppositions.

Consider her meditation on civil war and the "anthropological question of the world turned upside down": among the questions Greek discourse prompts us to ask, Loraux observes, is whether *stasis* should be understood—as Greek self-representations would have it—as an anomaly, a threat to civil society, as the essence in fact of the anti-civic, or whether *stasis* is better considered as constitutive of Greek civic life. Does *stasis* represent a "return to savagery," she wonders, with Françoise Frontisi-Ducroux's work in mind.[15] Or is *stasis* possible only within the heart of political life:

> *Anthrôpos* or *anêr*? A theological-anthropological reading or a purely political one? The question is complicated, because it

---

14 Loraux 1995:15.
15 Loraux 2001:56–57, citing the argument in Frontisi-Ducroux 1981, and Loraux 2002:20.

involves a tension internal to the Greek man... It is clear, however, that the dilemma runs through all of Greek thought, where it receives a variety of responses, not always unequivocal.[16]

Does *stasis* refer to man as *anthrôpos* or man as *anêr*, man as anthropological being or as political being? These questions revolve around discursive axes, as Loraux makes plain. The links between *stasis* and cannibalism would suggest that *stasis* marks a return to bestial existence. *Stasis* thus appears as an anthropological crisis, a disordering of the separation of men from beasts. Civil war would then appear, as Loraux puts it, "entirely within the realm of Greek anthropological discourse, of which it would be merely one figure. It would then be appropriate to situate *stasis* within the cultural realm of civilization rather than in the political realm, where citizens are not so much 'disciplined' (as the humanity of the *anthrôpoi* is in opposition to the animal kingdom) as *politicized*, as virile men (*andres*) are supposed to be."[17]

At the close of her essay, Loraux restates her central question: "*Anthrôpoi* or *andres*, *anthrôpoi* and *andres*: we will not attempt to choose between the two models, any more than the Greeks did."[18] It is characteristic of Loraux not only to raise these questions but to suspend them over the course of an essay, to rephrase, refine, and rediscover them over the course of an argument, to refuse prematurely to resolve them; her interest is, indeed, not to resolve but rather to identify the constitutive "dilemmas," to use her word, running through Greek thought. Hidden within her "or"s (e.g., *anthrôpoi* or *andres*) are always deeper recognitions of "and"s (*anthrôpoi* and *andres*), soon to be turned by "but"s or modified by "perhaps"es. Her style enacts what her methodological commitments enjoin, that is, a combination of rigorous hovering and surgical penetration. Let no one think this hovering bespeaks indecision: as numerous critics have remarked, Loraux's style is characterized by its authoritative tone as well as a syntactic precision and complexity that have dazzled and challenged many a translator and reader. In the words of a reviewer, "To summarize [Loraux's chapters] is to distort them, for Loraux's every paragraph qualifies, colors, or even contradicts the previous one, and nothing is more alien to her than simplification."[19] It is as if, through her pauses, her divagations, her sharp turns, her subjunctives, conditionals, "detours," and negations, she were performing—not theatrically but exem-

---

[16] Loraux 2001:67.
[17] Loraux 2001:57.
[18] Loraux 2001:67.
[19] Schaps 1996.

plarily—the texture of her thought: nuanced of course, but also interested in displaying the exact force of resistance that a trope, a concept, or a discourse might present to us.

A rigorous embrace of resistance, a refusal to dodge; considering the connections between civil war and *polemos* and *dikê*, Loraux observes, "These are disturbing connections, to be sure, but we must do justice to this straddling of boundaries that the Greeks were bold enough to imagine despite their preference for clear-cut distinctions. Otherwise, we risk depoliticizing the city through a 'mental dodge': by manipulating the horror that rivets the texts, thought prevents itself from thinking."[20]

Thought preventing itself from thinking: here is one pithy formulation of Loraux's recurring topic. The reduction of *stasis* to savagery and cannibalism—whether by Greeks or by us—is a "mental dodge" designed to keep us from thinking of the horror *within* the political, the horrors humans as political beings perpetuate and yet disown, or at least distance, through a discourse of "bestiality."

It is clear from this vantage that Loraux's work was always concerned with the politics of memory. What shall be remembered? How? By whom? For whom? These were some of the questions implicitly posed by *The Invention of Athens*, focusing as it did on the destination of the oration as much as on the topics central to it. Coordinating past, present, and future generations, the oration emerges in Loraux's account as a state genre and institution through which official memory is performed, cultivated, and transmitted. Throughout her oeuvre she returned to the problematic of memory and its institutions, perhaps most stunningly in her essay "Of Amnesty and its Opposite."

That the Greeks were expert technicians of memory—of owning and disowning—is clear; Loraux revivified some aspects of Athenian mnemotechnics, notably in her work on mourning mothers and on the concept and practice of "amnesty."

Consider, from the opening paragraphs of her essay, "Of Amnesty and its Opposite":

...[W]hat does an amnesty want...? An erasing from which there is no coming back and no trace? The crudely healed scar of an amputation hence forever memorable, provided that its object be irremediably lost? Or the planning of a time for mourning and the (re)construction of history?

[20] Loraux 2001:67.

We must arrive at some answer, but I shall abstain from providing any for now and suggest a detour, a way of taking a step back.[21]

Such a passage condenses the operations of Loraux's style, a style always inseparable from the argument, the "steps" always sure, whether taken forward or back. Having posed her central question, "What does an amnesty want?" Loraux offers a proliferation of possible answers, or rather a series of ramifying questions, responses over which she, and we, must hover: does an amnesty want erasure? A healed scar? A planning of a time for mourning? These alternatives, yoked by their "or"s—this, or that, or that—mark the paths we might take; but as always with Loraux, our next movement is a surprising one, a "detour," as she says, a "step back." Observe the detours of thought, the perpetual questioning, the surgical opening of the question of amnesty, which will involve us, as Loraux indicated, in matters of erasing, mourning, and history.

Let us stay with the question of amnesty; for, in its thinking through and around amnesty, the city offers us a history and an allegory of what Loraux calls "the uses of oblivion." In tragedy and in epic, in the funeral oration and in myth, the Greeks contemplate the pleasures and dangers of forgetting and equally those of its opposite, undying remembrance. Mourning is, as Loraux has shown us, a profound form of perpetual remembrance, vengeance another; and mourning modulates terrifyingly easily into wrath—a modulation Achilles perhaps best illuminates. Excessive mourning and excessive wrath threaten the polis, challenge cosmogonic order, and yet the polis ceaselessly meditates on such obsessive remembrance—to exorcise it? Or to remind the citizenry of another order?

Consider Loraux's account of the negations and operations encoded in "amnesty." The first amnesty she discusses was enjoined on tragedians after Phrynicus, in his drama about the capture of Ionian Miletus in 494, had reminded the Athenians of their own misfortunes. Herodotus tells us that the theater, viewing *The Capture of Miletus*, burst into tears, after which the Assembly forbade future productions of the play.[22] Loraux reads the Assembly's decree as the paradigmatic initial check, the initial prohibition, which tragedians thereafter observed—never to represent Athenians' own misfortunes to Athenians, never to traffic, that is, in "too current events."[23]

---

[21] Loraux 1998:83–84.
[22] Herodotus 6.21.
[23] Loraux 1998:85–86.

And then she considers another instance in her elaboration of amnesty, that is, the ban "on recalling the misfortunes" that seals the democratic reconciliation in 403.

I will not be able to recount in full the incredibly complex and deft arguments and sub-arguments Loraux then undertakes; suffice it to say—the risk of simplification all too present!—that in the problematic of "amnesty" Loraux identifies a predicament of ongoing political relevance, perhaps *the politically relevant predicament*. The amnesty of 403 is, in Loraux's words, "a double utterance [that] adjoins a prescription (*ban on recalling misfortunes*) to the taking of an oath (*I shall not recall misfortunes*)."[24] The political solution to civil war thus simultaneously inscribes a collective identity (those who have suffered misfortunes) onto each of the citizens, who assent to this inscription in the performance of the oath: I shall not recall misfortunes. What is clear is that such an amnesty is precisely *not* an amnesia, *not* a forgetting, a slipping away, a Lethean relief, a charm, a drug; the verbal structure of the amnesty reveals that amnesty must *announce* and *enforce* oblivion, that citizens as citizens must consent to bind themselves to this active forgetting, a politically constitutive forgetting. The civil war is too near for it to be forgotten; it must be promised to be forgotten, promised not to be recalled.

The negative construction underlying the amnesty—encoded linguistically in the privative 'a-mnesty', and in such semantically-related terms as 'a-lastor'—reveals that amnesty is, as Loraux suggests, a promise to refuse not only to recall misfortunes but indeed to refuse to "recall [misfortunes] against" an as-yet-unspecified object. As Loraux argues, to recall misfortunes would be, in this case, *to recall them against the city*; to promise not to recall misfortunes is to consent to the new, fragile self-representation the city offers itself in 403. When wounds are too near, forgetting is impossible. Amnesty is one solution—not the suppressing of memory but the performance of a suppression which in itself inevitably speaks the live presence of the suppressed matter. If it is dangerous to remember, it is also impossible to forget, and thus one announces, citizen by citizen, one's public commitment to forget. In the structure of amnesty, the Athenians illuminate for us the terror of a past not yet past enough, a past that, if acknowledged, would have to re-inaugurate the cycle of *stasis* and vengeance.

If we open ourselves to this terror, to a past not sufficiently interred to be decorously lamented or politely, silently forgotten, we see with Loraux how the problematic of amnesty speaks to our own use and abuse of the past.

---

[24] Loraux 1998:84.

Loraux herself reflected on Vichy France and the Dreyfus affair, both of which spectacularly raise the question of the politics of memory and the suppression of vengeance. Indeed the work of amnesty should make us ask, to paraphrase Loraux's reading of Charles Péguy:[25] when is it politically and ethically incumbent on us to be good haters; when should citizens risk disorder in the name of truth? At what price order? At what price justice? And what are the protocols for securing our consent to pay these prices?

Again, the trajectory of Loraux's analysis of amnesty and its opposites—amnesty always alluding to, if suppressing, its opposites—offers a decidedly non-curatorial reading of "the past." Making us feel the edges of every question the Greeks posed and surgically opening the body of Greek thought to discover endlessly new contours and edges, Loraux offered us not images of ourselves, but problems to think with, figures to think through.

Works Cited

Fisher, N. R. E. 1982. Review of N. Loraux, *L'invention d'Athènes. Histoire de l'oraison funèbre dans la 'cité classique'* (Paris 1981). *Greece and Rome* 29:93.

———. 1984. Review of N. Loraux, *L'invention d'Athènes. Histoire de l'oraison funèbre dans la 'cité classique'* (Paris 1981) and N. Loraux, *Les enfants d'Athéna. Idées athéniennes sur la citoyenneté et la division des sexes* (Paris 1981). *Classical Review* n.s. 34:80–83.

Frontisi-Ducroux, F. 1981. "Artémis bucolique." *Revue de l'histoire des religions* 1:29–56.

Loraux, N. 1984. *Les enfants d'Athéna: Idées athéniennes sur la citoyenneté et la division des sexes.* Paris.

———. 1986. *The Invention of Athens: The Funeral Oration in the Classical City.* Trans. A. Sheridan. Rev. 2nd ed. 2006. Cambridge, MA. Originally published as *L'Invention d'Athènes. Histoire de l'oraison funèbre dans la 'cité classique'* (1981). Paris.

———. 1998. *Mothers in Mourning.* Trans. C. Pache. Ithaca, NY. Originally published as *Les mères en deuil* (1990). Paris.

———. 1995. *The Experiences of Tiresias: The Feminine and the Greek Man.* Trans. P. Wissing. Princeton. Originally published as *Les expériences de Tirésias: le féminin et l'homme grec* (1989). Paris.

---

[25] Loraux 1998:92–93.

———. 2001. "Greek Civil War and the Anthropological Representation of the World Turned Upside-Down." Trans. A. Goldhammer. In *Antiquities: Postwar French Thought III*, eds. N. Loraux, G. Nagy, and L. Slatkin, 54–70. New York. Originally published as "La guerre civile grecque et la représentation anthropologique du monde à l'envers." *Revue de l'histoire des religions* 212:299–326.

———. 2002. *The Divided City*. Trans. C. Pache and J. Fort. Cambridge, MA. Originally published as *La Cité Divisée* (1997). Paris.

Schaps, D. M. 1996. Review of N. Loraux, *The Experiences of Tiresias: The Feminine and the Greek Man* (Princeton 1995). *Bryn Mawr Classical Review* 96.09.12 (1996), http://ccat.sas.upenn.edu/bmcr/1996/96.09.12.html.

Zeitlin, F. 1982. "Travesties of Gender and Genre in Aristophanes' *Thesmophoriazusae*." Reflections of Women in Antiquity, ed. H. Foley, 169–217. Reprinted as Chapter 9 of F. Zeitlin, *Playing the Other: Gender and Society in Classical Greek Literature* (Chicago, 1996), 375–416.

Index Locorum

Subject Index

Achilles, 103, 108, 117, 120, 123, 129–130, 132, 133–134, 159, 173, 183; absence, 100, 109, 116, 122, 181; comparison with Memnon, 33, 34 and nn6–7, 35n8, 40, 41; depiction of in vase paintings, 34; divine origins of, 32, 159; fate of, 159, 175; grief of, 72; in underworld, 140; lament for Patroklos, 50, 74; lineage, 101; mirror image of Hektor, 40n21, 171; *monomachia* with Hektor, 103, 125, 135, 175; mortality of, 35, 40–42, 43 and n24, 44, 47 and n31, 49–50, 81–83, 85, 159; parallels with Diomedes, 101; patronymic, 101; prayer to Thetis, 30–31, 56–59, 62n17, 82; pursuit of Hektor, 171; revenge of Patroklos, 179, 183

achos (ἄχος, grief), 72, 137; of Demeter, 75–76, 78, 80; of Thetis, 78, 83

adynaton, 211

Aegisthus, 139

Aelian, 153–154

Aeneas, 45–46, 53, 122–123, 173; encounter with Achilles, 67, 84n13, 124

Aeschylus, 65n23; *Prometheus Bound*, 65; *Psychostasia*, 34n7; treatment

of Thetis, 38, 66

Aethiopis, 32–35; immortality in, 28, 34; treatment of Thetis, 32–36, 45n28

Agamemnon, 101, 104, 106–109, 113, 123, 127, 130, 139, 143, 179, 183; rebuke of Diomedes, 112, 128–129, 131; rebuke of Odysseus and Menestheus, 129; revenge of Orestes, 144

Aglaia (wife of Hephaistos), 54n3

agorê, 120

Aiolos, 149

aisa (destiny), 41–42, 84

Ajax, 41, 104, 124, 133, 172–173, 178, 183; rebuke of Achilles, 180

Akamas, 135, 181–182

alaston (unforgetting), meaning of, 78

Alcman, 69 and n32, 70n34, 151

Alkathoos, 178

alkê, 132

Alkinoos, 146–147, 149–151

allusions, 86–88, 99–100; use in exhortations, 91

Amphiaraus, 110

Anchises, 37, 46, 53

andra (ἄνδρα), 160

anemôlia, 123

anti puros, 195, 197

Antilochos (son of Nestor), 35; death of, 33

CPSIA information can be obtained
at www.ICGtesting.com
Printed in the USA
JSHW032118150822
29286JS00004B/10

9 780674 021433